FIXING COLUMBINE

FIXING COLUMBINE

*The Challenge to
American Liberalism*

Doriane Lambelet Coleman

CAROLINA ACADEMIC PRESS
Durham, North Carolina

Copyright © 2002
Doriane Lambelet Coleman
All Rights Reserved

ISBN 0-89089-192-3
LCCN 2001099914

CAROLINA ACADEMIC PRESS
700 Kent Street
Durham, NC 27701
Telephone (919) 489-7486
Fax (919) 493-5668
www.cap-press.com

Printed in the United States of America

For my mother, Bluette Lambelet Dammond, who raised three children on her own and made extraordinary personal sacrifices along the way. It is because of her intelligence and pragmatism that we all are strong, and that we will forever feel the deepest love and respect for her and all that she has meant to us and to our children.

And for James E. Coleman, Jr., Alexander Coleman, Nicolas Coleman, Jacqueline Coleman, Tokya Dammond, Lalou Dammond, Cameron Greider, and Clara Dammond Greider. They are the family that nurtures me, and the village in which I am privileged to raise my children.

Contents

ACKNOWLEDGMENTS

Despite that my name is on the cover of this book, no such work can be produced without the support and assistance of family, friends, professional colleagues, and the communities in which one lives and works. And so it is my great honor here to acknowledge that I have been extraordinarily fortunate in the support and assistance I have received in the writing and production of this book.

For their invaluable substantive and editorial contributions to this finished product, I want to acknowledge my colleagues James E. Coleman, Jr., H. Jefferson Powell, David L. Lange, Paul Carrington, and Andrew Taslitz. Also invaluable were my research assistants—three years of them—Adam Miller, Kevin Anderson, Russell Powell, Matthew Field, Malia Herndon, Marina Mazor, Melanie Katsur, and Kerry Tynan. The personal care and enthusiasm I've received from the Carolina Academic Press has been amazing. Finally, there would have been no manuscript to call a book were it not for the time and care that Dawn Blalock provided throughout the process. I simply cannot thank my friends and colleagues enough for what they have contributed professionally to this project.

I also owe a great debt of gratitude to the Montessori Children's House of Durham and its extraordinary mission, and in particular to my children's unbelievably wonderful teachers, Carrie Benoit Salemi, Happy Sayre-McCord, Rachel Sulin, Chitra Alvarado, Pamela Milano, and Terri Epsten: Your devotion to Maria Montessori's fundamental principles, and especially to the children (including my own) contributed immeasurably both to the development of many of the ideas contained in this book, as well as to my practical ability even to contemplate its existence. I am certain that you will not agree with everything I have written here, but that does not change the fact that every child should have your counterparts in his or her village. Ultimately, that is one of the principal objectives of this project.

Last, but certainly not least, I want to acknowledge the immeasurable contributions made by my family and friends, and by my children's beautiful Daisy Ruth Tate. I respect and love all of you for your practical and emotional support, and for your own constant commitment to children. You have been a model for me, so that I might write this book and at the same time take the best possible care of my wonderful boys.

FIXING COLUMBINE

INTRODUCTION

*What happened at Columbine was ... the product of a culture that
cannot make up its mind between rugged, self-righteous individualism and the mutual cooperation necessary for a stable society.*[1]

The tragedy at Columbine High School in Littleton, Colorado—
in which two students killed twelve of their classmates and one
teacher before taking their own lives—has mesmerized the country since it occurred on April 20, 1999. This story has been so cap-
tivating in part because it reflects the apparent victory of evil over
innocence, and because it also poses the perplexing question
whether the society has struck a Faustian bargain with liberalism
that precludes a return to that innocence.* Before Columbine, the
notion was almost inconceivable that *children*—particularly affluent ones who appeared to "have it all"—would be so captured by
guns and murderous computer and Internet games that they
would defy the best intentions of their parents and the society, and
act out those games to the tune of fifteen lives.

And yet Columbine is only the proverbial tip of the iceberg. Recent studies conducted by the government and by scholars and
practitioners indicate that the severely disturbed boys who killed at
Columbine were merely two among an extraordinary number of
American children who are the victims of an unprecedented and
largely silent public health crisis. Specifically, these studies reveal
that approximately fifteen to twenty-five percent of American children—that is, between twelve and twenty *million* children—may
suffer from severe emotional dysfunction. This condition mani-
fests itself differently in different individuals, so that some will direct their scarred emotions outwardly, engaging in various degrees

---

* Throughout this book, unless it is otherwise indicated, I use the words
"liberalism" and "liberal" in their classic or historical sense, that is, referring
to a political philosophy centered on individual rights. Both contemporary
"liberals" and "conservatives" are adherents of liberalism in this respect.

of criminal assault and homicide, while others will engage in self-destructive thoughts and conduct ranging from severe depression to suicide. As Columbine illustrated so starkly, these children reside both within the traditional at-risk settings of the inner-cities *and* in the erstwhile "safe harbor" of the more affluent suburbs, and at all points in between.

The data are clear that this is a relatively recent phenomenon, dating from the 1980s by most estimates; during that period, the rates of homicide, suicide, severe depression, and related anxiety disorders have risen anywhere from one-hundred to four-hundred percent. The most important statistic in this regard involves suicide: Today, approximately 5,000 children in the United States kill themselves each year. This number represents an eight-hundred percent increase from the 1950s, and a four-hundred percent increase from the late 1980s. The data also are clear that American children are alone among their counterparts in other western and industrialized nations in the degree to which they are afflicted by these symptoms; for example, the United States has youth homicide and suicide rates that are approximately ten times that of Canada, our closest neighbor both culturally and geographically. And thus, as awful as it was, Columbine is only the most dramatic illustration of this larger public health crisis. Because of this, it also is the perfect metaphor for the problem that this crisis poses for our society.

There is general agreement among experts in child development that the ultimate causes of Columbine *writ small* and *large* are likely to be the same. They are inadequate parenting, the prevalence in other respects of a "socially toxic environment," both within and outside of the home, and the related "culture of violence" that is reflected in the media, games technology, and most recently on the Internet. Not surprisingly, however, the matter of inadequate parenting—primarily a result of parents, and particularly mothers, "choosing" to raise children from whom they are physically or psychologically disconnected—is, in the opinion of most experts, the more significant factor in the calculus.* This is

---

* Parents may "choose" to be physically or psychologically disconnected from their children because, for example, they work outside of the home or are otherwise absent (again physically or psychologically) for significant

because parents in general are viewed to be both the first and best caretakers of their children and, in the end, their last clear chance to avoid problems. Nevertheless, the causal contributions of the other factors are not to be discounted, and thus the rest of the society is not free of responsibility, as research consistently shows that the society we embrace also places children "at risk" for significant emotional problems. For example, children who are raised under these conditions are more likely to have low self-esteem, to fail to develop important social skills including especially empathy, to be incapable of trusting adults and the adult world, and to see violence—either inwardly or outwardly directed—as a viable solution to their problems.

Given that literally millions of American children are affected by these conditions, it is inevitable that the economic and cultural costs of Columbine *writ large* are likely to be staggering:

Depression alone is said to cost the economy approximately $44 billion each year. More generally, taking both the direct and indirect costs of mental health services and mental illness into account, the total cost exceeds $200 billion annually; and this is likely to be a conservative estimate. In total, mental illness, including suicide, accounts for over fifteen percent of the burden of disease in the United States, more than that attributed to all cancers combined. When the costs of violence also are factored into the equation, the full burden of emotional dysfunction reaches well into the hundreds of billions of dollars annually. While these data include individuals and conditions that are extraneous to the Columbine epidemic, they do provide a clear sense that the economy undoubtedly is and will continue to be taxed significantly as a result.

The cultural and philosophical implications of the Columbine epidemic match the economics in magnitude. It is cliche and yet absolutely correct that a society's children are its future. It is also cliche and equally true that the moral measure of a culture may be taken perhaps most incisively by the manner in which it takes care

---

parts of the day. In this context, I put "choice" in quotation marks because some and perhaps even most people do not choose voluntarily whether to work or not; for example, when these individuals are single parents, or couples with little earning capacity, it is the culture (rather than the parent or parents) that is "choosing" to allow children to be raised apart from them.

of its most vulnerable members. On both counts, the direction that the United States in general has chosen to take in the last thirty-to-forty years harks important social decay.

For the law and legal theory, the dilemma that is created by Columbine *writ large* is relatively clear, and at the same time quite unusual: As I argue in this book, despite that the law generally is a useful tool to resolve complex social problems, the most obvious solutions to Columbine are placed well beyond its reach by at least two constitutional doctrines that reflect deeply-held liberal convictions, the Fourteenth Amendment's right of parental autonomy, and the First Amendment's right of free speech.*

Specifically, the doctrine of parental autonomy precludes the government from remedying directly the problem of inadequate parenting, as it protects almost immutably the rights of parents to autonomous decision-making with respect to the rearing of their children. Abuse, neglect, and abandonment as traditionally defined are the only exceptions to this autonomy. Without redefining neglect, for example, to include the placement of children in deficient day-care programs—which by some estimates account for approximately ninety percent of existing centers—the doctrine will continue to act as a substantial bar to any law-driven solution to the crisis.

Similarly, the right of free speech precludes any obvious state action that would restrict in relevant ways a child's exposure to toxic Internet sites, television programs, and certain movies and

---

* It is worth noting with respect to my focus on these two doctrines, and thus my exclusion of others, that while there is significant agreement that restricting children's access to guns through background checks and trigger locks would pass constitutional muster, the doctrine of parental autonomy in combination with the Second Amendment (or at least Second Amendment politics) appears to preclude the government from banning outright the use of guns by children. Thus, there is an argument that the right to bear arms could or should also be included in this discussion. Indeed, if Columbine made anything clear, it is that when dysfunctional adolescents—and increasingly pre-adolescents—manage to obtain guns, the results are often the most catastrophic. As I explain below, however, I have chosen not to engage this argument here because guns are not an ultimate cause of childhood dysfunction, and thus gun control (while certainly useful as a proximate matter) is not necessarily an evident, first-line remedy.

games technology. This doctrine protects, again almost immutably, the right of adults to be free from content-based restrictions on protected speech; the only exceptions relate to material
that is not protected, that is, to material that is obscene for adults,
and material that would incite imminent violence. And current
doctrine makes no exception for restrictions that are designed to
protect children, unless the restrictions can be shown to have a
minimal impact on the access of adults to offending but otherwise
protected material. Moreover, it is unlikely that an effective restriction could be developed in the current climate that would meet
this standard.

Thus, together the doctrines of free speech and parental autonomy function as they were intended by the founders of American
liberal theory: They protect two of our most fundamental rights,
and bar all but the most minimal intrusion of government and society on their exercise.

It is likely because of these constitutional obstacles—and because of their own personal and philosophical commitment to the
liberal principles they embody—that public figures across the ideological spectrum were more-or-less stumped by the events at Columbine High School. For example, one reporter noted the "curi-
ous and altogether appropriate quiet [that] settled over American
politicians [of all persuasions] in the wake of the nightmare at Columbine High. Not absolute silence, mind you ... but quiet: a kind
of humility that suggested they knew they had come up against the
limits of their trade."[2] Even President Clinton, who generally was
"quick to launch a program for any problem, no matter how ob-
scure, with three points or five points or seven—the more the better ... dropped the wonkery and assumed the role of National
Grief Counselor" in the face of Columbine.[3] The same reporter
also noted the special irony that "activist liberal" politicians like
Clinton, "voluptuar[ies] of governmental solutions," would give up
on the law in this otherwise compelling context.[4] As I argue in this
book, this irony speaks volumes about the particularly lopsided
bargain the society has struck between individual rights and the
possibility of effective solutions to some complex and even debilitating social problems like Columbine.

A critical question that I seek to answer is whether it matters
that the law is an obstacle in circumstances such as Columbine that

implicate this bargain. Or, as some have suggested, are there adequate non-legal alternatives? President Clinton, President G.W. Bush, and others have strongly suggested, for example, that the Columbine problem could be solved or at least minimized if Americans voluntarily would adopt communitarian norms or at least become more devoted to religion and family values, both of which presumably incorporate such norms. While there is little doubt that children in particular benefit from social institutions and cultural values that are communitarian in nature—just as they tend to be harmed by certain liberal institutions and values—it is my view that these particular solutions are not viable precisely because they are voluntary. Most important in this regard is the fact that Americans already have made a different choice, even in the face of their suffering children. For example, many Americans (regardless of their religious proclivities) believe that individual self-fulfillment is best achieved in and through productive outside work, and that self-fulfillment is more important than anything else. Many of these same Americans also believe that the public has no responsibility to afford the poor an opportunity to make a different choice; that is, to choose not to work or to work part-time so that they personally can care for their children; that judgment is reflected in our most recent welfare reforms. So long as American culture continues to be dominated by and especially committed to these liberal values, suggestions that the solution to Columbine lies in a voluntary (re)commitment to an opposite (or communitarian) philosophy will ring hollow.

And so, how to fix Columbine? In this book, I argue that while we should never give up on the notion of parents as the children's first and best caretakers, the government affirmatively must assume that role where the evidence is clear (as it is today) that parents are not fulfilling their responsibilities. I argue further that the most effective—albeit clearly not comprehensive—way to accomplish this substitution is the establishment by the federal government of a mandatory curriculum for the public schools that creates a child-centered environment in the critical periods of a child's emotional and moral development. This curriculum would incorporate two elements designed specifically to alleviate and even to counter the conditions that ultimately cause children to become dysfunctional: the extension of the period of public education back to include pre-school, as well as the extension of the school year and academic day throughout that period; and the integration throughout the academic curriculum of a mandatory program of character education or values training.

Federal involvement is essential to assure that *all* children regardless of local funding problems and related politics, are afforded such respite and training. Currently, the public schools system is plagued with inequities among individual schools and school districts in facilities and programs. These inequities are largely a result of corresponding inequities in funding and wealth. We already know that unless these disparities are eliminated, the program I envision would be available only to children in wealthier districts, just as it currently is available only in certain private schools. That would be no solution to a nationwide public health crisis; indeed, to allow for such selective application given the scope of the problem would be akin to inoculating only of a small percentage of the population against a virus that had spread across the country and that would claim the remainder as its victims. On the other hand, federalization of the new curriculum would provide the necessary uniformity of treatment, which in turn would translate into the necessary social benefit, namely the amelioration of the public health crisis that motivates the proposal of this solution.

The reformation of the public schools curriculum to add the pre-school years is critical not only for children who are deemed at-risk for educational failure (who often already are the beneficiaries of such programs, most notably Head Start) but for *all children* who are at risk for the sorts of emotional dysfunction that characterize the Columbine epidemic. The point here is that the pre-school years should serve the function that the traditional, child-centered family home provided, and that is missing in *both* poorer *and* wealthier families today where single or both parents work outside of the home. The reformed curriculum also would include a lengthening of the school day and year from pre-school through high school, both to accommodate the values and character-building program that I will describe below, and to provide a safe haven for children (again from both relatively poor and relatively wealthy backgrounds) who otherwise would be subject to an emotionally toxic after-school environment.

There already is support among educators and politicians of both major parties for after-school and summer school programs to keep children safe and off the streets. While my proposal is not for such an extra-curricular program, but rather to permit the integration of character education and values training into the existing academic curriculum, the extension of the day and year that such a curriculum would require effectively would accomplish the same objectives. Importantly, while the schools as currently constituted sometimes are themselves a cause of childhood dysfunction—a part, for example, of some children's socially toxic environment—and that lengthening the period of time in which a child is at school might ordinarily exacerbate the problem, the opposite effect should be achieved if the curriculum simultaneously is reformed as I suggest, to make the schools a more nurturing environment. Certainly, the choice only to lengthen the exposure without also reforming the curriculum would create substantial additional concern.

The reformed curriculum would include a program of character education or values training that would target specifically those traits—both inwardly directed, or ego-building traits, and outwardly directed, or social-responsibility traits—that experts in child development agree are necessary for healthy emotional development and social interaction. While many policymakers—including perhaps most prominently, President G.W. Bush and former Education Secretary William J. Bennett—already have called for related programs, their approaches thus far have not been based on a child development model; nor have they emphasized the need for these programs to be integrated throughout the academic curriculum. Rather, they have focused almost exclusively on the need for children to develop outward or social responsibility, and they have suggested that such training could be accommodated in after-school programs, or special sessions during the school day. This "Sunday school" approach is insufficient from a developmental perspective, perhaps particularly because the systems that historically supported and extended the lessons learned on that day or the Sabbath are largely absent in the contemporary cultural context. This is in fact what got us to the place where we are today; or, things are worse than Bush and Bennett think they are.

In this context, it is important to note that whenever the subject of values or character-building is introduced with children as their intended recipients, political liberals begin to worry about the conservative agenda to indoctrinate their children in "Christian" beliefs, and conservatives worry about the liberal agenda to indoctrinate their children in "secular humanism." However, a core list of values along the lines of a secular "book of virtues" is rather easy to compile—with everyone at the table—when the objective is a clinical one rather than indoctrination into one or another ideological camp. Thus, for example, experts agree that it is essential for children's emotional health that they develop both a sense of self-worth *and* a sense of empathy, neither of which is indisputably innate or natural, and both of which traditionally were taught in the home but can be taught elsewhere—for example in an educational setting—in appropriate circumstances.

The schools are "the logical ... intervention point" for this crisis for two reasons.[5] First, as one commentator explained in a related context, it makes sense to use the schools in cases where the public health is at issue, for example to assure by vaccinations the inoculation of the populace, because "they are the one institution [in the society] in which everyone is mandated by law to participate."[6] Thus, the requisite compulsion—which is missing from the voluntary communitarian alternatives—is present in this solution. Second, the public schools since their origins have been used by the government for similar purposes; that is to ensure that children are raised consistently with the interests of the society or the community. Indeed, there is a significant argument, which I explore in this book, that the public schools were conceived—by Thomas Jefferson, Benjamin Rush, and others—in principal part to accomplish this non-academic objective. And, most importantly, the Supreme Court has consistently upheld the constitutionality of public school policies and programs that were designed to achieve communitarian ends, and in particular to achieve socializing objectives beyond the classic "three 'Rs'." It has done so in the face of the First and Fourteenth Amendments' promises of parental autonomy and free speech, and at least in partial reliance on the ironic rationale that the very success of American liberalism and its democracy depend upon the inculcation of its premises and fundamental values in its future citizens, the children. And thus, in this proposal there is also the necessary and rather unusual (if not unique) mandate for communitarianism, which has the clear potential to circumvent the otherwise strong liberal challenge to the more evident solutions to Columbine.

Apart from my premise that contemporary American parenting practices are largely responsible for the Columbine problem, my solution to federalize the curriculum of the public schools undoubtedly will be the most controversial aspect of this book. Indeed, in my review of the existing legal literature, I have found not a single commentator who has yet sought to make this case.[7] For the most part, this is because the suggestion appears to confront a longstanding tradition of "local control" of public elementary and secondary education that is firmly embedded at least in the minds of its proponents and to a lesser extent in federal statutory law. As I explain, however, once the rhetoric of local control is stripped away, it becomes quite clear that this tradition is neither intact nor practically viable in the contemporary context. For example, control of the curriculum of the public schools was long ago transferred from local school boards to the state boards of education of most if not all states in the country. As a result, local boards already are forced to accept the textbook series and the pedagogical objectives of a central authority. Moreover, the fundamental premise of local control—articulated most prominently by now-Attorney General John Ashcroft—that individual communities are best suited by virtue of their familiarity with regional employment prospects to determine the curricular needs of their students, is at best anachronistic where the relevant job market today is national, and increasingly international. For these and other reasons that I explore in this book, I suggest that the doctrine of local control is part myth, otherwise vincible, and ultimately a policy dinosaur.

Finally, it is clear that this proposal would be costly. For that reason, it is also likely to be controversial, because many taxpayers and their representatives persist in the belief that too much money already is being spent on a failed effort to prop up the existing public school system. I suggest, however, that the proposal is actually a partial response to this general concern, because it would have the ancillary benefit of curing some of the most important deficiencies of that allegedly failing or failed system, namely a poor educational environment and inadequate funding: It would ensure that the schools would become more effective and positive caretakers of the children; and these benefits would inure to all the children, regardless of the economics of the locale. In addition, and perhaps most persuasive, is the fact that the required expenditures are likely to pale in comparison to the costs of doing nothing. Indeed, in many respects we already are paying, albeit indirectly, for the effects of Columbine. The nation should seize this day of national introspection, community-building and relative prosperity finally to make this important investment in education. Terrorism and its subsidiary impacts on civil liberties are not the only dangers to the success and survival of our way of life.

Ultimately, the high national cost of Columbine also is the answer to what is perhaps the most perplexing question that arises from this book, namely why Americans would accept (voluntarily) legislation consistent with this proposal if they are not willing (voluntarily) to adopt the communitarian norms and practices that also would cure the children. My response is that they are likely to do so because, despite its admittedly steep price tag, the proposal has a real chance to fix Columbine at a *relatively* insignificant cost. That is, Americans would not have to give up what they consider to be their overriding interest in the liberties that matter, and, on balance—measuring the costs to the society of millions of dysfunctional individuals against the costs of the program—it is unlikely that the nation as a whole would be the poorer for it in financial terms. The fact that G.W. Bush won the presidency in significant measure based upon the issue of education reform, and that one of his principal successes to date has been in this area, suggests that my expectations in this respect are likely more true today than they may have been even in the immediate aftermath of the Columbine tragedy.

Part I of this book describes the Columbine problem, examining in depth the epidemic of dysfunctional children, its causes, and its costs to the society. Part II discusses the legal implications of Columbine, exploring in particular the fact that the Constitution and the liberal principles it enshrines are an obstacle to the adoption of the more obvious solutions to the problem. It is in this context that I review but ultimately reject the argument that has been made by politicians and others across the political spectrum that there are effective extra-legal solutions to the crisis, including what

I have called voluntary communitarianism and religion. In Part III, I argue that fixing Columbine requires at a minimum that we provide children with the environment necessary for healthy personal and social development, and that outside of the home, this environment can best be provided in the public schools. As part of this argument, I review relevant doctrine that establishes the schools as a special enclave of communitarianism within this otherwise staunchly liberal society. And, consistent with the treatment of other public heath issues of national concern, I argue that the Columbine problem requires a corresponding national solution, in this case the federalization of the public school curriculum to include those components necessary to ensure the creation of this beneficial environment. I conclude that while this "fix" will obviously be controversial—both because it confronts directly the doctrine of local control of public education and because it is likely to be costly—it is ultimately the most viable solution within the contemporary liberal landscape.

PART I

THE COLUMBINE PROBLEM

In this part of the book, I revisit the events that took place at Columbine High School, in Littleton, Colorado, on April 20, 1999. I also describe what is known about the two boys who created such havoc in that place and on that day. What follows is a contextualization of those events. I argue that Columbine as we know it is merely the most prominent example of a much larger national phenomenon which experts easily call an epidemic, and which has rendered dysfunctional millions of American children in the last few decades. As I noted in the Introduction, among these children are girls as well as boys, and they come from all walks of American life. No one is immune. I describe this epidemic, which I call the Columbine problem, including its characteristics and immeasurable costs to the society. Finally, I conclude this discussion with a substantial examination of the most important ultimate or original causes of the Columbine problem from the perspective of specialists in the field of child development: inadequate parents and parent-substitutes, and toxic media, peer, and school environments.

CHAPTER ONE

COLUMBINE HIGH SCHOOL, APRIL 20, 1999

On April 20, 1999, two students at Columbine High School in the predominantly white, upper-middle class town of Littleton, Colorado, armed themselves with a sawed-off double-barrel shotgun, a TEC 9 semiautomatic handgun, a sawed-off pump shotgun, and a 9-mm semiautomatic rifle, drove to the high school, and proceeded to kill twelve of their classmates and one teacher.[1] Before nineteen year-old Eric Harris and seventeen year-old Dylan Klebold ended their deadly rampage in a double suicide, they managed also to injure twenty-three others, to bring into the building one twenty-pound propane tank, assembled in the Harris family's garage and rigged "to blow up a sizable part of the school," and to plant approximately thirty pipe bombs (also home-made) which took "days" for the police to "find and defuse."[2]

Subsequently, police learned from the boys' diaries and web site that the killings and suicides were merely a small part of a grander and more destructive plan that evolved over a year, but in the end simply failed.[3] In fact, quite like a film script, the boys had conceived a plot that would have reduced the school to rubble, and that would have ended in an unimaginably prescient and dramatic airplane explosion over New York City.[4] The boys actually "wanted movies made of their story, which they had carefully laced with 'a lot of foreshadowing and dramatic irony,' as Harris put it ... 'Directors will be fighting over this story,' Klebold said—and the boys chewed over which could be trusted with the script: Steven Spielberg or Quentin Tarantino."[5] To assist with the production and for posterity, the boys videotaped themselves describing their plans and motivations, Harris armed with "a sawed-off shotgun ... [named] Arlene, after a favorite character in the gory Doom video games and books that he like[d] so much."[6] Indeed, Harris imagined that their rampage would mimic that game: "'It's going to be like f___g Doom ... Tick, tick, tick, tick ... Haa! That f___ing shotgun is straight out of Doom!'"[7] And then, quoting Shake-speare's *The Tempest*, Harris concluded, "'[g]ood wombs hath borne bad sons.'"[8]

Students who survived the ordeal say that the two boys—de-scribed as "brainy kids from seemingly stable, affluent homes"[9]—were part of a group of "school outcasts" called the "Trenchcoat Mafia"[10] whose members were continually and apparently viciously harassed by the "jocks" and other popular students at the school. According to one report, these "popular students"

> described [the Trenchcoat Mafia] as discarded, unwanted "stereotype geeks," who, like the jocks and the preppies, had their own table in the cafeteria, their group picture in the year-book ... "It's kind of like a rivalry with us," [explained a] hockey player ... "They hate us because we're like the social elite of the school." That rivalry had been smoldering for months. Some students say even the teachers picked on the Trench Coats, blaming them for things they hadn't done and letting jocks get away with anything because they were the crown princes. One athlete in particular liked to taunt them. "Dirtbag," he'd say, or maybe, "Nice dress." Others called them "faggots, inbreeds, ha-rassing them to the point of throwing rocks and bottles at them from moving cars." [11]

These were the students who were Harris's and Klebold's princi-pal targets, at least at the outset of the rampage.[12] One student re-called that "[t]he two moved through the room, calling out: 'All the jocks stand up. We're going to kill every one of you.'"[13] "[I]n the end," though, "the killings were ... blindly indiscriminate."[14] Ac-cording to one student,

> '[t]hey shot at everybody ... including the preps, the jocks and the people who wore Abercrombie & Fitch clothes. But it would be hard to say they singled them out, because everybody here looks like that. I mean, we're in white suburbia. Our school's wealthy. Go into the parking lot and see the cars. These kids have money. But I never thought they'd do this.'[15]

Harris and Klebold apparently also were obsessed with Adolf Hitler[16]—April 20, the date of the massacre, was Hitler's birth-day[17]—and to have hated "[various minority groups.]"[18] For example, according to a news report, "[s]ome members of Harris' and Klebold's clique ... had embraced enough Nazi mythology to spook their classmates. They reportedly wore swastikas on black shirts, spoke German in the halls, re-enacted World War II battles ... Harris and Klebold liked to bowl: when Harris made a good shot, he would throw his arms up, "Heil Hitler!"[19]

And while one year and much delving later, we still do not know a lot about their personal and family histories, we do know that both harbored deep resentment against people, primarily children, who had taunted them throughout their lives.[20] For example, in one videotape Harris "recall[ed] how he moved around so much with his military family and always had to start over, 'at the bottom of the ladder.' People continually made fun of him—'my face, my hair, my shirts.'"[21] And we know that Klebold similarly felt oppressed by "popular and athletic" jocks, including his brother, and that his feelings of oppression dated back to his time in day care when "he hated the 'stuck-up' kids he felt hated him. 'Being shy didn't help,'" Klebold added.[22]

The press did seek to examine more specifically the role that Harris and Klebold's parents might have played in the etiology of their particular disaffection, searching for "deep family dysfunction" but finding "nothing [tidy] in the first days of archaeology ... that explained something so massively wrong. These were parents who came to all the Little League and soccer games. They even came to practices."[23] What we do know of the Harris and Klebold families is certainly insufficient from which to draw any valid conclusions about their role in the tragedy. For example, we know that "Klebold's father Thomas is a former geophysicist who launched a mortgage-management business from his home. His mother Susan worked with blind and disabled kids at the local community college."[24] We also know that "Harris' father Wayne was a decorated Air Force pilot,"[25] and that the family apparently had moved at least a few times during the boy's childhood. And we know that on the day of the massacre "the barrel of a gun was clearly visible on the dresser of one suspect when investigators entered his room," and that the boys apparently turned the Harris family garage into a "bomb-making factory."[26]

The lawsuits that were filed by Harris's and Klebold's victims and their families against the boys' parents for "negligent supervision" of their children has at least temporarily sealed this dig for answers.[27] The plaintiffs' lawyer, Geoffrey Fieger, does assume that he will find evidence of parental neglect, or at least that it is out there. In his own words, "[i]n the 200 years of this republic's existence we never had children go into school and slaughter fellow children. What's going on here? Those parents know what happened. And the fact of filing a lawsuit gives me subpoena power to ask the questions we need to ask."[28] Despite his optimism, however, the fact of litigation assures at least that the boys' parents will not be voluntarily forthcoming with respect to any family or personal troubles they were aware of and thus that might implicate them in their sons' rampage, either legally or morally.

Whatever the hidden truths, in the end the boys did think about their parents and what their actions would mean for them. For example, the reporters who were given the exclusive rights to publish the contents of the boys' videotapes noted that

> [t]hroughout th[ose tapes], it seems as though the only people about whom the killers felt remorse were their parents. "It f___ing sucks to do this to them," Harris says of his parents. "They're going to be put through hell once we do this." And then he speaks directly to them. "There's nothing you guys could've done to prevent this," he says. Klebold tells his mom and dad they have been "great parents" who taught him "self-awareness, self-reliance … I always appreciated that." He adds, "I'm sorry I have so much rage." At one point Harris gets very quiet. His parents have probably noticed that he's become distant, withdrawn lately—but it's been for their own good. "I don't want to spend any more time with them," he says. "I wish they were out of town so I didn't have to look at them and bond more."[29]

On the very last videotape which Harris and Klebold made, on the morning of April 20, before they set off for Columbine High School, the boys said goodbye to their parents. Klebold said, "'[i]t's a half-hour before our Judgment Day … I didn't like life very much,' … 'Just know I'm going to a better place than here....'"[30] Harris concluded, "'I know my mom and dad will be in shock and disbelief … I can't help it.... That's it. Sorry. Goodbye.'"[31]

However shocked Harris and Klebold's parents might have been by the events of April 20, the American public was that and more. Mitchell Johnson, the father of a thirteen-year-old boy who just the year before had shot and killed four children and a teacher at a school in Jonesboro, Arkansas, perhaps best characterized the nation's reaction to Columbine when he wrote, "[t]o think anyone so young could create this kind of havoc, to be so callous about other people's lives, strains the imagination and makes us wonder and worry about what we are becoming as a country and a society."[32] The nation's initial obsession with this question continued for weeks, dominating the national news coverage in a period where one would have expected the presidential impeachment scandal to be the singular focus of our attentions.[33] Indeed, in the period between April 19 and April 30, 1999, there were approximately 8,600 stories about Columbine, and only eight hundred stories about the impeachment.[34]

The bulk of the Columbine stories in that period related to the development of the facts of the case—what exactly happened—and to the etiology of the perpetrators' deep disillusionment and propensity for such extraordinary violence. Many stories and commentary also focused on the growing and uncomfortable recognition that Columbine was (finally) irrefutable proof that the violence that many associate with the inner city was possible even the most affluent of suburbs. As one reporter wrote in that early period, "[t]he story of the slaughter at Columbine High School opened a sad national conversation about what turned two boys' souls into poison. It promises to be a long, hard talk, in public and in private, about why smart, privileged kids rot inside."[35] Less subtly, she also described how Columbine had, in one fell swoop, dashed the national illusion that such rot was confined to under-privileged children in the inner-cities: "Among the many things that did not survive the week was the hymn all parents unconsciously sing as they send their children out in the morning, past the headlines, to their schools: it can't happen here ... it could never happen here."[36]

Of course, when this reporter and others in that period thought about the awakening of "all parents" in this way, they certainly were referring only to parents outside of the inner cities, where violence has long been rampant, even if less dramatic or at least unnoticed by the public, and where parents have long and very publicly suffered from the anxiety (and the reality) of murdered children. Indeed, her instinctive reference revealed much about the subconscious division that most Americans who live outside of the inner-cities made before the events at Columbine between their relatively safe and peaceful world, and the war-zones that characterize many inner-city communities in the United States. And it also implied that they now understand that this division—albeit that it never was an equitable one—is not even factually viable.[37] Ultimately, this recognition that money (and perhaps even certain unspoken notions about race) does not insulate children from emotional dysfunction is Columbine's most important legacy. As I will describe in the following chapter, this is because it has exposed the depth and nature of what experts in child development have repeatedly called an "epidemic," a public health crisis that touches a surprising and extraordinary number of American children, and that is not bound by ethnicity, race, or wealth.

CHAPTER TWO

COLUMBINE *WRIT LARGE*: AN AMERICAN EPIDEMIC

The tragic events at Columbine High School were the most visible and dramatic evidence of what is clearly a much larger national epidemic of childhood dysfunction that plagues equally children in the inner-cities and those in more affluent circumstances. This epidemic has three distinctive characteristics.

First, it is personalized, manifesting itself in numerous ways, including in a propensity toward violence, but also in other less public ways, including in a tendency toward severe depression and suicide.

Second, as I have just noted, it is characterized by its extraordinary breadth. For example, almost all of the relevant analyses suggest that approximately fifteen to twenty-five percent of American children surveyed in any given period have exhibited at least one severe symptom that is generally associated with the epidemic. Based upon the most recent census data, which suggest that there are approximately 78,401,000 children in the United States, these percentages translate into an astounding 11,760,150 to 19,600,250 children who exhibit such symptoms.[1] (This number reflects the estimate for persons who are nineteen years old and younger, in the period "April 1, 1990 to July 1, 1999, with short term projection to March 1, 2000." The Census Bureau estimates that there were 70,354,000 children aged seventeen and younger in the same period.)[2]

Third, these numbers, and the illnesses they reflect, are a modern and uniquely American phenomenon. As the following statistics reveal, the numerical increases over time—ranging from one-hundred to seven-hundred percent in the relevant period—are simply astounding.

YOUTH VIOLENCE

Consistent with Columbine itself, the statistics on outwardly-directed violence have received the most attention. According to

James Garbarino—whose book, *Lost Boys: Why Our Sons Turn Violent and How We Can Save Them*, was published in 1999 immediately prior to the events at Columbine—serious assaults committed by juveniles have increased by seven-hundred percent since World War II.[3] Relying on statistics from the Centers for Disease Control and the Federal Bureau of Investigation, he notes also that from the mid-1980s to the mid-1990s, the youth homicide rate increased by one-hundred sixty-eight percent, and that from 1987 to 1996, juvenile arrests for violent offenses increased by more than fifty percent.[4] (Violent offenses are defined for this purpose as "possession of weapons, aggravated assault, robbery, and murder."[5]) Translating this data into raw numbers, Garbarino concludes that adolescents annually commit approximately 2,300 homicides.[6] More specifically, the Centers for Disease Control recently found that, in a given thirty-day period, eighteen percent of the students surveyed had carried a weapon, defined as a gun, knife, or club.[7] During the same period, approximately eight percent of students surveyed had carried such weapons onto school property; and five percent of them had carried a gun.[8]

In sum, "there has been an explosion in the rates at which adolescents commit and are victimized by serious crimes of violence."[9] It is true, of course, that "[t]he increase was concentrated among black males."[10] However, "the potential for trouble" in that group existed and was "realized" specifically because of "the secular decline in the quality of family life and parental resources devoted to socializing children."[11] As I will describe in Chapter Three, and as Garbarino has so forcefully argued, these are the very factors that today link inner-city children with their suburban counterparts. Moreover, while there is an indication that violent crime by children is no longer on the rise, and may even have tapered somewhat in the last decade, this "still leaves the rate more than 50% higher than it was in 1980," and certainly much higher than that which prevailed prior to the 1960s when the upward trend began.[12]

CHILDHOOD SUICIDE

The statistics on suicide in the United States are an eerie mirror image of these data. Recent congressional testimony suggests that approximately five thousand children and young adults kill themselves in this country each year.[13] According to Senator Christopher Dodd, who convened the first-ever Senate hearing on the subject in September of 2001, "[i]n 1998, more teenagers and young adults died of suicide than from cancer, heart disease, AIDS, birth defects, stroke, pneumonia and influenza" combined.[14] Suicide thus represents the "third-leading cause of death for young people in the United States" today, a rate of approximately ten in one-hundred thousand children annually.[15] These data are most startling because they represent an extraordinary rise in what was already an impressive incidence and increase from past periods in the nation's history.

According to Garbarino, statistics that were considered "recent" in 1999 showed that adolescent suicide rates at that time numbered approximately 2300 annually; and this already represented an increase of approximately four-hundred percent since 1950,[16] and a rise of two-hundred percent in the 1990s alone.[17] Perhaps even more disturbing is "the fact that younger and younger children have been trying to take their lives."[18] Finally, and again according to Garbarino, approximately fifteen to twenty percent of high school students seriously consider committing suicide in the United States each year;[19] approximately twelve to sixteen percent of high school students actually make a suicide plan;[20] and approximately five to eight percent of high school students actually attempt suicide.[21]

Finally, the statistics concerning self-destructive behavior or symptoms that fall outside of these first two categories also are staggering, ranging from ten to twenty-five percent of American children depending upon the study. For example, is has been reported that approximately twenty percent of children aged three to seventeen have some sort of developmental, learning, or behavioral disorder.[22] The Surgeon General has confirmed these numbers, indicating that "[a]bout 20 percent of children are estimated to have mental disorders with at least mild functional impairment," including both "mental or addictive disorders," and "[c]hildren and adolescents with [serious emotional disturbance] number approximately 5 to 9 percent of children ages 9 to 17."[23] Some have suggested that even these numbers are low.[24]

DEPRESSION IN CHILDREN

Depression is one of the most significant impairments affecting children. The figures vary rather widely depending upon the manner in which depression is defined and the relative seriousness of the dysfunction; what is clear, however, is that it is an enormous problem. Thus, the National Institutes of Health found that

> up to 3 percent of children and up to 8 percent of adolescents in the U.S. suffer from depression, a serious mental disorder that adversely affects mood, energy, interest, sleep, appetite, and overall functioning. In contrast to normal emotional experiences of sadness or passing mood states, the symptoms of depression are extreme and persistent and can interfere significantly with the ability to function at home or at school.[25]

Eric Mash and David Wolfe write that "[a]lmost all children and teenagers experience some symptoms of depression, and as many as 5% of prepubertal children and 10% to 20% of adolescents experience significant depression that may not get better on its own."[26] Moreover, and consistent with the suicide statistics, Mash and Wolfe note that rates of childhood depression also are on the rise, so that "[i]ndividuals born in the latter part of the 20th century have a greater risk for developing depression than those born earlier."[27] The largest estimates come out of "[r]esearch by psychologist Ronald Kessler at Harvard Medical School [which] reveals that the rate of serious depression among American youth has increased from 2 percent in the 1960s to almost 25 percent in the 1990s."[28] Garbarino emphasizes that, unlike in the past where primarily poor children were afflicted by depression in large numbers, current research shows that "these high rates of depression are now being found equally among affluent and poor youth."[29] Finally, according to Mash and Wolfe and again consistent with the suicide statistics, "[n]ot only is depression increasing, it also is occurring at a younger age, with individuals born in the later decades of the 1900s reporting progressively younger ages of onset for their first episode of major depression than those born in earlier decades."[30]

ANXIETY DISORDERS

Apart from depression, the "anxiety disorders," including generalized anxiety disorder,[31] obsessive compulsive disorder,[32] panic disorder,[33] post traumatic stress disorder,[34] phobias,[35] and other disorders such as separation anxiety,[36] are said to account for most mental health problems suffered by children in the United States today.[37] For example, "[a]ccording to one large-scale study of 9 to 17 year olds ... as many as 13 percent of young people had an anxiety disorder in a year."[38] Other significant problems include attention deficit hyperactivity disorder (ADHD), which is said to be "the most commonly diagnosed psychiatric disorder of childhood,"[39] accounting for "3 to 5 percent of school-aged children;"[40] and eating disorders including anorexia nervosa,[41] bulimia nervosa,[42] and obesity.[43] Both ADHD and eating disorders significantly impair the individual's ability to function socially and academically. For example, ADHD is associated with "impaired functioning in peer relationships and multiple settings including home and school ... [with] long-term adverse effects on academic performance, vocational success, and social-emotional development."[44] And the eating disorders, "[i]n addition to causing various physical health problems, ... are associated with illnesses such as depression, substance abuse, and anxiety disorders."[45]

CONCLUSIONS ABOUT THE DATA
AND THEIR GENDER EFFECTS

Certainly some of these numbers are the product of different and perhaps better diagnostics in the relevant period; however, it is equally clear from current homicide and suicide rates that diagnostics alone cannot provide the answer to these epidemic numbers. Indeed, as Patricia Hersch explains, "study after study points to problems and inadequacies in *today's* kids," problems caused by "a vortex of *new* risks ... almost unknown to their parents or grandparents."[46] Moreover, the resulting "deluge of [particularly] adolescent dysfunction sweeping the nation, manifesting itself in everything from drugs, sex, and underachievement to depression, suicide, and crime" is "[m]ost threatening," according to Hersch, because these indicia of dysfunction are being seen in increasingly younger children.[47] And thus, while there is some recent good news indicating, for example, that children in the past few years have begun to engage in slightly fewer high risk behaviors and commit slightly fewer violent crimes, the overall rates in all of the categories that I have described continue to be extraordinarily high in comparison with rates thirty years ago.[48]

There are often stark differences between boys and girls with respect to all relevant manifestations of the epidemic. For example, according to Mash and Wolfe, "behavior problems such as aggression, noncompliance, and rule breaking seem more common among boys than girls, whereas emotional problems, such as sadness, anxiety, and withdrawal, seem more common among girls than boys."[49] These authors explain further that

> [g]ender differences ... interact with age, meaning that boys show a pattern of behavior different from girls as they grow older.... boys typically have more difficulties than girls during early or middle childhood ... Girls' problems are more likely to increase during adolescence, with higher prevalence rates for depression and dysphoric mood from mid-adolescence through adulthood.[50]

Furthermore, "[f]or girls, emotional problems such as anxiety or depression are more likely to persist over time, whereas boys with either behavior problems or emotional problems as children are more likely to end up with behavior disorders in adolescence."[51] Thus, while the literature shows that all children are in crisis, experts in child development have recently begun to focus on these differences, creating what is, in essence, a "new" gender-based model of emotional disease.

For example, in her book, *Reviving Ophelia: Saving the Lives of Adolescent Girls*, Mary Pipher takes on the subject of the many, seemingly "confident, well-adjusted girls [who were] transformed into sad and angry failures" in the1990s.[52] She elaborates that "girls are having more trouble now than they had thirty years ago ... and more trouble than even ten years ago.... Parents, teachers, counselors and nurses see that girls are in trouble but they do not realize how universal and extreme the suffering is."[53] Consistent with the data that I have previously described, Pipher sees this suffering manifested in dramatic rises in rates of depression, eating disorders, the use of drugs and alcohol, problems with sexuality and sexual predation, and violence.[54]

William Pollack also adopted this gendered approach with the 1999 release of his book, *Real Boys: Rescuing Our Sons from the Myths of Boyhood*, in which he explains that

> [b]oys today are in serious trouble, including many who seem "normal" and to be doing just fine. Confused by society's mixed messages about what's expected of them as boys, and later as men, many feel a sadness and disconnection they cannot even name. New research shows that boys are faring less well in school than they did in the past, and in comparison to girls, that many boys have remarkably fragile self-esteem, and that the rates of both depression and suicide in boys are frighteningly on the rise. Many of our sons are in a desperate crisis.[55]

Pollack follows with some specific distinctions between boys and girls:

> [I]n the educational system, boys are now twice as likely as girls to be labeled as "learning disabled," constitute up to 67 percent of our "special education" classes, and in some school systems are up to ten times more likely to be diagnosed with serious emotional disorder—most especially attention deficit disorder—(for which many boys will receive potent medications with potentially serious side effects.) ... Boys are experiencing serious trouble outside school as well. The rate of depression among today's boys is shockingly high, and statistics now tell us that boys are up to three times more likely than girls to be the victims of violent crime (other than sexual assault) and between four to six times more likely to commit suicide.[56]

Finally, he notes that

> [w]hile the significant gaps in girls' science and math achievement are improving greatly, boys' scores on reading are lagging behind significantly and continue to show little improvement. Recent studies also show that not only is boys' self-esteem more fragile than that of girls and that boys' confidence as learners is impaired but also that boys are substantially more likely to endure disciplinary problems, be suspended from classes, or actually drop out of school.[57]

Pollack's book is joined by others, also of recent vintage, that address with equal alarm the concerns about these statistics in particular, and about the sharp rise more generally in the numbers of American boys who suffer emotional dysfunction.[58]

There are, of course, faces and stories behind these data and generalizations. The tragedy at Columbine High School is only one of these stories, representing a very few of these faces. Others are set out in books, including in those that I have just described, and the more incendiary appear in the daily news. Yet others, certainly the vast majority, are likely to remain private, forever the exclusive property of those who own them. I obviously could not even begin to describe these other children and their stories here; indeed, given their anecdotal nature, these stories are not necessary or even particularly valuable in evidentiary terms. What is important, however, is that Columbine *writ small* clearly was not an aberration. There undoubtedly are other children today who live in inner cities *and* suburbs, who share Eric Harris and Dylan Klebold's lack of empathy and their desperation, and who are victims of the epidemic that I have called the Columbine problem.

THE ECONOMIC COSTS OF COLUMBINE

Columbine is remarkable not only for these extraordinary impacts, but also because its magnitude is unique to this country. Thus, while other countries also saw a rise in childhood dysfunction during the late twentieth century, the rise was paltry in comparison with that which characterized the same period in the United States.[59] For example, the Centers for Disease Control (CDC) note that "the United States has the highest rates of childhood homicide, suicide, and firearm-related death among industrialized countries."[60] Its conclusion was based on a comparative study of the twenty-five countries, including the United States, that make up the "high[est]-income group" in the World Bank's 1994 World Development Report.[61] This study found that in 1994, when the rates of suicide especially were substantially less than they are today, there were "a total of 2872 deaths [attributed to homicide, suicide, and fire-arms] among children aged less than 15 years;" that "homicides accounted for 1995 deaths;" and that "1464 (73%) of these occurred among U.S. children."[62] In particular, the study found that suicide "accounted for the deaths of 599 children, including 431 (72%) in boys and 168 (28%) in girls," and that "321 (54%) [of the total number of child suicides] occurred among U.S. children."[63] Astonishingly, even in this earlier period, "[t]he suicide rate for children in the United States was two times higher than in the other 25 countries combined."[64] To the extent that suicide is an indicator of underlying emotional dysfunction in general, it may be surmised that rates of depression and anxiety disorders are commensurately lower in these countries as well.[65]

No one can doubt that these data represent enormous economic costs to this society. Indeed, just as economists are able to calculate the losses that would result from an Internet virus, so too they are able to estimate the costs of one or more dysfunctional (or abnormally dysfunctional) generations, using both direct and indirect or downstream costs associated with the occurrence or phenomenon at issue.[66] Direct costs would include the costs of treatment, for example, and indirect costs would include such items as "lost productivity at the workplace, school, and home due to premature death or disability."[67] To my knowledge, no one has yet used this standard analysis to estimate the "costs of Columbine" specifically; and it is not my task here to attempt that calculation.* Nevertheless, it is possible to gain a good sense of the likely economic impact of the epidemic from related estimates that have been devel-

---

* According to the National Institute of Mental Health at the National Institutes of Health, the "economic costs of children's mental illnesses" have yet to be calculated. E-mail from Margaret Strock, Information Resources & Inquiries Branch, Office of Communications & Public Affairs, National Institute of Mental Health (May 11, 2001) (on file with author). All of the work that has been done to date on the issue has been on adults. Ultimately, estimating accurately the "costs of Columbine" will require the development of good data on the costs (both direct and indirect) of emotional dysfunction in children. It also will require an evaluation of the proportion of childhood dysfunction that continues on into adulthood. Finally, it will require an assessment of the difference between the national "bill" for dysfunction before and after the Columbine epidemic began, or before and after a particular manifestation of the epidemic first appeared. As I will argue in Part III below, engaging this effort will be important for any arguments like mine that would call for the investment of substantial new societal resources into programs to enhance the lives of American children.

oped, for example, from the direct and indirect costs of some of its most important manifestations.

Thus, it was reported in 1993 that depression cost the United States approximately $43.7 billion annually, accounted for primarily in lost earnings and efficiency, and in the costs of associated medical and other care.[68] In 1990, anxiety disorders were reported to have "cost the U.S. $46.6 billion [in direct and indirect losses] ... nearly one-third of the nation's total mental health bill [in that same year] of $148 billion."[69] Other studies estimate that "if addictive disorders and alcoholism are included" in the total figures, "the economic costs to society [of individuals with dysfunctions in these categories] exceeds $185 billion per year."[70] In all, "mental illness, including suicide, accounts for over 15% of the burden of disease ... [in] the United States. This is more than the disease burden of all cancers."[71]

Moreover, given "projections that show that with the aging of the world population [including the U.S. population] and the conquest of infectious diseases, psychiatric and neurological conditions could increase their share of the total ... disease burden by almost half."[72] This statistic likely already has increased and will continue to increase substantially in the future.* Finally, such increases are likely to be compounded by the effects of the separate continuous rise in childhood emotional dysfunction in these same categories.[73]

Violence and violent individuals also have an adverse impact on the national economy. Thus, it is useful to note the estimates that have been derived for some of the violent acts associated with Columbine. Much of the data relate to children in the inner cities who were affected by the Columbine problem before the rest of the society. However, as Garbarino explains, the etiology of their dys-

---

* Of course, this increase in the share of the total disease burden does not itself signify that there is more mental dysfunction. This is because the increased share is largely the result of medical advances in addressing purely physical disease. Despite this, there is ample evidence separately that mental dysfunction is claiming an increasing number of victims not only in the U.S. but also globally. In addition, even if it were the case that the absolute incidence of mental dysfunction remained the same, and the increased share of the total disease burden was uniquely the result of medical advances, my point that society needs to declare war on mental dysfunction as it has declared war on cancer and other organic illnesses remains the same.

function largely mirrors that which lies at the heart of the larger problem. It is because of this that he urges that we "move beyond the surface differences between the two groups of violent individuals—principally class and race—to see the profound emotional and psychological similarities that link [inner city and suburban children] together."[74]

For example, hospital fees and related expenses associated with gun violence are reported to cost the national economy approximately four billion dollars annually.[75] According to a comprehensive study undertaken by Philip Cook and Jens Ludwig, the total cost of gun violence—taking into consideration lost productivity and the emotional impacts on relatives and the larger society—is estimated to be much higher, approximately one-hundred billion dollars annually.[76] Relatedly, because dysfunctional children often become dysfunctional adolescents and adults who act out against members of their own families, it is significant to note the Inter-American Development Bank's estimates that domestic violence costs the United States somewhere in the range of $10 to $67 billion annually, depending upon what is included in the analysis.[77] Finally, the Minnesota Department of Health reports that rape victims cost the society approximately $127 billion on an annual basis. This figure does not include the costs of child sexual abuse, which that Department puts at $71 billion annually; nor does it include the costs of law enforcement, criminal prosecution, and incarceration associated with this conduct.[78]

Of course, these data describe estimated economic costs of childhood and adult dysfunction combined, and thus do not accurately describe the economic impact of dysfunction affecting only children. This is in part because "[n]ot all mental disorders identified in childhood and adolescence persist into adulthood, even though the prevalence of mental disorders in children and adolescents is about the same as that for adults (i.e., about 20 percent of each age population)."[79] Nor are they an accurate assessment of "costs of Columbine" alone, since childhood dysfunction has persisted throughout history, albeit to varying degrees depending upon the children's circumstances.

There are three important considerations, however, that justify reliance on these numbers to describe the impact of the Columbine epidemic. First, despite the fact that some children "grow out of" their early dysfunctions, more often than not dysfunctional children become dysfunctional adults unless they die prematurely; the seeds of adult dysfunction are often if not always planted in childhood.* Second, given this relationship, the number of dysfunctional adults is likely to increase (dramatically) from the base numbers that I have set out above, in direct proportion to the increase in the number of dysfunctional children. This is especially true since I have only sampled the dysfunctions that characterize Columbine, and since researchers have yet to assess the full costs of childhood emotional disease. Third, the dramatic increases in the number of dysfunctional children—from one-hundred to seven-hundred percent, for example, depending upon the manifestation used—suggest that current economic data already reflect the epidemic to a great extent. For these reasons, it is defensible to suggest that the "costs of Columbine" are likely to be in the hundreds of billions of dollars annually.

THE CULTURAL COSTS OF COLUMBINE

Culturally, its costs are equally significant. As the Chief Justice of the United States Supreme Court, William Rehnquist, has suggested,

> [f]ew could doubt that the most valuable resource of a self-governing society is its population of children who will one day become adults and themselves assume the responsibility of self-governance. "A democratic society rests, for its continuance, upon the healthy, well-rounded growth of young people into full maturity as citizens, with all that implies." Thus, "the whole community" has an interest "that children be both safeguarded from abuses and given opportunities for growth into free and independent well-developed ... citizens."[80]

To the extent that such large numbers of dysfunctional children have entered and continue to enter adulthood, where they are ex-

---

* Recall that I am not describing normally troubled adolescents who in the main have tended to overcome their troubles to become functioning adults. Rather, I am describing children who are clinically dysfunctional in the ways that this diagnosis is meant by the psychiatrists and psychologists who work with them.

pected to begin to contribute directly and indirectly to the well-being of the society, the eventual impact on our country will be devastating.[81] This much was confirmed by developmental experts in earlier stages of the Columbine epidemic, indeed "[a]s early as 1989," when the Carnegie Council on Adolescent Development issued its report *Turning Points: Preparing American Youth for the Twenty-first Century*.[82] That report warned that "'by age 15, substantial numbers of American youth are at risk of reaching adulthood unable to meet adequately the requirements of the workplace, the commitments of relationships in families and with friends, and the responsibilities of participation in a democratic society.'"[83] (I assume that, in general, individuals will continue to create families, and that this will not be the issue.) Thus, the conclusion is inescapable that "our most cherished values, moral and cultural,"[84] as well as "the future welfare of the commonwealth,"[85] all are in jeopardy. This will be true so long as, in the words of the Supreme Court, the family is "the institution by which 'we inculcate and pass down'"[86] these values and ensure that future against "the forces that make for social disorder and civic decay."[87]

Finally, it also is basic that the manner in which a civilization cares for its children (and more generally for its innocent or most vulnerable members) reflects its moral stature. As Marian Wright Edelman described, it is a "measure of [its] success."[88] Such sentiments are not confined to those who advocate for children. Indeed, mainstream religious and political literature is replete with such references. For example, as Edelman has noted, at the turn of the century, the theologian G. Campbell Morgan wrote that "[i]f the child is safe everyone is safe."[89] And Winston Churchill later added that "[t]here is no finer investment for any country than putting milk into babies."[90] Ultimately, societies that conscientiously care for their children given their means are perceived by history and even contemporary comparisons to be the most ethical. On the other hand, Edelman is absolutely correct that societies that are relatively wealthy but that prefer to sacrifice the children to other (adult) values tend to be viewed as "spiritually impoverished," "morally lost," and "ethically confused."[91] To the extent that the United States has chosen *consciously* to bear these labels, it has and will continue to suffer the indictments of those in this country and in the international community who would view the nation's success most holistically. It is no defense to such an indictment that we sacrifice our children because, on balance and weighed against other important objectives and ideals, their welfare is somewhat less significant; indeed, this calculus is simply further proof of the nation's moral, ethical, and spiritual fall, and of its ultimate folly.

Given the circumstances that I have just described, Columbine begs for a meaningful explanation of its ultimate or original causes. As one of the FBI investigators of the events in Littleton, Colorado, opined, "'I think I know why they did it,' ... 'It was because they were so filled with hate.' ... 'But the real question is why they had so much hate inside them.'"[92] Unless this "real question" is answered, both with respect to the immediate tragedy and the larger crisis of which it is merely one manifestation, no viable solution is possible. Any proposals that address only its most proximate or superficial causes will only delay a viable remedy, and, in the interim, mask the true nature of the problem.* Thus, the following chapters review the cultural revolutions that in the past three decades have transformed the lives of our children, and the developmental significance of these changes. In order of importance, the chapters explore the novel parenting experiment that has characterized the last twenty-to-thirty years of American history, and that for the first time has separated large numbers of children, including infants, from their mothers and other consistently caring

---

* Child development specialists are clear that "[u]nderstanding [the social and environmental context of a child's development] requires a consideration of both proximal (close-by) and distal (further-removed) events, as well as those that impinge directly on the child in a particular situation at a particular time." Mash and Wolfe at 52. Steven Tisch, a movie producer, made the most of precisely this point in the aftermath of the Columbine massacre when he cautioned the public and policy-makers to look beyond its proximate causes: "It's not just movies. Lots of other wires have to short before a kid goes out and does something like this. It's a piece of a much bigger, more complex puzzle." Richard Corliss, "Bang, You're Dead: Revenge fantasies are proliferating in movies and on TV. But should they be blamed for Littleton?" Time, May 3, 1999, at 50. Id. Although clearly correct, Tisch's statement was also clearly self-serving. Indeed, Tisch and other media advocates used the inherent complexity of the Columbine problem as an argument against regulating their industry.

adults; the development of a virtual-reality in the media, in games technology, and on the Internet, that is often extraordinarily violent and anti-social, and that is used by many as a "babysitter" for children; and a real-life toxic environment that thrives today in communities and schools across the country, both within and outside of the inner-cities, that is characterized by anti-social and sometimes violent forces.

CHAPTER THREE

THE GENETICS OF VIOLENCE
AND DEPRESSION

As a threshold matter, it is critical to dispel the notion, prominent in the aftermath of the Columbine tragedy, that dysfunctional children like Harris and Klebold were the products of genetic propensities rather than environmental adversity. Quite a lot of research has been done on this subject, using both traditional (Mendellian) genetic analyses and modern (molecular) genomics technology. While it continues to be true in general that "surprisingly little is known on the role of genetic factors in the causation" of "crime and on childhood disorders of conduct,"[1] both kinds of research have revealed the existence in some subjects of a genetic predisposition to negative affect or emotional dysfunction.[2]

Specifically, "[g]enetic factors have been implicated in a number of childhood disorders, such as autistic disorder, ADHD, conduct disorder, mood disorders, and schizophrenia."[3] And "[g]enetic influences play a role in forming children's basic temperaments as well, influencing, for example, the degree of behavioral inhibition and emotion regulation children may show."[4] Analogous studies also have demonstrated the likelihood that in some families there is a genetic predisposition to certain forms of anti-social conduct.[5] And, using modern genetics technology, it is known that mice that are engineered to lack certain genes—particularly those that regulate serotonin, the neurochemical that is principally responsible for, or linked to emotional response—are predisposed to aggression, and that humans with analogous serotonergic (mal)function also may be prone to exhibiting negative affect, including *both* depression *and* aggression.*

---

* Mouse models are particularly useful analytic tools for research on humans because they are in relevant respects biologically compatible organisms. See Collins F.S., Patrinos A., Chakravarti A., Gesteland R., Walters L., New Goals for the U.S. Human Genome Project: 1998–2003, Science 282(5389):682–9, Oct. 23, 1998. Indeed, "[t]he mouse is currently the best mammalian model for studies of a broad array of biomedical research ques-

Thus, based upon these studies and others along the same lines, there always is the possibility that a particular individual has a genetic predisposition (rather than one that is uniquely driven by environmental conditions) to the sorts of disorders that characterize the Columbine epidemic. However, the question remains as it was framed in the post-Columbine discussions about Eric Harris, whether the epidemic itself can in any substantial sense be attributed to genetics, making unnecessary any need for further discussion of the conditions in which Americans nurture and raise their children.* The clear answer based upon current science is "no."

This is primarily because, while geneticists who study the issue apparently are "on the track" of a genetic link to aggression in humans, the record nevertheless is clear that whatever its characteristics, such a link will not be fully deterministic since all of human behavior is likely to be multifactorial.[6] That is, research shows that human behavior, including aggression and depression, is complex, accounted for by a necessary combination of nature and nurture: "[V]iolence is [not simply] in the genes, or murder in the folds of the brain's frontal lobes."[7] For example, the literature is relatively clear that individuals with a genetic predisposition to psychopathology "carry a greater risk for antisocial behaviour" particularly when as children they are exposed to "environmental hazards" including "low social status" and "parenting breakdown."[8] Interestingly, with respect to "parenting breakdown," it has been noted that "early separation from a parent was a risk factor for boys from average-or high-income families but a protective factor for those from low-income families."[9]

Many scientists in the field have noted the "now substantial evidence for genotype-environment interactions."[10] This is an impor-

---

tions. The complete mouse genome sequence will be a crucial tool for interpreting the human genome sequence, because it will highlight functional features that are conserved, including noncoding regulatory sequences as well as coding sequences." Id. This is because "mice and humans have many homologous genes mapped to homologous chromosome regions." Cecilee Price-Huish, "Born to Kill? 'Aggression Genes' and Their Potential Impact on Sentencing and the Criminal Justice System," 50 S.M.U. L. Rev. 603 (1997). Serotonin itself is known as a "mood manager" among other things.

  * Eric Harris was reported to have been taking anti-depressants or to have had them prescribed in the period preceding April 20, 1999.

tant reason why "not every child with access to guns becomes an Eric Harris or a Dylan Klebold, and why not every child who feels ostracized, or who embraces the Goth esthetic, goes on a murderous rampage."[11] Using the work of Debra Niehoff, author of the book *The Biology of Violence*, Sharon Begley provided a useful example of the ways in which nurture can tilt the scales one way or another:

> A baby who is unreactive to hugs and smiles can be left to go her own natural, antisocial way if frustrated parents become exasperated, withdrawn, neglectful or enraged. Or that child can be pushed back toward the land of the feeling by parents who never give up trying to engage and stimulate and form a loving bond with her. The different responses of parents produce different brains, and thus behaviors.[12]

Some in the field have characterized this genetic effect as creating a "sensitivity to the environment," explaining further that "individuals at a genetic risk are more likely than individuals not at a genetic risk to react maladaptively to psychosocial stresses."[13] Concomitantly, as the previous discussion shows, genes likely play a role in explaining why "many kids drink [from the 'venomous cultur[al]'] waters without turning into mass murderers."[14] Thus, at most, genetics may permit us to identify a certain risk or probability of future dysfunction, which generally will be "activated" only in the context of certain external conditions.

Second, and perhaps more importantly, developmental experts note that "very few specific genetic causes have been isolated or identified as the underlying cause of child psychopathology."[15] Since much of the relevant genetics research is ongoing and based upon new technology, this conclusion could change, so that over time we may come to understand that genes in fact do play a greater role. It may turn out, for example, that genetic predispositions to negative affect comprise a larger percentage of a given population than contemporary experts imagine based upon previously and currently available research tools.

However, what is critical here is that even this would not begin to explain the sheer number of individual children who are caught up in the Columbine epidemic, simply because genetic predispositions tend to manifest themselves in the population over a long period of time, and they generally are not confined by political or cultural boundaries.[16] For example, one researcher on the biology of violence notes "that [the massive and] sudden rise [in crime in most western countries since the middle of the twentieth-century] is most unlikely to be due to genetic factors directly, if only because the genetic pool cannot change quickly enough to account for a rise of that speed and degree."[17] He suggests further that "genetic factors are [also] most unlikely to account for the fact that the murder rate in young people today is over 10 times higher in the USA than in the UK."[18] One reporter put this point most poignantly in the aftermath of the Columbine tragedy: "It isn't the brains kids are born with that has changed in half a generation."[19] And thus, with what are likely to be a few exceptional individuals aside, we are required to explore the developmental and environmental causes of Columbine.

CHAPTER FOUR

THE DEVELOPMENTAL SIGNIFICANCE OF PARENTING

The most important of these developmental causes is the rise of inadequate parenting during the relevant period—a direct result of mothers entering the workforce and skyrocketing divorce rates—*and* the concurrent failure of the society as a whole to develop and implement an alternative child-rearing or care-giving model that adequately substitutes for parents. While developmental experts view these failures to be principal causal contributors to childhood dysfunction, the tendency of the society generally has been to reject or discount this explanation, on feminist or political grounds, on the assumption that children are resilient,[1] and because the circumstances do not amount to the sorts of abuse and neglect traditionally thought to cause serious or severe emotional dysfunction.

Despite this tendency towards denial, the general consensus among child development experts is clear that while emotional dysfunction usually has a complex and multifactorial etiology,[2] "the roots of the most serious and persistent forms of antisocial behaviour [are known to] lie in early childhood,"[3] and more specifically, in a childhood lacking in adequate parental care.* With re-

---

* The dispute about what constitutes adequate "parental" care is complicated by the fact that this it is often characterized as "maternal" care, particularly in the earlier years of a child's life. There is today broad agreement among developmental experts that appropriate care in many respects can be provided both by mothers and fathers, and also by suitable alternative caregivers. See Elizabeth S. Scott, "Pluralism, Parental Preference and Child Custody," 80 Cal. L. Rev. 615 (1992) (describing the literature that "emphasizes the importance of the mother-child relationship to the child's healthy development," and that which "suggest[s] that the role of fathers in their children's lives has been undervalued and that attachment theory exaggerates the uniqueness and exclusiveness of the primary caretaker-child bond.") However, this consensus position has not managed to squelch the original discussion (which continues to thrive particularly among neurobiologists) about the special role that human mothers may play in the lives of

43

spect to children who are beyond the "tender years" of emotional and neurological development—now pegged at approximately birth to three years—experts generally agree that, while multiple forces clearly influence children's emotional health, the fact of inadequate or dysfunctional parenting continues to dominate the equation. Thus, the literature and inevitable extrapolations from the literature reveal the inherent fallacy of assumptions about children's resiliency in the face of their unfulfilled emotional needs, and about the nature and the measure of the neglect that can cause serious dysfunction.

CHILDREN FROM BIRTH-TO-THREE

For many people, it is likely intuitive that children (and particularly young children who are unable to delay their gratification) need constant love and attention to secure an emotionally healthy present and future.[4] Margaret Talbot has noted, for example, that "[i]t might seem self-evident that human babies, notoriously help-

---

their babies. See, e.g., Myron A. Hofer, M.D., "On the Nature and Consequences of Early Loss," 58(6) Psychosomatic Medicine 570–581 (November/December 1996) (results of studies on maternal deprivation show "a number of discrete sensorimotor, thermal, and nutrient-based events that have unexpected long-term regulatory effects on specific components of infant physiology and behavior"); K.J. Anand and F.M. Scalzo, "Can Adverse Neonatal Experiences Alter Brain Development and Subsequent Behavior?" 77(2) Biology of the Neonate 69–82 (Feb. 2000) ("Self destructive behavior in current society promotes a search for physiobiological factors underlying this epidemic.... We propose that lack of N-methyl-D-aspartate (NMDA) receptor activity from maternal separation and sensory isolation leads to increased apoptosis in multiple areas of the immature brain"); C.M. Kuhn and S.M. Schanberg, "Responses to Maternal Separation: Mechanisms and Mediators," 16(3–4) International Journal of Developmental Neuroscience 261–70 (Jun.–Jul. 1998) ("Consequences of disrupting mother-infant interactions range from marked suppression of certain neuroendocrine and physiological systems after short periods of maternal deprivation to retardation of growth and behavioral development after chronic periods.") It remains to be seen whether the results of these biological studies will generate a more integrated consensus among the relevant experts.

less creatures that they are, need mother love or something much like it in order to thrive and develop emotionally and cognitively."[5] Whatever the evidentiary value of this intuition—for example, some might charge that it focuses inappropriately on a social rather than a biological (or true) construct of the parent-child relationship—its substance is confirmed by the work of developmental experts, including psychologists, psychiatrists, and neurobiologists, whose conclusions are backed by clinical research.[6] Specifically, such research shows that "[c]hildren's successful adaptation, and perhaps their very survival, depend on [the existence and sufficiency of care-giving] relationships."[7] And, while the nature of those relationships are important throughout childhood, "[e]arly experiences seem to be especially powerful" in the etiology of emotional disease.[8]

Thus, Eric Mash and David Wolfe explain that

[i]nfants and children are keenly attuned to the cues they receive from care-givers, and they are especially sensitive to signs of indifference. Responsive, sensitive parents inspire trust in their children, giving rise to attachment. Insensitive or withdrawn parents, on the other hand, can foster insecure attachments that affect future relationship formation and regulation in significant ways. Thus, a relationship, or attachment, with a parent or other care-giver is as essential to normal child development as learning to walk and talk. If the relationship with the attachment figure has been consistent and reliable, children are able to regulate their emotions and cope with stress more effectively. Conversely, lack of such a relationship creates the breeding ground for a number of stress-related disorders.[9]

Indeed, "the damage caused by early neglect—or even by physically adequate but emotionally indifferent care—can be deeply intractable, not the least because it may have neurological as well as psychological dimensions."[10]* In this regard, biologist Michael

---

* For example, Margaret Talbot discusses the work of Harry Chugani, "a neurologist at the Children's Hospital of Michigan," who has "compar[ed] PET scans of the brains of eight apparently healthy Romanian children adopted by Americans with a control group of children reared in normal family settings. Although the results [at the time of her writing were]

self physically, and his emotional and intellectual memory is not sufficiently matured to enable him to use thinking to hold on to the parent he has lost.[20]

Goldstein, Freud, and Solnit extrapolated from this and related findings (about children's need for continuity) that care-giving "[d]iscontinuities can evoke different responses at different ages as well as among children of the same age."[21] Infants, for example, have negative reactions, including "food refusals, digestive upsets, sleeping difficulties, crying, or withdrawal states ... even if [daily] care is divided between parent and baby-sitter," because "[s]uch moves bring with them changes in the way the infant is handled, fed, put to bed, and comforted.... The attachments of infants and toddlers are as upset by separations as they are promoted by the constant, unrationed, consistent presence and attention of a familiar adult."[22]

Ultimately, what this research shows is that if the child's care-giving experience provides her with a reasonable substitute for the attentive parent, the child will suffer the least; on the other hand, if her caregivers are "unresponsive and emotionally unavailable," the child will initially protest, "actively tr[ying] to recover his or her mother;" then despair as his or her "hopes ... fade" that his mother will return; and in the end, he or she will become detached, "as a defense against painful feelings ... [and will] seem to forget his or her mother so that when she comes for [the child, she or] he remains curiously uninterested in her and [depending upon the duration of her absence] may not even recognize her."[23] This last development is crucial, because "[w]hen ... children feel themselves abandoned by their parent, their distress leads to weakening their next attachments. Where continuity of such relationships is interrupted more than once ... the children's emotional attachments become increasingly shallow and indiscriminate. They tend to grow up as persons who lack sustained warmth in their relationships."[24]

Many if not most of the experts working in this field have traditionally seen this cause-and-effect relationship through the prism of what is known as "attachment theory."* Attachment theory "fo-

---

* Over the past century, researchers have developed several other theories to explain the particular prominence of parents, and especially mothers, in this calculus.[106] However, most if not all of these alternatives are re-

cuses on parental separation and disruption of an attachment bond as predisposing factors for depression" in children.[25] It holds that "[a] parent's consistent failure to meet the child's needs is associated with the development of an insecure attachment, a view of self as unworthy and unloved, and a view of others as threatening or undependable [all factors which] may place the child at risk" for future emotional dysfunction.[26]

Despite its predominance, however, attachment theory has important detractors. They appear to be primarily and in many instances appropriately concerned about what Diane Eyer—who is said to have "made a career of denouncing attachment theory and its more simplistic variants"—explains is "too much emphasis on the early relationship between mother and child … [which] allows society to abdicate responsibility for its role in shaping children."[27] However, in its contemporary iteration there is no question that attachment theory remains the most probabilistic explanation for disorders that originate in childhood, including especially depression and anti-social personality disorder.

Indeed, whatever their differences, child development experts generally agree with the theory's central tenet that "the lack of an emotional connection with a consistent caretaker can be deeply damaging," to the point of "'hav[ing] grave and far-reaching effects' on a child's 'character and so on the whole of his future

---

dundant of attachment theory in that they also focus on disruptions in the family, and the unavailability of the child's mother or parents.[107] Importantly, as Margaret Talbot explained in 1998, until that time the experts could do no more than theorize however they ultimately came out. Neurological research did not yet support attachment theory, and no one would dare publicly to perform the "diabolically perfect experiment" that would be necessary to prove or disprove its inherent truth.[108] For example, "[t]o test the effects of maternal and sensory deprivation on infants, you cannot take a population of newborns and confine them to cribs in a gloomy, ill-heated orphanage with a small, rotating staff of caretakers who might spend an average of 10 minutes a day talking to them or holding them." Talbot at 24. In addition to these "real-life" situations which can be observed and analyzed, however, and as I already have described, there also is ongoing physiological research that is designed to "prove" the theory or to get the "facts" through analyses of neurobiological changes that would be based on "maternal deprivation" and other parental neglect.

life.'"[28] Significantly, this contemporary iteration acknowledges that the attachment figure who provides the requisite "maternal care" need not necessarily be the child's mother, but any nurturing individual who is consistently available to the child, and thus with whom the child can bond. It acknowledges that a child may have a group of attachment figures, albeit that it is likely hierarchical.[29] And, it has increasingly begun to acknowledge that there is an intersection among genetics, neurological development, and the external environment that accounts for the different reactions of children to the same stressful conditions. The most crucial development from a purely evidentiary standpoint, however, has been the scientific validation of attachment theory that has resulted from current (and ongoing) research in the area of neurobiology, some of which I already have described.

CHILDREN BEYOND THE TENDER YEARS

Assuming that they are at least relatively well-adjusted, children who are older than three tend no longer to require the minute-to-minute care and attention from an attachment figure that is required by an infant or toddler. Nevertheless, while the parental role changes, children continue to need their parents to nurture and guide them, and to facilitate their relationships with others and the world outside of the home. This period is often divided by child development experts into three parts: early childhood, middle childhood, and adolescence.

Penelope Leach explains that "early childhood," or the "preschool period," spans the years from approximately three until approximately five years old, and it has "its own developmental agenda."[30] Specifically, "the vital education of early childhood is concerned with managing feelings, emotions and relationships."[31] It is in this period that the child gains (or not) "self-consciousness and therefore the beginnings of shame and pride, the capacity for empathy and the potential, at least, for altruism."[32] Leach explains that "[f]inding words for feelings and language, and a more or less reliable match in feelings for other people's words, takes many more hugs and yells, smiles and frowns, and all of early childhood."[33] And it requires that the adults who provide this nurturing and guidance must also supplement the developmental process "with richly varied and largely social play,"[34]* play which "stimulat[es] persistence and practic[e of] problem solving, provid[es] 'preliteracy exercise' and encourag[es] 'communication skills.'"[35] In large measure, this includes facilitating the beginnings of peer relationships. Parents who neglect these essential needs, either because they do not (or cannot) provide them personally, or because they do not (or cannot) provide them through appropriate day care programs or preschools, place their children at risk.[36] Moreover, parents who spend adequate physical time with children, but who are otherwise passive "babysitters," or parents who focus upon their children's intellectual or academic development to the exclusion of their emotional needs are equally culpable in this respect.[37]

"Middle childhood" follows "early childhood" and spans the years from about six until about nine years old.[38] It is this period that "meshes th[e] individual into his society."[39] Leach explains that "[w]hether the focus is on children's feelings, understanding or thoughts, their judgments, beliefs or reasoning, the beginning of middle childhood promises new maturity and a new desire to learn that is recognized in every culture."[40] And, "because children are, above all, social animals, they do all that learning within the context of social value systems and come to behave as others in their social group behave."[41]

Obviously, unless we can assume that children can develop positive or beneficial values on their own, this means that adults must mediate the children's behavior or enforce its comportment with such values. Thus, Leach writes that

> far from being [the] well-earned rest pause in parenting [that many believe it to be], these are the years that give parents vital opportunities to influence the children they have made toward being the kind of people they want them to be.... Children's identification with parents or parent figures is the basis of all social bonds and at least as important in middle childhood as it was early on. The relationship that was the basis for the child's

---

* Leach explains that "it was recognition of the difficulty of providing for play in small families and urban homes that inspired the first preschool play groups." Id.

development of socialized behavior now becomes the basis for
her dawning social morality, and the simple guidelines—such as
"do as you would be done by"—that were useful in early childhood are no longer adequate.[42]

Because of this, Leach is concerned that in contemporary society,
"those opportunities are not being fully exploited."[43] She surmises
that this is likely because "they [are] not recognized," or "they are
personally demanding and difficult," or "that, unlike the urgent demands of the baby or toddler, or the potentially dangerous excesses
of the adolescent, the latency child's socio-intellectual demands
can be ignored, in favor of her 'busyness' with skills and school and
peers."[44] In any event, she explains that when parents abandon
their responsibility to inculcate the children with a positive, values-
laden morality—because they are too busy, because it is too difficult, or because it is not "politically correct" to identify a right and
a wrong—they in fact are abandoning their children to others who
will fill the vacuum: "If parents withhold deliberate input, children
will be exposed both to untempered influences from the outside
world and to *unintended* influences from their parents."[45] If these
"others"—peers, teachers, the media—are inadequate to the task,
then the children are left without those beneficial values that are
critical to emotional health and successful integration into the
larger society.

The adolescent period continues to be characterized by the
process of engaging relationships, but here the emphasis clearly is
on relationships with those outside of the home: peers and the external culture. The period also is characterized by increasing self-
awareness. This process is rendered in many instances exceedingly
complicated by the increases in hormone activity and sexual
awareness that also characterize this developmental phase. The
ability of a child to negotiate it successfully depends to a large extent upon whether he or she is guided and supported by understanding, caring adults who function as positive role models: If
this is the case, the child is likely to be relatively healthy emotionally. On the other hand, if this phase and the emotional and physical turmoil that accompanies it are ignored or exacerbated by disengaged and absent adults, the child is at significant risk of
mild-to-severe emotional dysfunction.

John Rosemond describes the early adolescent period as one of "great psychological vulnerability" where "[t]he young person's self-concept is ambiguous, and therefore fragile."[46] In particular,

[His] mind, after ten years of grappling with the logic of concrete, measurable relationships, is beginning to grasp the abstract, the hypothetical ... Add an overdose of hormones, put the mixture under ever-increasing peer pressure, and you've got a guaranteed two or three years of [relative chaos.] ... [These] years are a time of transition ... [which] involv[e] the whole child and dramatically alter[] his definition of himself and his world.... Changes in the structure and chemistry of the child's body and corresponding upheavals in his emotional nature bring him face to face with his emergent sexuality.... [and his] brain begins to process and organize information in a radically different manner, adding new dimensions to his perception of the world and further complicating his view of himself.[47]

The process of individualization that takes place in this period is especially significant from an emotional standpoint:

[Children at this age] tend to be introspective; that is, they think a lot about themselves, sometimes to the point of obsessiveness. They reflect upon and evaluate their own behavior, feelings, and even their own thoughts. This ability to look within brings into clearer focus not just the person-that-is, but also the person-that-could-be–the *ideal self.* Comparisons between the real (present) and ideal self generate either aspiration or anxiety, depending upon factors which include how much discrepancy there is between the two and whether the preadolescent has basically positive or negative self-regard.[48]

Because the culture today is saturated with media images of a certain and usually unattainable version of aesthetic and behavioral perfection, depending upon the individual child, this process of comparison may be exceedingly difficult.

Perhaps most important, it is "[d]uring this critical period [that] the child transfers most of his security needs from parents to peers. The peer group bridges childhood (when the child relied on his parents) and adulthood (when the healthy individual is primarily self-reliant); it is a social laboratory where rules and roles can be

Despite this consensus position, the debate goes on as to whether children are better off if their parents stay together or get divorced.[63] Note, however, that to the extent there is such a debate, it is premised upon the assumption that the parents in any event would be engaged in a dysfunctional relationship of their own; there is no sense in this context that parents might choose to "stay together for the kids" and at the same time patch up their differences sufficiently so that their own relationship was a healthy one of sorts.[64] In other words, the argument for divorce does not claim that the children of divorce do not suffer, and it is premised exclusively on the relative happiness of the parents as individuals who do not find their principal fulfillment in the happiness of their children.

THE ABSENCE OF ADEQUATE PARENTING
IN THE LIVES OF AMERICAN CHILDREN

Set against this basic developmental literature is the stark reality that, because of the massive exodus of *both* poor (or "welfare") *and* wealthier mothers from the home and into the workplace, an extraordinary number of American children in the past thirty years have lost their connection with their traditional caregiver. Moreover, the society that has fostered or at least accepted this revolution in child-rearing practice has failed appropriately to compensate for their historically novel absence from the lives of children: Fathers have not, in general, stepped in to "do their share" of the child-rearing; to the contrary, they have either stayed at work or, courtesy of liberalized sexual mores and divorce laws, they simply have left their children (emotionally if not financially) and moved on. Women have not, in general, opted for or been permitted as an institutional matter to carve out positions that would enable them to continue "mothering" their children when they are not in school. And, adequate alternative care-giving models either have not been developed, or have failed because Americans (again in general) have not been committed to the extent necessary to make them work. Ultimately, these factors are the most important and fundamental cause of the Columbine problem.

It is indisputable that in the United States in the last two-to-three decades "we have witnessed the massive movement of women and young mothers into paid employment," and that this movement has wrecked havoc on children's traditional childcare arrangements.* For example, "[i]n 1995, 64 percent of U.S. married mothers with a preschool child were in the workforce, compared with 30 percent in 1970."[65] The numbers for single mothers, who today account for approximately 50 to 65 percent of all mothers, are most likely much higher. Relatedly, in 1996, "half of mothers [were] back at work by 6 months after the child's birth."[66] As a result, in the same period, "60 percent of children aged 1 to 5 years, or 13 million children, were in nonparental child care or early education programs."[67] The numbers are much higher for older children: "In 1995, of the 36 million children in the United States between the ages of 5 and 14, about two-thirds lived in families with [two] working parents."[68†] Given the comparative data on childhood dysfunction that I described in the previous section, it is especially interesting that while "labor force participation in developed countries such as Sweden is very high, few mothers with infants are actually working."[69] In the end, the result of these

---

* Suzanne Helbrun explains that the "[c]ommodification of goods previously produced at home and the invention of home appliances, along with the declining birthrates and increasing levels of education, have made it increasingly expensive for women to stay at home. Given the reduced demands of housework, they can manage a greater contribution to family income and [economic] well-being through paid work." Helbrun at 8. See also Tamar Lewin, "It's Not Just for Mothers Anymore," The New York Times, May 13, 2001, at 14 (noting that "[i]n the 1960s when women began pouring into the work force, the changes in family life were profound. By 1990, with 70 percent of the nation's children living in households where every parent was in the labor force, millions of families were groping for child care that could accommodate overtime or night shifts—or work schedules that could bend for teacher conferences, sick children, school holidays, or ailing grandparents.")

† Another study, conducted in 1997, broke the numbers down this way: 32 percent of children under 5 were in "center-based care"; 16 percent were placed with "non-relatives"; 23 percent were placed with "relatives"; 6 percent were placed with "nannies/babysitters"; and 24 percent stayed with "parents." Susan H. Greenberg and Karen Springen, "Back to Day Care," Newsweek, Oct. 16, 2000, at 62.

American trends is that "children in large numbers are deserted to a destiny of living with an overburdened mother, inadequate financial support, and lack of parental attention."[70]

The concurrent epidemic of divorce and non-marital births in the United States in this same period has had a particularly significant impact on these statistics. And while divorce rates have declined slightly since the 1980s, because the rates of "breakups more than doubled between the 1960s and the late 1970s," approximately fifty percent of all marriages continue to end in divorce.* Suzanne Helburn explains, based upon data collected more than ten years ago, that "[r]ising divorce rates and the increasing percentage of female-headed households make more families dependent upon the mother's earnings; 21 percent of all children lived in these families in 1988, compared to only 8 percent in 1960."[71] The direct result of this is that today, about half of American children live in a single-parent family at some point or during the entirety of their childhoods, and on average, approximately thirty percent of American children under eighteen are "living with only one parent" who is likely to be working full time.[72] Significantly, this is the case whether the children's primary caretakers are their mothers or fathers, since divorce increases rather than decreases the likelihood that both parents regardless of their custodial status will enter the workforce.

Having said this, it is important to emphasize that whatever the evidence is with respect to children's biological need for their mothers, the fact remains that culturally, mothers are more likely to raise and spend time with their children than fathers are. Moreover, there also is no question that men generally have not heeded the progressive call to involve themselves as women do in the lives of their children; nor has the society acted to facilitate such involvement. Again, to understand the tremendous numbers of American children today who live without a father in their lives, these perennial facts must be coupled with the relatively new (in

---

* Indeed, "[a]ccording to the National Center for Health Statistics, parents are getting divorced at twice the rate they did twenty years ago, and more children than ever are involved in marital dissolution: 1.18 million in 1979 as compared to 562,000 in 1963." Neil Postman, The Disappearance of Childhood at 138 (1994).

historical terms) facts of a divorce rate that rests at fifty percent, and an out-of-wedlock birth rate that rests at sixty percent in the inner cities and twenty-eight percent nationwide.[73] The result is that approximately 31 percent of children in the United States today live either with their mothers alone, their fathers alone, or with neither parent.[74] Moreover, despite a recent surge in single-parent households headed by fathers, a full 23 percent of non-marital homes (out of that 31 percent) are headed by single mothers.* Indeed, "only a small percentage of divorced and unmarried fathers [even] provide any regular child support."[75] Translated into gross figures, these percentages mean that approximately "14.5

---

* The Census Bureau reports that "in 1998, sixty-eight percent of children under eighteen lived with both parents, twenty-three percent lived with mother only, four percent lived with father only, and four percent lived with neither parent." Jacoby, Sullivan, and Warren at 375; see also Laura W. Morgan, "The Federalization of Child Support, A Shift in the Ruling Paradigm: Child Support as Outside the Contours of 'Family Law,'" 16 J. Am. Acad. Matrim. Law 195, 209 (1999). The number of female-headed households may be even higher than that which is reflected in the Census report. See Patrick McKinley Brennan, "Of Marriage and Monks, Community and Dialogue," 48 Emory Law Journal 689, 714 (Spring, 1999) (providing that "[i]n 1970, 13 percent of all households were headed by single mothers; today, the number stands at more than 30 percent.") Finally, "the proportion of female headed households (both family and non-family households) is increasing slowly over time." Bruce L. Dixon and Daniel M. Settlage, "Consumer Bankrupcy Filings in the U.S. and Arkansas: Growth Rates and Possible Causes," 1998 Ark. L. Notes 13, 17 (1998). According to these authors, "[i]n 1980 the figure was 26.2 percent of households and in 1996, the last year for which such data were available, the figure was 29.3 percent with 1994 having the highest percentage, 29.4 percent, over the 1980–1996 span." Id. For a discussion of the surge in households headed by single-fathers, see Dan Chapman and Maurice Tamman, "More single dads are kids' primary parent," The Atlanta Journal and Constitution, May 18, 2001, at A1 (noting that "[t]he number of U.S. households headed by single fathers with kids under 18 increased a whopping 62 percent during the 1990s;" that "[s]ingle men with kids headed 2.2 million households," and that "[t]en years earlier, only 1.4 million houses were male-run"); Marsha Ginsburg, "More U.S. fathers raising families by themselves; Single dads in 1 of 45 households," The San Francisco Chronicle, May 18, 2001 (providing these same statistics from the U.S. census and noting that today—even with this surge—only one in forty five households is run by a single father).

million children under the age of eighteen live in a female-headed family, almost triple the number in 1960; 65 percent of absent fathers contribute no child support or alimony; [and] only 5.5 percent of absent fathers contribute as much as $5,000 per year."[76] And in cases where mothers and fathers share formal custody after a divorce, "[t]he basic pattern of children residing with their mothers and visiting periodically with their fathers remains the rule."[77] According to one estimate, "[c]ustodial mothers head households for more than 90 percent of the children of divorce."[78]

It is perhaps not surprising that among the many statistics I have described in this book, these on the involvement of fathers in the lives of their children are not in any respect exclusive to the United States. For example, a 1994 United Nations report explains that among several trends relating to the family is the "increasing percentage of female-headed households"; this at the same time that "the balance of financial responsibilities for family support [shifts] onto the shoulders of women as their share of the labor market increases and the share of men decreases."[79] And generally around the world, including in the United States, "women's lives [continue to be] characterized primarily by motherhood, [while] men's lives are characterized largely without reference to fatherhood."[80] *

None of this means of course, that the United States and societies around the world should abandon the project that is developing boys into men who will be present and participating fathers in their children's lives. Indeed, as I suggest below, this project is critical for women and for children, as well as for the men who do and

---

* Ted Peters supports this proposition by citing to "[a]n ethnographic look at 186 different societies [which] reveals that in only 2 percent of societies do fathers have 'regular close relationships' with their babies, and in only 5 percent of societies do they have such close relationships with their toddlers during early childhood." Peters at 15. Social construction and theories about patriarchy in particular have provided most of the popular explanations for this ubiquitous cross cultural dynamic. Peters and others also have explored its biological basis. See id. at 19–21 (exploring the problem using evolutionary biology); Jared Diamond, Why is Sex Fun? The Evolution of Human Sexuality (Basic Books, New York, 1997) (same); Timothy H. Goldsmith, The Biological Roots of Human Nature, Forging Links Between Evolution and Behavior (Oxford University Press, New York, 1991) (same).

who will find their own lives enriched by such presence and partic-ipation. Nevertheless, it would be naive to believe that this is a short-term endeavor. The fight to turn even most men around is against centuries of socialization—and perhaps even biological in-fluences—to the contrary. As I argue below, in the meantime, it is self-destructive for the society to put women to work (for whatever reason) without finding an adequate replacement for their role in the lives of the children.

This is clear also from the developmental literature, which em-phasizes that equal to the impact of absent parenting in a child's life is that which fills in the void. This literature shows that if the parental replacement is a positive force in the child's life, the effects of parental deprivation will not be so significant. On the other hand, if the replacement is inadequate in the respects that I have just described, the resulting deprivation will have an enhanced toxic effect. Thus, the quality of alternative caregivers, compan-ions, and environments is critical.

Unfortunately, the news on this front is almost uniformly nega-tive as well: The prevalence of mothers in the work force, coupled with the dearth of good child care options has created "a silent, voiceless crisis,"[81] where too often, "no one is left to care fully for the children."[82] Helburn explains that the crisis is "silent" because "[t]hree-, 4-, and 5-year-old children cannot speak for themselves. Low-and middle-income children and mothers, those most di-rectly affected, have little economic or political power."[83] Addition-ally, she suggests that "[t]he mundane work of raising children is a task that every society has managed one way or another. The crisis does not present an immediate danger to our way of life or our na-tional security. It is not dramatic enough to occupy much space in the news."[84]

While Helburn may be correct in certain respects, Columbine and the extraordinary statistics on childhood suicide and related dysfunction are in fact dramatic evidence that this should be top of the news. Indeed, according to Sheila Kamerman, the circumstances in this country are distinguished from those in "[a]ll other major in-dustrialized countries ... [that] manage to afford decent family pro-grams."[85] Specifically, "European family-care programs ... 'put our country to shame'" with respect to the accommodations—including especially the duration of paid parental leave and alternative child

Not surprisingly, one of the most severe effects of day-care appears to be on the all-important parent-child relationship itself. Thus, "[f]ederally funded research indicates that mother-child interaction is 'less harmonious' when children spend more than 10 hours a week in day care."[99] Specifically, "mothers whose children receive extensive day care 'are a little less sensitive in the care they provide, and even slightly more negative.' By the age of 3 ... 'children seemed to be less positively engaged when interacting with their parents.'"[100] According to the researcher responsible for these findings, the cause of this disconnection is that

> [i]t simply takes time to get to know your child well.... Parents come home, they're tired, and it goes on day in and day out— and all of a sudden you have, not quite two ships passing in the night, but the capacity to synchronize and coordinate is reduced because of these other stresses and strains.[101]

As Goldstein, Freud, and Solnit reported years ago, such synchrony and coordination are crucial to the development of a healthy emotional profile, both in terms of the child's sense of time, and his need for physical and emotional attention.

At the same time, "families [today] make less use of arrangements for the out-of-school time of school-aged children."[102] For example,

> [i]n 1991, of the 36 million children in the United States between the ages of 5 and 14, about two-thirds [approximately 23,800,000 children] lived in families with working parents, but fewer than 2 million were enrolled in formal before or after-school programs. About a third [or approximately 13 million] were latchkey children.[103]

Thus, while a substantial number of American children continue to be cared for either in their own homes or in the homes of rela-

---

Dangerous Experiment in Child Rearing?" (noting the results of some studies that "children '... who had spent more time in day care suffered proportionately greater ill effects, regardless of the quality of day care;' the most extreme case being the kibbutz-raised children of Israel '... who received 24-hour day care, [and who] were at significantly greater risk of developing schizophrenia and other serious mental disorders.'")

tives, many are either in critically deficient day care programs, or are not in the care of any adult at all for an important part of most of their days. There are recent signs, particularly since the events at Columbine High School, that some American parents (both mothers and fathers) have begun again to arrange their schedules to spend slightly more time with their children.[104]* There also are

---

* A study conducted by the University of Michigan's Institute for Social Research revealed that in 1981, mothers in marital households spent an average of 21 hours each week with their children, but that today, they spend an average of 31 hours a week with their children. The same study showed that in 1981, fathers spent an average of 19 hours each week with their children, and today, they are with their children for an average of 23 hours a week. Transcript at 1–2. The rate for single mothers has not changed: In 1981 and today, they spend an average of 21 hours a week with their children, approximately the same amount of time that fathers in marital households spend with theirs. Id. at 4–5. The study also revealed that the extra hours that parents in marital households spend with their children often involve driving "highly scheduled kids ... to and from all those activities." Id. at 2. Counted as part of these extra hours was time spent by the child playing video games while the parent was otherwise occupied in another room. Id. at 2.

Family income, both in the abstract and as a proxy for race, may or may not influence the amount of time parents spend with their children; the evidence in this category is literally all over the place. For example, there is good evidence that "hispanic" fathers spend more time with their children than parents in other racial or ethnic categories, despite that they also tend to make less money. Id. at 16–19. Also, lower income parents may have less money to spend on babysitters and adult activities, and thus may spend more time with their children. Id. On the other hand, there is evidence that low-income parents spend less time with their children because they work more hours. Id. The same results sometimes are found for high income families where both parents work. Id.

Finally, while many parents today (particularly in higher income categories) feel that the culture has become child-centered and that as a result, they are "hyper-parenting"—that is, freeing up time and spending all of that free time arranging for their children's activities—the fact is that this time is likely to be unhealthy for both parents and children in general. See id. at 7–8 (noting that hyper-parenting generally involves time-shifting, which makes the parent tired and not necessarily available psychologically to their child); see also Barbara Kantrowitz and Pat Wingert, "The Parent Trap," Newsweek, Jan. 29, 2001, at 49–53 (exploring the problem of "hyper-parenting," noting that it is largely a phenomenon of that demographic seg-

signs that in some demographic groups, women who are mothers have begun to reconsider the merits of full-time employment, particularly when their children are very young and during adolescence. However, these trends are not dramatic, and most important, they apply uniquely to individuals in two-parent households who can manage or afford the flexibility that is required to accommodate parenting in this manner.[105] In the end, we are left with the overall trends that I have just described. And what they suggest in child development terms is clear and devastating: The critical developmental needs of millions of American children throughout the period of their childhood are not being met. Indeed, to the contrary, these children have been left in various circumstances that place them at great risk of serious emotional dysfunction.

---

ment of the society that wants to pad "resumes for Harvard" and ensure "big bucks [for their children] forever," and explaining that when children are highly scheduled everyone is exhausted); David Noonan, "Stop Stressing Me," Newsweek, Jan. 29, 1999, at 54–55 (explaining that "highly scheduled" children are generally overwhelmed by their schedules and "burn out.").

CHAPTER FIVE

VIRTUAL REALITY AND THE SCHOOL ENVIRONMENT

There is an inevitable connection between the psychological and physical absence of parents from their children's lives and the influence on these children of the media and their peers. Indeed, while parents traditionally mediated their children's relationships with outside influences, their relative absence today ensures that these influences are incrementally substantial. Most importantly, because the media—television, movies, the Internet, and games technology—and children's peers themselves are widely believed to be harmful in several respects, this novel and substantial influence in many instances amounts to bad childcare, with all of the developmental ramifications that this indictment implies.

THE INFLUENCE OF MEDIA TECHNOLOGIES

As a threshold matter, and even before the substance or content of television programming and other media are considered, it is important to understand that, in some respects, this technology is inherently detrimental to a child's development. As Neil Postman explains with respect to television, viewers "watch ... dynamic, constantly changing images, as many as 1,200 different ones every hour.... the average length of a shot on a network television program is somewhere between three and four seconds, the average length of a shot on a commercial, between two and three seconds."[1] John Rosemond explains that the result of this "constant perceptual shift, or 'flicker'" is that

> the television-watching child isn't attending to any one thing for longer than a few seconds. As a result, television-watching is a strangely paradoxical situation for the young child. The more time he spends watching television, the shorter his attention span becomes. Lastly, but by no means least, because the action

on a television set shifts constantly and capriciously backward, forward, and laterally in time (not to mention from subject matter to subject matter), television fails to promote logical, sequential thinking, which is essential to an understanding of cause-and-effect relationships. This causes difficulties in both following directions and anticipating consequences.[2]*

Rosemond concludes that these difficulties are likely tied closely to children's intellectual and behavioral or emotional difficulties, including the increased propensity of children to violence; indeed, with respect to the latter, he suggests that seeking a definitive causal link between the content (rather than the nature) of television programming and violence may be "exercises in barking up the wrong tree. The relationship between television and aggressive behavior in children may have more to do with process than content—more to do with the watching that with what's being watched."[3]

The issues raised with respect to games technology and the Internet are slightly different, but equally important. As David Walsh explains, games technology in general—*Pokemon*, even—can be "a gateway to more dangerous obsessions."[4] This is because

[t]he technology behind most video games ... is based on a psychological principle called "operant conditioning"—essentially, a stimulus-response-reward. "Research has shown that operant

---

* Rosemond concludes, rhetorically, "[i]f a young child spends significant time staring at a fixed and flickering electronic field, is it not reasonable to assume that this experience is interfering with the establishment of key neural skills, including a long attention span and certain reasoning abilities? Might this not go a long way toward explaining the epidemics of learning disabilities (LD's) and attention deficit disorder (ADD)?" John Rosemond, "Book: TV inhibits brain growth, Learning disabilities linked to TV-watching," The Charlotte Observer. His (and Postman's) assumptions are supported by important evidence that "television's electronic environment is actually altering the brains of children, both functionally (how the brain works) and structurally (its construction.)" Id. (describing the conclusions of psychologist Jane Healy's book, Endangered Minds: Why Our Children Don't Think, and the work of Yale University's Jerome Singer, who is described as "this country's leading researcher into the effects of television on children.")

conditioning is a powerful shaper and influencer of behavior ... The obsession is not about violence; it's about how engrossing the game becomes."[5]

The same concerns have been raised about the use of computers and even educational computer products by young children. Thus, "a growing number of educators, child development experts, and doctors are beginning to speak out against early computer use, especially when coupled with regular television watching. Too much 'screen time' at a young age, they say, may actually undermine the development of the critical skills that kids need to become successful, diminishing creativity and imagination, motivation, attention spans, and the desire to persevere."[6] As a result of these concerns, several prominent experts have called for "'an immediate moratorium on the further introduction of computers in early childhood and elementary education' until it can be determined what effect they have on young children."[7]

The reason that computer use appears to cause these effects is that even games directed at the youngest audience operate on the "stimulus-response-reward" system, and thus captivate, engross, or addict the user so that he or she is no longer as interested in engaging the real world relationships and activities that are essential to the development of these skills and traits.[8] For example, children who spend time playing computer games and watching television often "have withdrawn socially, passing up friends in favor of computer games."[9]*

Similarly, "obsessive Internet use"—again regardless of content—is linked by several studies to "social isolation, depression,

---

* It is clearly possible to mediate the negative effects of computer use, just as it is possible to mediate the negative effects of television by setting strict guidelines regarding the onset of initial use, and then limits on the time and quality of the products and programming to which children are exposed. The messages in these respects are mixed, however. For example, experts differ on when children should begin to use the computer, some indicating that limited use at aged 3 is not harmful, others suggesting that waiting until a child is 7 or even 10 is least detrimental; and explaining that there are "quality" products that minimize the risks and enhance the beneficial effects of computer use. Given that much of children's media usage is unmonitored, however, the problems that I have identified are likely to continue to exist in any event.

and failure at work or school" as well as other "serious mental disorders."[10] This is because obsessive use of the Internet functions like any other addiction for those individuals who may be predisposed to these behaviors.[11*] Thus, individuals including children who are lonely and unfulfilled in their real world relationships are most likely to become negatively absorbed in virtual ones. There is some popular disagreement about whether this is truly good or bad; for example, one Internet user explained his view that "[r]elationships online can be just as powerful and moving as real-life ones."[12] Nevertheless, there is little doubt amongst psychologists that children's Internet use is to be carefully monitored to avoid these conditions, particularly where a child is at-risk in other developmental respects.[13]

With some vocal—primarily industry-related—opposition, it also is generally accepted that much of the content of the media technologies, whether or not the products are targeted at a childhood audience, are likely to contribute to emotional dysfunction in at-risk children.[14] With respect to television in particular, Postman explains that this is because that medium uniquely and continuously exposes even the youngest children to the developmentally damaging secrets of adulthood: sex, violence, and illness.[15] He emphasizes that "[f]rom the child's point of view, what is mostly shown on television is the plain fact that the adult world is filled with ineptitude, strife, and worry."[16] Indeed, television programs, including the news and commercials, routinely depict illness, nat-

---

* Of course, most Americans do not describe themselves as "obsessive" or unhealthy users of the Internet, and thus do not apparently experience the depression, social isolation, and other affect disorders that are described here as being signs of addiction. See "Study suggests Net does not create isolation,"USAToday.com, available at http://www.usatoday.com/life/cyber/tech/cti715.htm (last visited May 2, 2001) (describing results of survey conducted by the University of California, Los Angeles, that found that "[n]early two-thirds of all Americans have ventured online, and the majority of them deny the Internet creates social isolation.") Indeed, for those "healthy" users of the Internet, it appears that the technology and forum actually "improves communication with friends and family," rather than "encouraging social isolation." "Survey disputes notion that Internet encourages isolation," CNN.com, available at http://www.cnn.com/2000/US/05/10/internet.study/ (last visited May 2, 2001).

ural and man-made disasters, wars, violence, financial and environmental crises. The same is true of many movies that are available to the childhood audience. These depictions can have a substantial effect on children, particularly where the exposures are repeated and unmediated by an adult who is able appropriately to contextualize them.

Thus, for example, the American Psychological Association concluded that "[w]atching television can lead to antisocial behavior, obesity, gender and racial stereotyping, bad grades, and a lack of self-esteem for families."[17] Not surprisingly, the most serious damage is to the "youngest and oldest Americans, minorities and women ... population groups with 'restricted mobility,' ... 'Many of the poorest and most vulnerable groups in our society are also the heaviest users of television, in part because television is a default option used when other activities are not available.'"[18]

Violent content clearly has drawn the most attention. This is largely because "[m]ounting evidence suggests that aggression is to a great extent learned,"[19] and related evidence "accumulated ... from both laboratory and field studies has led most reviewers to conclude that aggressiveness and viewing violence are interdependent to some degree."[20] As John Rosemond explains,

> [t]he *Report to the Surgeon General on Television and Social Behavior*, published in 1972, verified that children can, and often do, act on the suggestion, inherent in the themes of many television programs, that violence is an acceptable way of handling conflict and other problem situations. The idea that violence on television can stimulate violence on the playground has since become a generally accepted belief. But that tie that could forever bind television violence to aggressive behavior in children has yet to be found. The so-called "smoking gun" theory is still just a theory.... [Nevertheless,] [t]here's definitely reason to suspect a link between television and aggressive behavior among children. Since the early 1950s, when television first moved into our homes, the number of violent crimes attributed to juveniles has increased more than tenfold. Over the same period, big-city public schools have become a battleground, where students fight not only among themselves, but also with their teachers. Even without a final answer from the scientific establishment, the anecdotal evidence strongly sug-

gests that the "television generation" is also a more violent generation.[21]*

The most comprehensive scientific study of this subject likely is *Television and the Aggressive Child: A Cross National Comparison.*[22] Its editors, L. Rowell Huesman and Leonard Heron, conclude there is "little doubt that in specific laboratory settings exposing children to violent behavior on film or TV increases the likelihood that they will behave aggressively immediately afterwards."[23] They also agree that there is a clear indication outside of the laboratory that "more aggressive children watch more television, prefer more violent programs, identify more with TV characters, and perceive violence as more like real life than do less aggressive children."[24] In fact, their own work in the United States has demonstrated that "early TV habits significantly predicted the aggressiveness of children at the end of the study even when the children's initial aggressiveness was statistically controlled."[25] And again in this respect, "the United States seems to lead the world" in the amount of "violent [television] programming per week."[26] In the end, as one commentator

---

* Neil Postman's work, supported by research that shows that affect and behavior are largely modeled, also argues that reality-based programming including perhaps especially the news is detrimental to children. His emphasis is on the fact that children, particularly younger children, simply are not ready as a developmental matter to integrate the messages that such programming conveys. He writes, for example,

[t]here can be no denying that human beings spend an inordinate amount of time and energy in maiming and killing each other.... [Nevertheless, it makes sense] to keep this knowledge from children because for all of its reality, too much of it too soon is quite likely dangerous to the well-being of an unformed mind. Enlightened opinion on child development claims it is necessary for children to believe that adults have control over their impulses to violence and that they have a clear conception of right and wrong. Through these beliefs, as Bruno Bettelheim has said, children can develop the positive feelings about themselves that give them the strength to nurture their rationality, which, in turn, will sustain them in adversity.... Without [this sustenance] children find it difficult to be hopeful or courageous or disciplined.

Postman at 93.

noted, "[o]ur generation is far more desensitized to violence than any other generation. TVs raise children now more than parents do, and television caters to children's violent fantasies."[27]

These same authors emphasize that

[t]he relation [demonstrated by their work and that of others in their field] is not strong by the standards used in the measurement of intellectual abilities, but the relation is highly significant statistically and is substantial by the usual standards of personality measurement with children. More importantly, the relation is highly replicable.[28]

Because of this, they conclude that the evidence is sufficiently strong that it should have "had more of an impact on viewing habits and programming policy in the United States."[29] They also suggest that this has not happened because in this country

an equally important factor may have been the economic importance of media violence. Just as the tobacco companies have demanded virtually unobtainably strong evidence that smoking causes lung cancer, so the television programmers have demanded impossibly strong evidence linking television violence to aggression.... we do not yet have an adequate psychological model to explain the process by which television violence viewing engenders aggression.[30]

In the end, and despite that these studies establish only a "scientifically reliable correlation" rather than insurmountable scientific or even legal causation, their conclusions have been sufficiently strong to cause various organizations, including the American Medical Association, the American Psychological Association, the American Academy of Pediatrics, and the National Institute of Mental Health, to conclude that virtual violence is sufficiently linked to real world aggression that it should be controlled.[31]

Coupled with this strong link between virtual violence and at least a "desensitization to violence" if not outright violent behavior is the fact that television and movie production increasingly involves violent content, and that content itself is increasingly violent; again, this has been the case whether or not the productions are marketed to children.[32] Thus, for example, a 1998 report indicated that today "[t]here are 16 acts of violence per hour of children's television programming, with very few peaceful solutions to con-

material. For example, in a poll conducted among adolescents, forty-four percent reported that they had used the Internet to view "websites that ... [a]re X-rated or have sexual content;"[46] twenty-five percent said they had viewed sites that "[h]ave information about hate groups;"[47] fourteen percent had viewed sites that "[t]each how to build bombs;"[48] and twelve percent had viewed sites that "[s]how where or how to buy a gun."[49]

There also is good evidence that these exposures are substantially and substantively different from the "illicit" material that was hidden from, but nevertheless often found, by children in the past. As Okrent also has noted, "[w]here an earlier generation of children sneaked hygiene texts off library shelves to giggle over drawings of the human reproductive system, our kids can now cruise through unspeakable swamps" including "recipes for pipe bombs or deranged rants about white supremacy."[50] In other words, the very breadth that makes the Internet an extraordinarily positive communications concept for adults is responsible for extraordinarily dangerous communications potential for children.

In fact, what makes the Internet especially dangerous for children is that "they are plunging into a whole world of influences and values and enticements that is, most of the time, hidden from our [adult] view," and that world is often (although certainly not always) inconsistent with their capacities and developmental needs.[51] As Michael Thompson explains, this phenomenon is rendered all the more problematic because the children themselves do not "think of themselves as imperiled. 'Because there's a lot of omnipotent thinking in adolescents ... and because the dangers are somewhat more abstract than climbing trees ... they [do not] perceive the dangers in anything like the way adults do."[52] The fact that parents are often not available to cull the wheat from the chaff compounds the damage that accompanies children's own inability to engage in self-selection.

In light of these process and content concerns, it is clear that many children today are spending an inordinate amount of time using media technologies. Television continues to be the children's technology of choice, "in spite of the proliferation of new media."[53] Thus, in *Kids & Media @ the Millennium*, a 1999 report sponsored by the Henry J. Kaiser Foundation, it was reported that "on average [children] watch nearly 3 hours of television ... each day."[54]* Further, "[a]n alarming one-third of children between the ages of 2 and 7—and two-thirds of kids 8 and older—have their own television set in the bedroom."[55]

These data are generally supported by similar studies. For example, John Rosemond reports that "[b]etween birthdays two and six, the average American pre-school child watches thirty hours of television a week" which averages "slightly more than four hours a day ... 1,560 hours of television a year, for a grand total of 6,240 hours between the ages of two and six. Based on a fourteen-hour day, this means that preschool children spend roughly one-third of their daily discretionary time sitting in front of a television set."[56] And he offers that these numbers have "been confirmed by Nielsen survey after Nielsen survey since the early 1970s."[57] The numbers obviously go down once children are in school; nevertheless, as the Kaiser Family Foundation study indicates, they still remain at approximately 21 hours per week. Moreover, that study also found that "much of children's media use goes unsupervised by harried or guilt-ridden parents. 'We know that parents aren't exercising control,' said one of the study's authors."[58] And, the report concluded that "there is every reason to assume that [children's] media use and exposure will continue to increase."[59]

The time that children spend using games technology is more difficult to measure. Nevertheless, we might derive some sense of the magnitude—and surmise responsibly that it is quite large—from the fact that the "electronic-games industry posted sales of $5.5 billion in the U.S. in 1998, and was the second-most popular form of home entertainment after TV."[60] This surmise is bolstered by data from research, also reported in *Kids & Media @ the Millennium*, which shows that "more than two-thirds [of American homes with children] have video game players," and that children in

---

* The researchers found that the average child in the U.S. today watches television for two hours and forty-five minutes each day, and that this number increases to three hours and fifteen minutes daily if taped television programs and movie or other program videos are included. Broken down by age, the report provided that children from two to four watch an average of two hours of television daily; children at the end of grade school watch an average of three hours and thirty minutes daily; and children in later adolescence watch an average of two hours and forty-five minutes daily.

those homes spend approximately 20 minutes per day using them.[61]* Similarly, with respect to the Internet, *Time* magazine reported that "[i]n 1998, 17 million kids ages 2 to 18 were online," and this "number is expected to grow in five years to more than 42 million."[62] Contrary to reports that show that older children in particular are replacing their television viewing with Internet use hour-for-hour, *Kids & Media @ the Millennium* reports that on average, American children spend twenty minutes daily on the computer, and in later adolescence, the number rises to 30 minutes daily.[63] Whatever the real amount of daily computer use by children, polling number suggest that approximately forty-three percent of children have parents who "don't have rules" about their use of the Internet, and twenty-six percent had parents who have rules that the children "don't always follow."[64]

THE ECOLOGY OF THE SCHOOLS

While it is impossible cleanly to separate the parental and other causes of contemporary childhood dysfunction, there is little doubt that "[t]he world is becoming a much more dangerous place for children."[65] It has long been recognized that many streets and schools in the United States today, particularly in the inner-cities, are littered with drugs and real life violence, and that such environments can have devastating effects on the children who survive them.[66] Most recently, developmental experts have come to understand that contemporary life outside of the inner-cities also can be emotionally toxic for children, with similarly devastating effects.[67] In this respect, the focus of their attentions has been on the peer

---

* According to the report, this is the average for children ages two to eighteen. Broken down further, the numbers are as follows: Children from two to seven play video games on average 11 minutes daily; from eight to thirteen, an average of 50 minutes daily; and from fourteen to eighteen, an average of 52 minutes daily. There are stark gender differences in the use of video games technology by children. Thus, the researchers found that video games equipment was found in the homes of 77% of boys, but only 64% of girls. And while 33% of all children reported having video games equipment in their own bedrooms, by gender that broke down to 43% of boys and 23% of girls.

group, and on "the cliquish environment in many schools in which unpopular students are ostracized."[68] Indeed, this has been described as part of the root of the problem that is Columbine.

Because it is in so many instances overtly violent, it is the latter, cliquish environment of the schools, that has received the most recent and prominent attention. Elliot Aronson explains that this environment is characterized by

> rejection and humiliation that makes a very significant minority of students, ... 30 percent to forty percent of them, very, very unhappy. If the kids at the top of the pyramid start calling a kid a nerd, then the kids in the second tier of cliques tease him because that's one way of identifying with the powerful group. Next thing you know, everybody's teasing him. Everybody in school knows what group everybody belongs to. They know whom they can get away with taunting. Most of the kids who are taunted suffer in silence. Some of them seriously contemplate taking their own lives. A handful—and it's going to be more than a handful in the next few years—lash out at their fellow students almost randomly.[69]

Aronson's research and conclusions are confirmed by, among other studies, a finding of the National Threat Assessment Center, which is operated by the U.S. Secret Service, which "found that in more than two-thirds of 37 recent school shootings, the attackers felt 'persecuted, bullied, threatened, attacked or injured.'"[70] For example, "[e]xcessive bullying has been offered as motivation for Eric Harris and Dylan Klebold to kill."[71] And the same was true more recently, in the case of Charles Andrew Williams, who "shot up his high school in Santee, California."[72] Short of such dramatic consequences, but still quite significant is the finding of the National Association of School Psychologists that "bullying is why more than 160,000 children skip school every day" in the United States.[73]*

---

* For example, according to *Time* magazine, 41% of children polled indicated that they had been "picked on" by other children; 32% reported that they "haven't been picked on"; and 27% allowed that they "usually do the bullying." Gibbs, "It's Only Me," at 12. Based in part on such numbers and the views of developmental experts as to their significance, schools and legislatures across the country are beginning to discuss "anti-bullying" policies that would both prevent and punish individual or group bullying of socially unpopular children. For example, "[n]ew laws in Georgia, New Hampshire

Given that cliques and a certain degree of teasing or bullying always have been part of the schools' environment, Aronson and others accept that "forming cliques is a natural part of being a teenager"; however they reject as unhealthy and unnecessary the sort of exclusion that is accompanied by "taunting and humiliation."[74] Indeed, these anti-social behaviors are rare in environments where children are taught early on to respect one another, and where it is clear that the responsible adults will not tolerate them. Most important for purposes of defining the Columbine phenomenon, however, is that many experts believe that the kind and degree of taunting and humiliation have in fact changed, apparently substantially, in the past several years. According to one report, for example, while "[p]art of the story is old: the embittered outcasts against the popular kids on campus,"

> the worst of high school fringe groups do seem more disturbed than in the past.... [For example, s]ome high schools have white supremacist cliques. Then there are groups like the Straight Edge, a presence at schools like Salt Lake City's Kearns High School. They are puritanical punkers who are anti-drug, anti-alcohol, and anti-tobacco—and they are violent. If you smoke or drink in their presence, some Straight Edgers will attack you with a baseball bat.[75]

It is not popular to view Harris, Klebold, Williams, and the other recent school shooters, as victims. Nevertheless, it is undoubtedly true that their personal circumstances, the bullying and ostracism to which they were subjected before they became ultimately violent themselves, reveal the pervasiveness of this deep disturbance and perhaps even something about the different nature of the taunting and clique mentality that exists in American schools today. Thus, for example, in the days following April 20, 1999, high school compatriots of Harris's and Klebold's noted without

---

and Vermont require them, and Colorado ... is debating a [related] measure." Id. Aronson, for one, finds it "outrageous that there needs to be legislation for such a thing. Clearly," he says, "schools should be trying to prevent bullying." Id. I agree. Indeed, as with much of the discussion in this area, I find it odd at best that our national or cultural intuition does not itself provide for such interventions.

apparent discomfort that the two boys who belonged to the Trenchcoat Mafia were viewed by their peers as "discarded, unwanted 'stereotype geeks,' ... even the teachers picked on the Trench Coats ... [students] called them 'faggots,' inbreeds, harassing them to the point of throwing rocks and bottles at them from moving cars." Said one hockey player, "'It's kind of like a rivalry with us ... They hate us because we're like the social elite of the school.'"[76] Similarly, before his rampage at Santee High School outside of San Diego in March of 2001, Williams was constantly called names and "picked on by the bigger, more streetwise kids ... [who would] burn their lighters and then press the hot metal against his neck.... [and] 'walk up to him and sock him in the face.'"[77]

It is in spite of the views of experts like Aronson that ordinary adults tend to question whether these acts of humiliation and ostracism truly are different in kind or degree from those that children have faced in other periods. Indeed, the history and literature of childhood are replete with examples of vicious and excruciating relationships among children. Many of us who grew up in generations before Columbine have our own personal stories of peer torture that rival even those of Harris, Klebold, and Williams. On the other hand, our individual experiences may have been so impacting that we cannot imagine things being worse, even though—as the experts suggest—they might indeed be so. For example, the increases in youth depression and violence during the period that characterizes the Columbine epidemic, coupled with children's access to and use of increasingly violent and anti-social media products, certainly support the supposition that there are likely to be an increasing number of more effective bullies in school today than there were in the past.

Ultimately, however, what is important is that my argument is not dependent upon a finding that contemporary peer relationships are in fact substantially harsher than those that existed in the past. Rather, it is simply that in their unmediated harshness, contemporary peer relationships are *particularly* likely to contribute to events like Columbine because children today are generally different from children in the past in that they are *particularly* and *abnormally* vulnerable to such harshness. In other words, for all of the reasons that I previously have described, many children today

CHAPTER SIX

CONCLUSIONS ABOUT THE ULTIMATE CAUSES OF COLUMBINE

In the past thirty years, many Americans scrapped almost all that they knew instinctively, culturally, and personally about what it takes to raise emotionally healthy children, children who are most likely to succeed as adults in their own lives and in their contributions to the society. All along, we have proceeded, assuming that this revolutionary disengagement from our children was viable, without a shred of real evidence that it was, armed with and empowered by a flawed theory of childhood resilience, a conviction that in any event the cause of substantive (gender) equality was separately worthy, or a belief in the superlative nature of an ever more expansive marketplace of ideas and economy. If this experiment had involved the intentional manipulation of the children's physiology (rather than their psychology) it likely would have been criminal.

For perhaps the first time in human history, the United States at least implicitly has proceeded on the assumption that children do not need their mothers, even in the earliest days and years of life. Legally and culturally, we have sought to rid "mothering" and "motherhood" of its inextricable linkage to the women who bear children, and we have sought instead to tie these concepts in a gender-neutral fashion equally to these women, to men who would be fathers, and to assorted others who might be, somehow and for minimal pay, adequate substitutes for both. Along the way, as mothers went to work and fathers remained there, we forgot or at least permitted ourselves to ignore that children have irreducible needs that simply cannot be put on hold for the duration of the business day, needs that cannot be met by fatigued parents when they happen to be free.

We forgot or ignored that children need (not just want) nurturing in deeds rather than only in words; that as infants and toddlers, they need to be constantly touched, smiled at, and talked to by a person who loves them; that as toddlers and thereafter, they need appropriate discipline and guidance from the few adults they know they can trust; and that all the children need their trusted adults to instill in them the values, particularly self-worth, personal restraint, and empathy, that will provide the building blocks for their relationships with their peers and with the external environment throughout their lives. The fact that we (as individuals and as a society) have acted this way for ostensibly good reasons does not compute for the vulnerable and appropriately self-centered three-year-old child; she cannot understand the value to an adult of individual self-fulfillment outside of the home, and the value to the larger society of primacy in the global marketplace. It also does not compute for the equally vulnerable and self-centered adolescent who comes home to an empty house every day where he must resolve his emotional and physical struggles on his own, in consultation with similarly confused peers, or with the assistance of a stranger in an Internet chat room.

Coincidentally, at the same time that the society abandoned large numbers of children to themselves or to inadequate parental substitutes, it also allowed them generally unrestricted access to real and virtual worlds where they remain unprotected from what Neil Postman so aptly calls the secrets of adulthood: the capacity of humans for extraordinary hate and violence, the devastation wrecked by natural and unnatural disasters, debilitating and deadly illness, and all forms of sexuality. While such exposure is not unprecedented in the history of childhood, which is largely characterized by such openness, it is nevertheless a dramatic shift in the theology of childhood that has prevailed in the United States since at least the mid-to-late nineteenth century.

To the extent that this model is still the aspiration, it is clear that today we are failing many American children. Today, for example, it is not unusual to find two and three-year-olds who, by virtue of their access to the streets and to television, are panicked by and then reconciled to the fact that guns exist, that familiar-seeming humans use them to kill, and that sometimes even mothers and children are killed. Similarly, it is not unusual to find seven and eight-year-olds who believe, because of their time on the streets, in front of the television or playing video games, that in circumstances of conflict acting with "courage" requires violence rather than avoidance or mediation. It is also not unusual today to find adolescents who are so numb from seeing and understanding all of this that even at the dawn of their adult lives they have no hope.

None of this is surprising, since childhood is defined not only as that period in our lives when we ordinarily should be shielded from these secrets, but also as the period in which we are developmentally incapable of fighting the hopelessness that comes inevitably from premature exposures to their particulars. None of these facts is altered by the abiding belief of the society in individual responsibility and an unfettered marketplace of ideas. In other words, the children will react as they do without regard to the political philosophy or expedience that undergirds our decision to leave them exposed and unprotected.

The belief that children are resilient has been critical to Americans' fealty to the twin revolutions that spawned this extraordinary negligence. After all, as a society we still love our children and hope that we are doing what is necessary for them to succeed emotionally and otherwise. In other words, this experiment may not ever have been launched, even given its personal and collective payoffs, if parents and others who think about the health of the nation believed that they would be sacrificing the children as a consequence. Most Americans today, however, do not believe that they are being negligent, or that the children are being sacrificed. They think that like children throughout history who have faced adversity of various sorts, the children in our generations and in the future also will survive. Life and perhaps especially childhood have always been hard, and despite that, children have tended to make it through to adulthood, not so much intact but alive and generally able to find some measure of happiness.

The problem is that these assumptions about children's resilience have turned out not to be true for many American children. In fact, the data show a literal explosion in rates of emotional dysfunction in the years following the cultural and legal devaluation of women's roles as mothers and of mothering more generally, and in the years following the beginning of the revolution in media technologies, particularly in the television industry. Extraordinarily, this explosion was almost unnoticed (at least outside of child development circles) until the events at Columbine High School in the spring of 1999. Following those events, however, it became impossible to ignore: A serious assault rate that has risen seven hundred percent since World War II; a suicide rate that has risen by some estimates eight-hundred percent since 1950; a risk of serious depression that is commensurately higher in this period than it was in that earlier era; and anxiety disorders that today strike approximately thirteen percent of American children in a given year. Clearly, resilience can no longer be taken for granted. Or, resilience is relative.

Following Eric Harris and Dylan Klebold's rampage through Columbine High School, it became something of a national pastime for those in the spotlight—parents, educators, schoolyard bullies, media representatives, and the gun groups—to point fingers at one another, suggesting that, but for the other's negligence, Columbine would never have happened. Each sought in the process to absolve itself from direct blame, by distancing in time and value their own contributions to the immediate disaster. The fact is, however, that individuals in all of these groups share some of the blame: But for many decisions they made, Columbine in our minds would have remained a beautiful mountain flower rather than a horrific carnage in a children's house. In the end, though, however much some may prefer the most proximate causes (they are much easier to work with in many respects) there is little doubt that the complex etiological stew that lies at the core of Columbine *writ large* involves mostly absent parents, inadequate parental substitutes, and the quite toxic real and virtual environments that would fill the void.

The data that I have marshaled to support this discussion are controversial, not because they lack validity, but rather because of their implications, particularly for women and the advances we have made in the past thirty years toward substantive equality. Juxtaposed with the arguments that I have made that women are critical to the emotional well-being of their children, is the wildly successful contemporary perspective that views as positive (albeit for very different reasons) the exodus of both relatively rich and poor women who are mothers from the home and into the workplace. In its pragmatic recognition that, whatever our best intentions, men have largely failed to step in to fill the gap that the women's absence has ensured in the lives of the children, the data and my argument are similarly at odds with contemporary progressive orthodoxy that allows for a new and special place for men in the home, as nurturing fathers. Nevertheless, I stand by both unequivocally because the developmental literature and related statistics allow for no other rational position. As Postman has written on this point exactly, it

> cannot be denied that as women find their place in business, in the arts, in industry, and in the professions, there must be a serious decline in the strength and meaning of the traditional patterns of child care. For whatever criticisms may be made of the exclusive role of women as nurturers, the fact is that it is women, and women alone, who have been the overseers of childhood, shaping it and protecting it. It is unlikely that men will assume anything like the role women have played, and still do, in raising children, no matter how sensible it might be for men to do so.[1]

The fact that the women's movement unintentionally has contributed to the Columbine problem does not negate that "men, even more than women, shirk their family responsibilities to pursue self fulfillment."[2] Indeed, even beyond individual men and women, as I already have suggested, there is ample blame to go around: The society and corporate interests that have devalued motherhood, and at the same time encouraged or found a private benefit in the women's movement as well as in the continuing (relative) absence of fathers in the lives of their children, also are an integral part of the calculus. In my argument there is thus no call to "return to a time when women had fewer [legal] rights on the pretense of saving the family."[3] Rather, it suggests that the evidence of a national crisis cannot be ignored simply because it may be difficult politically and personally to face it. And it suggests that this crisis begs for a solution that each of these groups might contribute to, a solution that has a real chance of reversing the downward slide we currently are experiencing. In the end, it is both naive and arrogant to believe that the future of this society is secure when such a large number of its children, the future guardians of the democracy, are so fragile. Most importantly, however, it is a moral abomination for the society to define happiness and success in a manner that leaves out the well being of children.

PART II

THE CHALLENGE OF
AMERICAN LIBERALISM

I have just argued that the ultimate causes of the Columbine epidemic are inadequate parenting, children's relatively unfettered access to media technologies, particularly television, and an otherwise toxic environment in the schools, among peers, and in the external world generally. At the outset of this next discussion, I suggest that to be viable, any solution to the problem must address these ultimate causes and be applicable generally across the United States. There may be some temporary or slight benefit to be derived from an attack on its more proximate causes, for example, we might see fewer shootings if we found ways to ensure that children did not have easy access to guns, and fewer shootings in schools if we installed more metal detectors in that environment. In the end, however, because children shoot out of deep seeded anger, depression, and incapacity, and not merely because they happen to have guns, these approaches and others that would target similarly incidental causes of childhood dysfunction will serve only as bandages on what is clearly a gaping wound.

Lest I be misunderstood in this respect, I would like to make it perfectly clear that in rejecting an attack on guns as a useful solution to the Columbine problem, I am not subscribing to the National Rifle Association's public position that "guns don't kill people, people kill people." This position is simplistic, and disingenuous at best. It is a fact that both the gun and the person generally are necessary to cause a death by gunfire. If Eric Harris and Dylan Klebold had been armed only with knives or their fists when they launched their assault on Columbine High School, it is quite unlikely that at the end of the day, fifteen people would have died. That they had guns made all the difference. On the other hand, it is also a fact that emotionally stable individuals with a well-developed sense of (positive) values do not so easily pick up a gun and shoot people, unless it is in self-defense or in the context of a war. The fact that there might be guns lying around does not change this. Thus—and this is my own bottom line—while it certainly will help to reduce the number of gun deaths caused by children if we can ensure that children do not have unsupervised access to those weapons, this attack alone will do little to resolve the underlying emotional dysfunctions that lie at the heart of the Columbine problem. In other words, without guns, Harris and Klebold may not have managed to kill so many people, but they would have remained (if they survived themselves) extraordinarily angry and dysfunctional young men.

Finally, because Columbine is a public health crisis that is national in scope, it is also essential to assure that the greatest number of American children are "treated" or afforded the opportunity to escape its clutches. Again, anything less, such as the amelioration of the crisis only among the relatively few children whose parents can afford to create the requisite environment, will make no more than an incidental dent in the problem. In this part of the book, I explore the obstacle that liberalism throws into this entire equation. Lawyers and others in the society who understand the institutional role that the law plays in ordering human relations tend to expect that there is or should be (if one is sufficiently creative) a law-based or at least a lawful solution to most national crises. The notion is that law provides a principal framework to consider issues that threaten the success, or the "health, welfare, and morals" of the society. In the case of Columbine, however, we face the extraordinary irony that the law in its highest (constitutional) sense both enabled the problem and stands as an arguably immutable obstacle to its resolution.

Specifically, if it matters that we address how individual adults parent their children and who or what they choose as parental substitutes, we run headlong into the brick wall that is the doctrine of parental autonomy. And if it matters that we address the nature and content of the media technologies that are available (legally or in fact) to the children, we hit the wall of free speech. While there are strong moral and pragmatic arguments that the jurisprudential trends in these areas are flawed and thus should be reconsidered, ultimately they stand firm, precluding these most obvious attacks on Columbine. Finally, because these liberal values also are entrenched in the culture, they render relatively meaningless the politicians' recent calls to community, religion, and family values as alternative solutions.

CHAPTER SEVEN

AN INTRODUCTION TO AMERICAN LIBERALISM

As a liberal democracy, the United States subscribes to the doctrine of constitutional liberalism, which holds that "human beings have certain ... 'inalienable'... rights and that governments must accept a basic law, limiting its own powers, that secures them."[1] The basic law that secures these rights is, of course, the federal Constitution, which limits the power of government in those provisions that define restrictively the positive or "enumerated" authority of the national government, and in the Bill of Rights, which more specifically tells the national and state governments what it is that they cannot do.[2] The Bill of Rights in particular prohibits the government from intruding into areas that traditionally have been viewed as encompassing the private realm of the individual, including individual speech, religion, association, private property, and privacy.[3] At the same time, however, American liberal theory as it is ensconced in constitutional law is not so impractical that it assumes that individual rights are absolute; despite their original significance, the government is permitted to fetter their exercise where it has a "compelling interest" that justifies the intrusion, and where that intrusion is "narrowly tailored" so that no unnecessary deprivations of liberty result.[4]

Some liberal theorists suggest that the government may intrude on individual liberty only according to the "harm principle," that is, where their exercise endangers the well-being of other individuals within the society or in some instances of the society itself. Thus, for example, according to John Stuart Mill,

> [t]he sole end for which mankind are warranted, individually or collectively, in interfering with the liberty of action of any of their number, is self-protection. The only purpose for which power can be rightfully exercised over any member of a civilised community, against his will, is to prevent harm to others. His own good, either physical or moral, is not a sufficient warrant. He cannot rightfully be compelled to do or forbear because it

will be better for him to do so, because it will make him happier, because, in the opinions of others, to do so would be wise, or even right.[5]

Of course, the first and most evident respect in which the government will be permitted to intrude on individual freedom to act is in the criminal context. Indeed, "[a]s a matter of Lockean political theory, on its most fundamental level government exists to protect the life, liberty, and property interests of the people who have consented to its jurisdiction ... 'citizens owe allegiance to their government in exchange for the government's grant of protection to them'... the criminal law is one tool government uses to serve this protective function."[6]

While Mill is said to have vacillated on the question of the sorts of harms that might properly invoke state action to restrict liberties, and late in life is said to have been "more favorable to government authority," Lockean liberalism is believed by some to be faithful to the purest version of the theory, which holds that the state is only entitled to promulgate criminal laws, again according to the harm principle: "Any broader role for the state, on this view, threatens people's freedom by allowing the state too great a say in what people's life choices should be."[7] The ultimate issue in any event is always whether a particular circumstance constitutes a sufficient need for self-protection so that governmental interference with an individual's rights is appropriate; and relatedly, whether a particular mode of analysis is appropriate to make this determination. In the law, this question translates directly into the three levels of scrutiny—rational basis, intermediate, and strict—that are used to determine when the government may interfere with the otherwise legitimate exercise of constitutional rights.[8]

Just as Mill and John Locke may have disagreed, so too there is a range of views within contemporary society on this question. It is largely on this question that we see the principal contemporary political divides, including in particular the split among democrats, republicans, and libertarians. Thus, Jean Hampton writes that "today, Locke's descendants are invariably committed to markets and market-based solutions, both because of their economic efficiency and because, these Lockeans say, markets best realize freedom.... This style of liberalism has inspired libertarianism and other 'right-wing' political parties and movements."[9] Hampton also notes that "'left-wing'" [but still obviously liberal] opponents of the Lockeans" also thrive in the United States.[10] Consistent with the philosophies of John Rawls and Jean-Jacques Rousseau, for example, these liberals "focus on the danger to liberty that comes from a society that is distributively unjust and unequal" and thus they "tend to emphasize equality."[11] "Sometimes they are also more collectivist in outlook. However, [they] remain committed to the individual as the basic unit of political justification."[12] This latter point is particularly important for purposes of this book because, whatever differences exist amongst the parties in general, American jurisprudence in the areas of free speech and parental rights today is strictly aligned with the Lockean's perspective on liberalism.

That is, in recognizing that the government might appropriately override individual freedoms, the Constitution is said to embody the principle of "ordered" (rather than absolute) liberty. As I have explained in a related context,

> [o]rdered liberty provides for freedom within assumed societal goals and values as opposed to freedom from assumed goals and values. Specifically, ordered liberty permits [individual] and cultural pluralism within boundaries that the majority is willing to tolerate, so that the liberty we are afforded is not unfettered, but rather bounded by prevailing social dictates.[13]

Today, these "prevailing social dictates," are increasingly liberal. Indeed, Mary Ann Glendon argues—and the evidence strongly supports her analysis—our "rights talk" is both unprecedented in scope and degree. By way of comparison, it "is set apart from rights discourse in other liberal democracies by its starkness and simplicity, its prodigality in bestowing the rights label, its legalistic character, its exaggerated absoluteness, its hyperindividualism, its insularity, and its silence with respect to personal, civic, and collective responsibilities."[14] For example, "[n]either in England, nor even in Canada (where conditions historically were more similar to ours) is the idea of property or the discourse of rights so extravagant."[15] Glendon is particularly struck by the disjunction between what contemporary Americans perceive their rights to be and what they are in fact. She explains that "American rights dialectic" is especially "remarkable when we consider how little relation it bears to reality" which necessarily requires that "common sense restrictions

[be] placed on one person's rights when they collide with those of another person."[16]

There are myriad examples that illustrate Glendon's point. One of my own favorites involves the Elian Gonzales case. There we saw Americans of all political stripes convinced that the six-year old castaway from Cuba had a "right" to be raised in our liberal democracy rather than under the communist regime of his birth, despite the wishes of his only parent to the contrary. For example, one commentator argued that "an escapee from Cuba deserves asylum because of the nature of the government there," and that "[i]n Elian's case, the issue isn't life in a poor country versus life in a rich country, but rather slavery versus freedom."[17] Some even argued (quite loudly) that Elian's relatives in Miami had a "right" to raise him in place of his father who is communist and a resident of Cuba, because they are capitalists and live in the United States.[18] Finally, some argued that the Miami relatives had a "right" to be free from governmental intrusion into the sanctity of their home, even after these relatives had holed up there with the boy in defiance of a lawful United States government order to return him to his father.[19] Lawrence Tribe himself was oddly in the latter camp for a moment, pronouncing in an editorial in *The New York Times* that the government raid on the Miami home of Elian's relatives "strikes at the heart of constitutional government and shakes the safeguards of liberty."[20]

In each of these instances, the people were absolutely wrong about the scope of the "rights" they insisted upon; indeed, the law was always to the contrary, well-established, and not controversial.[21] Ultimately—and this is Glendon's point—what this "rights talk" in the culture signifies is that Americans generally are inclined to be more liberal (as in subscribing to a particularly permissive version of liberal theory) than even the law supports. Likely, this cultural perspective reflects what Fareed Zakaria has explained is the "tradition, deep in Western history, that seeks to protect an individual's autonomy and dignity against coercion, whatever the source—state, church, or society."[22]

Accordingly, and consistent with the notion of ordered liberty, the Supreme Court has embarked upon a clear trajectory in the area of individual rights that Glendon calls "the central legal drama of the times."[23] Indeed, today, the Supreme Court infrequently finds any governmental intrusions on these fundamental rights to be justified. And it is ever more wary of communal interests or group rights (particularly under the Fourteenth Amendment's equal protection clause) that are in conflict.[24] In this sense, legal liberalism today is in many important respects perhaps more liberal than ever before in the nation's history. Whether any of this will change in the wake of events of September 11, 2001, has yet to be seen: In the meantime, though, we are left with the law as it stands.

The liberal theory and trajectory that I have just described stand as a backdrop to the examination in the next two chapters of the particular constitutional doctrines that are relevant to the Columbine problem. Indeed, it is the point of this next discussion that liberal theory enabled both the specific tragedy called Columbine and the larger epidemic for which it now stands. Because the Bill of Rights protects the individual exercise of rights that are primarily implicated by the crisis, liberal theory also inevitably is an obstacle to fixing it. More specifically, the behaviors, environments, and technological freedom that lie at its roots inherently reflect the profound and unwavering commitment the society has in particular to two of the doctrines that flourish in liberalism's wake: the Fourteenth Amendment's right of parental autonomy, and the First Amendment's right of free expression.

CHAPTER EIGHT

THE CONSTITUTIONAL DOCTRINE OF PARENTAL AUTONOMY

The right of parents to raise their children as they see fit is a fundamental one in American political philosophy. Indeed, according to liberal theory, it is one of the most important of the natural, inalienable rights that individuals bring with them into their relationship with the state, and thus that the state must respect at its origins. In what has become a classic statement of this doctrine, the Wisconsin Supreme Court in 1922 wrote that

> [a] natural affection between the parent and offspring, though it may be naught but a refined animal instinct and stronger from the parent down than from the child up, has always been recognized as an inherent, natural right, for the protection of which, just as much as for the protection of the rights of the individual to life, liberty and pursuit of happiness, our government is formed.[1]

The Wisconsin court went on to emphasize its

> trust that it will never become the established doctrine that the state shall say to the parents, and particularly to the mother, she who doth travail, and in great pain bring forth her child and after labour doth rejoice that the child is born, that there is but a mere privilege and not a right to the subsequent affection, comfort, and pride of and in such a child.[2]

Consistent with this longstanding commitment to parental autonomy as an aspect of liberal theory, courts ruling in this area frequently begin their opinions with language much like this one from the United States Supreme Court's decision in the case *Parham v. J.R.*:

> Our jurisprudence historically has reflected Western civilization concepts of the family as a unit with broad parental authority over minor children. Our cases have consistently followed that

course; our constitutional system long ago rejected any notion that a child is "the mere creature of the state" and, on the contrary, asserted that parents generally "have the right, coupled with the high duty, to recognize and prepare [their children] for additional obligations."[3]

Children themselves are not respected as individual rights holders in this tradition.[4] In fact, as others—in particular Barbara Bennett Woodhouse—have noted, American culture and law generally have treated children as if they were the chattel of their parents.[5]

The doctrine of parental autonomy formally resides in the Fourteenth Amendment. The boundaries of the doctrine were most recently articulated in the so-called "grandparents' rights case" *Troxel v. Granville*.[6] According to Justice Sandra Day O'Connor, who wrote the opinion for the plurality, the Due Process Clause of the Fourteenth Amendment "includes a substantive component that 'provides heightened protection against government interference with certain fundamental rights and liberty interests.'... [Among these interests is that] of parents in the care, custody, and control of their children."[7]* Consistent with liberal theory, the Court has "consistent[ly] recogni[zed] ... the principle that 'the parents' claim to authority in their own household to direct the rearing of their children is basic in the structure of our society."[8] Indeed, Justice O'Connor emphasized that this "is perhaps the oldest of the fundamental liberty interests recognized by this Court."[9] Elaborating on this history, she wrote that beginning

> [m]ore than 75 years ago ... we held that the "liberty" protected by the Due Process Clause includes the right of parents to "establish a home and bring up children" and "to control the education of their own."... [Subsequently] we held that the "liberty of parents and guardians" includes the right "to direct the upbringing and education of children under their control."... [Later still, we emphasized that] "[i]t is cardinal with us that the

---

* A plurality opinion is one "in which more Justices join than in any concurring opinion (though not a majority of the court) ... [it is] distinguished from a majority opinion in which a larger number of the Justices on the panel join than not." Black's Law Dictionary, 6th Ed., at 1154 (1990).

custody, care and nurture of the child reside first in the parents, whose primary function and freedom include preparation for obligations the state can neither supply nor hinder."[10]

Troxel itself represents the Court's most recent reaffirmation of its commitment to this version of parental rights. Indeed, although no single rationale commanded a majority in the case, and although three justices dissented, in the words of Justice Anthony Kennedy, they all were otherwise "unanimous" in their view that "the custodial parent has a constitutional right to determine, without undue interference by the state, how best to raise, nurture, and educate the child."[11] Because of this, and notwithstanding their disagreements, the justices ultimately rejected an effort by the paternal grandparents of two children to obtain visitation rights over the objections of their single mother.[12]

The practical relationship between parents and the state that exists as a result of this doctrine was described as early as 1840 by Heman Humphrey in his book *Domestic Education*.[13] In that treatise, Humphrey explained that

> [e]very family is a little state, or empire within itself.... Every father is the constituted head and ruler of his household. God has made him the supreme earthly legislator over his children ... amenable to no other power, except in the most extreme cases of neglect, or abuse. The will of the parent is the law to which the child is bound in all cases to submit, unless it plainly contravenes the law of God.... Nor has civil government any right to interfere with the head of a family, unless it be where he is guilty of extreme neglect, or abuse.[14]

Of course, many things have changed since Humphrey wrote these words. The relevant parental authority has become gender neutral.[15] The rationale for the doctrine itself has been, at least in the law, divorced from its religious underpinnings.[16] And, most important for present purposes, the Supreme Court has explored the boundaries of parental autonomy and the states' often competing authority to enact abuse and neglect laws pursuant to its own constitutional police and *parens patriae* powers. The earliest and most significant of these cases (in terms of the development of these boundaries) were those that involved the regulation of child labor, the imposition of mandatory school attendance requirements, and mandatory inoculation of children against disease that would threaten the larger society.[17] Ultimately, however, all that these cases have done is to define the kind and quantum of "abuse and neglect" that will be considered "extreme" enough for the state to intervene in the family. In doctrinal terms, they have established the sort of proof that is necessary to show that the state has an interest that is compelling enough to override the parents' fundamental right to raise their children as they wish. Thus, Humphrey's original proposition continues to animate contemporary jurisprudence.[18]

Having said this, those who have an interest in a more absolute doctrine of parental autonomy argue that the changes I have just described have eroded their natural and traditional rights in significant ways, so that a parent's autonomy is no longer consistent with liberal theory. After all, parents have almost no liberty at all to school their children outside of an externally-prescribed curriculum; or to exclude their children from vaccination; or to discipline them beyond what others deem to be the limits "reasonable" parental authority; or to make them work and to leave school before others deem that they are old enough. Thus, for these parents it is perhaps appropriate to talk about the "demise of liberty" rather than about any clear jurisprudential trajectory toward increasing liberty. However, for those individuals who agree with the relatively few and specific restrictions that are imposed by virtue of the abuse and neglect laws, parental autonomy is otherwise virtually unlimited. That is, apart from the extreme circumstances that those laws ordinarily contemplate, there is no governmental bar at all to the various exercises of parental liberty that are important to the vast majority of Americans. And, for purposes of this book, these laws as they currently are interpreted impede any law-based solution to the Columbine problem.[19]

For example, although all states have mandatory school attendance requirements and ordinarily find parents neglectful who do not assure their children's education consistent with those requirements, parents nevertheless are permitted to send their children to private schools to assure, among other things, that they are not "mainstreamed."[20] In most jurisdictions, parents may even home school their children if they wish, for the same reason; and, in a few of these states, there are no restrictions whatever on the parents' qualifications, the curriculum, or the child's progress.[21] In

Wisconsin v. Yoder, the Supreme Court went so far as to permit a group of Amish parents to remove their thirteen and fourteen-year-old children from school entirely, without any guarantee that their formal education would be continued or resumed. This decision was rationalized on the grounds that there was little evidence that Amish children would later become a burden on the society, and that it was necessary to assure the survival of the parents' religion and community.[22] The ruling reversed the decision of the state court that the parents were neglectful for having failed to assure their children's attendance at school.[23] Together, this line of education cases assures that parents have the almost unfettered right to determine the ideas to which their children will and will not be exposed, the books their children will and will not read, and the individuals with whom their children will and will not associate.[24]

Outside of the schools, parents also have the unfettered right to determine the extent of their children's ability to view whatever materials or use whatever technology—including music, magazines, books, television programs, Internet sites, and video games—that they do not themselves choose to censor. The states have in some cases sought to restrict children's access to pornography or to subjects or treatments that were deemed by the legislature to be otherwise unsuitable for children.[25] And in some cases, particularly where pornography was at issue, these restrictions have been upheld by the courts against First Amendment challenges. But, as I will explain in the next chapter, these decisions were reached in principal part on the ground that the restrictions were necessary to assist parents to restrict or to screen objectionable material that their children can obtain when they are not physically under their control.[26] At the same time, no statute has survived constitutional scrutiny which has not permitted parents to override the restrictions to allow their children access to the material. *Ginsberg v. New York* is perhaps the most provocative in this respect, because the Court in that case opined that the anti-pornography statute at issue likely would not have survived constitutional scrutiny (as it did) if it had prohibited parents themselves from giving their children access to the otherwise restricted material.[27]

Parents also are free—in the first instance, and short of conduct that would constitute neglect—to make medical decisions for their objectively ill or handicapped children, including whether they will be treated at all. They also are free to determine (again in the first instance) the source and nature of the treatment their children will receive. Thus, for example, a parent's decision to treat a child using a spiritual healer rather than a conventional medical doctor has frequently been sanctioned, even in life-threatening emergencies where it is objectively doubtful that the spiritual healer would be successful and almost certain that the doctor would be.[28] Similarly, a parent's decision to medicate a child rather than to address her problems behaviorally, or to institutionalize a child rather than to care for her at home, has consistently received judicial and cultural sanction. Indeed, the case *Parham v. J.R.*—in which the Supreme Court ruled that the state need not require an adversarial proceeding in circumstances in which a parent wishes to institutionalize a child in a state mental hospital—stands in part for the proposition that the law presumes that parents act in the best interests of their children when they choose a particular approach to a child's medical and emotional problems. While this presumption is rebuttable in an individual case, the burden on the state is high to prove both that the parent or parents are not in fact acting in the child's best interests, and that the child is suffering from abuse or medical neglect. In other words, the courts have very rarely acted against the wishes of a child's parent or parents in circumstances where there was no clear and convincing evidence that the child was at risk of imminent and severe harm.[29]

Finally, there is a consistent line of federal cases which holds unconstitutional most efforts by the state to intervene in the family where it believes that parents are abusive or neglectful in the manner in which they watch over (or have others watch over) their children. While such interventions theoretically are permitted in "extreme" cases of abuse or neglect, in general, the courts have not found many circumstances that meet this standard. Thus, for example, the courts have denied states the authority to intervene in the family or to remove children from their homes when parents do not clean and supervise them according to majoritarian standards, unless there is strong evidence that the children are at risk of serious physical injury as a result of the unorthodox practices.[30] These cases often involve circumstances in which young children of five years and older also are left alone for various periods of time.[31]

Closely related to these federal cases are state law decisions which hold that parents generally have no duty in tort to watch over their children with any particular degree of attentiveness; that is, there is (again in general) no such tort as negligent supervision of a child. This majority rule applies both with respect to injuries that might be suffered by the child herself,[32] or to injuries or property damage that the child might cause to others.[33] It is premised on the view (which itself is derived from the doctrine of parental autonomy) that parents are entitled to exercise judgment in the fulfillment of their right and duty to raise their children.[34] According to the New York Court of Appeals in the case *Holodook v. Spencer*, for example, any other rule would "circumscribe the wide range of discretion a parent ought to have in permitting his child to undertake responsibility and gain independence."[35] The existence of such a wide range of discretion is deemed in the law to be particularly important given the traditional and even increasing pluralism of American society:

> [C]onsidering the different economic, educational, cultural, ethnic and religious backgrounds which must prevail, there are so many combinations and permutations of parent-child relationships that may result that the search for a standard would necessarily be in vain—and properly so.[36]

A few jurisdictions have rejected the *Holodook* rationale and adopted some variation of a "reasonable parent" rule that allows for an injured child or a third party who is injured by a child to hold responsible a "negligent" parent. However, even these decisions are weakened (almost to the point of being useless) by the express exclusion of any ordinary exercise of parental discretion from consideration as a basis for liability.[37] (Given that the doctrine of parental autonomy is paramount—constitutional doctrine trumps conflicting state law—this exclusion is required to keep the rule constitutional.) Thus, according to the *Restatement of Torts*, "the standard of a reasonably prudent parent ... recognize[s] the existence of that discretion and thus ... require[s] that the [parent's] conduct be *palpably* unreasonable in order to impose liability."[38] Moreover, according to the treatise *Prosser and Keeton on Torts*, "it is not possible to state an exact rule as to the scope of 'parental discretion,'" in part because "it is clear that the parent-child relationship remains a special one and that not every act or omission by a parent will be regarded as actionable negligence, even if, as to some other persons, negligence might be found to exist."[39]

For example, in adopting the "reasonable parent" rule in the case *Gibson v. Gibson*, the California Supreme Court recognized that the rule could not abrogate the right and duty of parents to exercise authority over their children.[40] Thus, the court explained that it was intended to extend only to those situations in which parents were negligent in ways that did not implicate that authority. Included among those situations were car accidents, where an insurance company was the real party in interest and thus where the parent actually instigates the lawsuit; negligent maintenance of household equipment, which has practically nothing to do with parental discretion; and willful, malicious, and intentional injuries, which in any event are not protected by the doctrine of parental autonomy.[41] Thus, despite the hypothetical intrusions that might be conceived based on the notion of the "reasonable parent," the few courts that subscribe to it have been careful to assure that the economic, ideological, and ethnicity-based diversity of child-rearing patterns in the United States are protected from any more intrusion than results from existing abuse and neglect law more generally.

This broad view of parental autonomy is unheard of outside of the United States, where parents are almost if not always either directly or vicariously liable for their children's circumstances and behavior. In a purely private context, where there is no state action involved, parents in this country are literally free from any restraints whatever on their ability to make such decisions. The Supreme Court of Arizona notes, for example, that "[t]he doctrine of parental immunity is an American phenomenon unknown in the English common law.... Courts in Canada and Scotland have held that children may sue their parents in tort."[42] On a personal note, I have for several years taught Torts as part of a program on United States law for foreign lawyers, and this point—that parents in this country are not in general directly or vicariously liable for the torts of their children—always is the principal source of the students' sense that Americans are bent much too far toward liberty and away from responsibility; indeed, the traditional rationales for this rule—that the children belong to all of society and thus that society should pay for their wrongs, and that we are not prepared as a liberal democracy to prescribe a particular parenting approach—bear little-to-no weight for them in this discussion.

One last corollary to this discussion is the existence in some states—including in the majority of jurisdictions that do not allow the general claim of negligent parental supervision—of the possibility that a parent might be found culpable of negligent supervision where the child injures another person or the property of another in circumstances where the parent knew or should have known that her child had violent or destructive propensities.[43] This is analogous to the "one bite free" rule that governs liability for damage and injuries caused by domestic animals or pets.[44] Thus, for example, the state of Colorado—where the events at Columbine High School took place—allows recovery from parents for damages caused by their children in circumstances where the parents knew or should have known of their tendency to be violent or destructive, and nevertheless failed reasonably to supervise them.[45] Victims of the shooting at Columbine have brought suit against the parents of Eric Harris and Dylan Klebold under this theory.[46] What is unclear from the facts that are publicly known today is whether the victims will be successful in proving that Harris's and Klebold's parents had actual or even constructive knowledge that their sons might try to kill someone. Ironically, it is because of the contemporary parenting practices that I described in Chapter Four that this rule is unlikely to be useful: Parents who are not there for their children in the ways that count developmentally are the least likely to know of their children's violent, anxious, or depressive tendencies.[47]

CHAPTER NINE

THE RIGHT TO FREE SPEECH

Like the right of parental autonomy, freedom of speech "is one of the preeminent rights of Western democratic theory, the touchstone of individual liberty."[1] Writing in the case *Palko v. Connecticut,*[2] Justice Benjamin Cardozo described the "freedom of thought and speech" as "the matrix, the indispensable condition of nearly every other form of freedom."[3] He explained further that "[w]ith rare aberrations a pervasive recognition of that truth can be traced in our history, political and legal."[4] Perhaps the most important aspect of this right to free speech is the right to speak about an infinite variety of subjects, indeed, whatever is on one's mind. Thus, for example, the right is inclusive "not only [of] political discourse, but [also of] the infinite range of artistic, scientific, religious, and philosophical inquiries that capture and cajole the human imagination."[5]

Freedom of speech has been justified by at least three liberal theories:

The first and most prominent is the so-called "marketplace theory," which holds that a free market in ideas is necessary to assure that "the truth" ultimately prevails.[6] The marketplace theory was perhaps first and most famously articulated by Justice Oliver Wendell Holmes, who wrote that "the best test of the truth is the power of the thought to get itself accepted in the competition of the market."[7] According to Rodney Smolla, "[t]he 'marketplace of ideas' is perhaps the most powerful metaphor in the free speech tradition."[8]

The second rationale is that which holds that free speech is crucial to assure human autonomy and dignity and individual fulfillment, not least because speech is the externalization of the most profound aspect of autonomy, namely human thought.[9] Thus, Smolla writes,

> [t]he marketplace theory justifies free speech as a means to an end. But free speech is also an end itself, an end intimately intertwined with human autonomy and dignity. In the words of Justice Thurgood Marshall, "The First Amendment serves not only the needs of the polity but also those of the human spirit—a spirit that demands self-expression." Free speech is thus specially

the ideas expressed. Content-based regulations are presumptively invalid."[24] Based upon this view of the wide swath of permissible speech, and of the corresponding narrow range of governmental authority to regulate it, the Court historically has been thrifty in its acquiescence to specific content-based restrictions on speech; indeed, it has allowed such restrictions in only two circumstances.

The first comprises the category of speech that is considered "unprotected" under the First Amendment, or not "First Amendment speech," because it is " 'of such slight social value as a step to the truth that any benefit that may be derived from [it] is clearly outweighed by the social interest in order and morality.' "[25] William Van Alstyne explains that "unprotected speech" is speech which is not considered subject to the inherent protections of the First Amendment, that is, it is speech about which the First Amendment is not concerned.[26] Speech that falls into this category is speech that is obscene from the perspective of adults,[27] child (but not other) pornography,[28] speech that constitutes "fighting words"[29] or that incites "imminent lawless action,"[30] and speech that is defamatory.[31] Material that falls into these categories may be regulated without regard to the otherwise strong protections provided by First Amendment doctrine.[32]

The second circumstance in which the Court has permitted restrictions on speech involves otherwise "protected speech" that the government can show nevertheless deserves to be regulated, because the society has a compelling interest that is endangered by its presence in the public discourse.[33] Where the government seeks to act in this situation, it must meet the strict scrutiny standard applicable to all restrictions on fundamental rights; that is, it must also tailor its regulation narrowly to assure that it is the least restrictive alternative possible.[34] By negative implication, all speech that does not fit within the few narrowly circumscribed categories of "unprotected speech" is subject to such strict scrutiny. Among other things, this second category includes "hate speech,"[35] speech which can be characterized as violent or antisocial,[36] and speech that is otherwise considered "indecent" or "offensive" for all or particular segments of the society.[37] Critical for purposes of this book is the rationale used to justify inclusion of these latter sorts of speech in the category of "protected speech."

Thus, according to Justice William O. Douglas, speech often is "[v]icious, irresponsible, and depraved."[38] However, "the [American] constitutional remedy is not censorship. The antidote is education, pinning our faith to the Jeffersonian creed that by education we may in time become mature people."[39] In this regard, Douglas explained that "[i]f society does such a poor job of educating itself so that four letter words and explicit pictures are dangerous, the remedy is to improve the educational process, not to outlaw certain publications."[40] Indeed, he opined that objectionable but otherwise "protected" speech is purposefully off limits to most content-based restrictions in part *because of* the disturbing effect it may have on the populace:

> [A] function of free speech under our system of government is to invite dispute. It may indeed best serve its high purpose when it induces a condition of unrest, creates dissatisfaction with conditions as they are, or even stirs people to anger. Speech is often provocative and challenging. It may strike at prejudices and preconceptions and have profound unsettling effects as it presses for acceptance of an idea. That is why freedom of speech, though not absolute, is nevertheless protected against censorship or punishment. There is no room under our Constitution for a more restrictive view. For the alternative would lead to standardization of ideas, either by legislatures, courts, or dominant political or community groups.[41]

This rationale survives intact today; indeed, as I noted above, there is clear evidence that in this respect also, First Amendment free speech doctrine is becoming ever more liberal in its orientation. A good example of this can be found in the Court's most recent decision in the case *United States v. Playboy Entertainment Group, Inc.*, which invalidated on First Amendment grounds a federal statute designed to block children's access to pornography on cable television.[42] According to Justice Anthony Kennedy, writing for the majority, the First Amendment does not incorporate a "relativistic philosophy or moral nihilism."[43] Rather, in his words, "[t]he Constitution exists precisely so that opinions and judgments, including esthetic and moral judgments about art and literature, can be formed, tested, and expressed. What the Constitution says," explained Kennedy, "is that these judgments are for the individual to make, not for the government to decree, even with the mandate or approval of a majority."[44] Perhaps most significant for present purposes was Kennedy's further nod to the information revolution: "Technology expands the capacity to choose; and it denies the potential of this revolution if we assume the Government is best positioned to make these choices for us."[45]

It is against this jurisprudential landscape that the Court has recognized what intuitive individuals and experts in child development have long known, namely that children may be differently and detrimentally affected by speech that is generally deemed appropriate or "protected" for adults.[46] (Of course, even for adults, pornography that is "hard core" also may be obscene, it which case it is no longer "protected speech" under the First Amendment.) Simultaneously, the Court also has recognized that parents—under the doctrine of parental autonomy—have the right and the obligation to determine the circumstances in which their children can hear or view speech that involves the secrets of adulthood, most importantly, sex and violence. (Children themselves have a heavily circumscribed right to free speech, but obviously no right whatever as against the wishes of their parents who in this respect are "the[ir] supreme earthly legislator[s].")[47] Finally, the Court traditionally has recognized that the government has a compelling interest in protecting children from harm, either as individuals in its *parens patriae* role, or collectively in its police power role.[48]

Despite these recognitions, however, the Court has acquiesced only to a very few restrictions on adult speech to protect children; all of these involved pornography or material that was deemed obscene for children.[49] Thus, in the case *Ginsberg v. New York*, the Court upheld a state statute designed to limit children's ability to purchase pornographic magazines from a drug store;[50] in *F.C.C. v. Pacifica Foundation*, it upheld a federal administrative order designed to assure that children did not hear profanity on the radio, at least during the time of day when they were most likely to be listening;[51] in *American Booksellers Association, Inc. v. Virginia*, it upheld a state law that prohibited bookstores from knowingly permitting children to view or purchase books that were deemed "harmful" to their interests;[52] and in *Board of Education v. Pico*, it upheld a state statute designed to prohibit children from obtaining books of an arguably prurient nature from the public school libraries.[53] These restrictive measures were upheld even though all but the last also to some degree restricted adult access the material at issue. That is, after the restrictions were upheld by the Court, pornographic material intended for adults was moved to a different part of the store or wrapped in special paper; and adults were able to hear "dirty words" on the radio and on television only at certain times of the day.

However, as I will describe below, the Court apparently has begun to move away from a sense that limited restrictions on adult speech are acceptable under the First Amendment, having recently refused to restrict children's access to pornography on the Internet,[54] on cable television,[55] and on the telephone.[56] Additionally, First Amendment doctrine has played a significant role, even if indirectly, in frustrating efforts to restrict other primarily violent and antisocial speech that is believed to be noxious for children. The most critical factor in cases challenging such efforts, regardless of how the cases were decided, was the impact the challenged regulation might have had on the right of adults to access the same material. As Catherine Ross has explained,

> [t]he pace of social change and the emergence of new modes and styles of communication have long inspired calls for censorship designed to shield children from contamination.... But whether or not such adult concerns are justified ... the Speech Clause [consistently] restricts the ability of the body politic to regulate speech that is protected for adults.[57]

In the most significant of the recent decisions, *Reno v. American Civil Liberties Union*,[58] the Court struck down certain provisions of the federal Communications Decency Act (CDA) that were designed "to protect minors from 'indecent' and 'patently offensive' communications on the Internet."[59] Proponents of the legislation imagined the CDA as "a sort of 'cyberzoning'" that would secure certain parts of cyberspace for the children by prohibiting and penalizing the placement of pornographic material in that realm.[60] In doing so, they "[a]cknowledg[ed] [the CDA] as a potential abridgment of First Amendment rights, ... [but they] consistently claimed that they were championing the Act for the compelling interest of protecting children from pornographic material."[61] Rejecting the government's approach, and brushing aside analogies to past zoning decisions,[62] as well as to prior rulings upholding restrictions designed to promote the welfare of children,[63] the Court found that the challenged provisions of the CDA were both vague and over-broad; as such, they impermissibly restricted adult speech.[64] Writing for the majority, Justice John Paul Stevens explained the Court's ruling in language that reaffirmed its strong commitment to liberal theory:

> In order to deny minors access to potentially harmful speech, the CDA effectively suppresses a large amount of speech that adults have a constitutional right to receive and to address to one another. That burden on adult speech is unacceptable if less restrictive alternatives would be at least as effective in achieving the legitimate purpose that the statute was enacted to serve.... It is true that we have repeatedly recognized the governmental interest in protecting children from harmful materials. But that interest does not justify an unnecessarily broad suppression of speech addressed to adults. As we have explained, the Government may not "reduc[e] the adult population ... to ... only what is fit for children." ... "[R]egardless of the strength of the government's interest" in protecting children, "[t]he level of discourse reaching a mailbox simply cannot be limited to that which would be suitable for a sandbox."[65]

Significantly, the Court also noted the legal impermissibility of such provisions, which by their terms would prohibit even a parent from choosing to allow her child to access otherwise restricted material.[66] In this respect, and as one commentator noted, the Court's liberal bent also overcame both utilitarian and communitarian arguments that were made in favor of the CDA. Specifically, "[i]n declaring the CDA unconstitutional, the [lower courts] tacitly acknowledged that the Act contravened a more fundamental American ideology—that of liberalism."[67] Indeed,

> [i]n deferring to First Amendment values in the face of what they conceded to be a compelling governmental interest, the judicial panels reconfirmed the primacy of rights in the American political landscape. In doing so, they declined to accept teleological communitarian arguments which suggest that society must define the scope of a right (e.g., free speech) in light of its conception of what is good (e.g. pristine family values necessitating an indecency-free Internet).[68]

The Court's concerns about the breadth of the CDA's operative terms were clearly legitimate; after all, the statute on its face failed to define with any specificity either the term "indecent" or the term "patently offensive." Thus, if one could conceive a way (semantically and technologically) to refine these terms so that they were the equivalent of hard copy pornography—to which children's access could be restricted under existing doctrine—this case would not be so significant in the long run, and the constitutional demise of the CDA in particular could be chalked up to bad legislative drafting or to antiquated technology. There are two flaws in this analysis, however, both of which point to the real significance and impact of the case. First, the Court itself acknowledges the practical problem that technology does not currently exist that can simultaneously block a child's access to "indecent" and "offensive" material on the Internet and permit such access to adults using the same computer terminal.[69] (Existing child filters were found not to be effective for this purpose.)[70] Second, current technology is incapable of discerning the difference between "decent" and "indecent" material, and between "inoffensive" and "offensive" material.[71] As a result, if the statute had prevailed, even children would have been denied access to legitimate material.[72] While it is possible that both of these circumstances could be overcome as the technology develops—useful filters might be conceived assuming that the more substantial definitional problem could be resolved—until then, they render the Internet essentially "off limits" to restrictive regulations of the sort that would be required to protect children from harmful access.

Most telling on this overriding point was the Court's obvious approval of the lower courts' characterization of this medium as the ultimate free speech soap box because of its uniquely participatory nature.[73] Indeed, the Court spoke directly of "the vast democratic fora of the Internet,"[74] and noted that "[t]hrough the use of chat rooms, any person with a phone line can become a town crier with a voice that resonates farther than it could from any soap box."[75] Based upon the record below, the Internet itself was described by the Court as "a ... wholly new medium of worldwide human communication" involving approximately 200 million people, who "are engaging in conversations on a huge range of subjects ... as diverse as human thought."[76] In turn, the CDA was described as "threaten[ing] to torch a large segment of the Internet community" that would participate in such democratic chat rooms.[77] All of the powerful free speech code words were invoked by the Court, embedded in the opinion as a not-so-subtle warning that the Congress in treading into this area had invaded the most hallowed First Amendment ground.[78] In the end, the message was loud and clear that as things stood, the Court did not want to deny that potential for anything, even for the children.

The second and most recent decision of the Court with which I am particularly concerned because it continues along this increasingly liberal trajectory is *United States v. Playboy Entertainment Group, Inc.*[79] In *Playboy*, the Court found unconstitutional that part of the federal Telecommunications Act of 1996 that required

> cable television operators who provide channels "primarily dedicated to sexually-oriented programming" either to "fully scramble or otherwise fully block" those channels or to limit their transmission to hours when children are unlikely to be viewing, set by administrative regulation as the time between 10 p.m. and 6 a.m.[80]

This restriction was designed to ensure that children did not inadvertently view pornographic material as a result of the "signal bleed" that might occur from the less precise scrambling methods that were favored by the industry.[81] The congressional means to achieve this would have forced adults who wished to view the programming to act affirmatively; that is, it placed the burden on them to call the programmer to request the broadcast, and unless they did so, the programming would be blocked.[82]

Writing for the Court, Justice Kennedy first rejected the government's compelling state interest argument. That is, for him and the majority, the government did not prove that children were exposed to pornographic signal bleed in numbers that were significant enough to warrant the restriction. In his words,

> [t]here is little hard evidence of how widespread or how serious the problem of signal bleed is. Indeed, there is no proof as to how likely any child is to view a discernible explicit image, and no proof of the duration of the bleed or the pictures or sound. To say that millions of children are subject to a risk of viewing signal bleed is one thing; to avoid articulating the true nature and extent of the risk is quite another.... The First Amendment requires a more careful assessment and characterization of an evil in order to justify a regulation as sweeping as this.[83]

This finding taken in isolation was not particularly noteworthy, since it was based on a data set that might well have been lacking in objective or scientific content. On the other hand, and as I will discuss further below, it was truly revolutionary in a doctrinal sense because it was the first time that the Court has refused to accept the government's argument in any context that it has a compelling interest in protecting children.

Next, the Court found that the statute was defective in any event because it was not "narrowly tailored" and did not employ the "least restrictive alternative" available to achieve the desired ends.[84] The Court found that placing the expensive and complicated scrambling technology that would be required to achieve this blockage would in many instances result in a programmer's inability to provide the programming at all, even to adults who would wish to see it. It also found that programmers who could not obtain this technology would be left only with the option of foregoing daytime programming, which would again result in a dearth of such programs for adults who wished to view them. Because either option would effectively diminish the availability of this programming for consenting adults at least during certain portions of the day, the majority also found the relevant provisions to be an unconstitutional denial of the right of adults to view the offending material. Thus, the majority accepted the industry's argument that the government could have protected the children and left access for adults otherwise intact by shifting the burden to act away from adults who wished to view the programming and onto parents who wished to block their children's access to the offending material. In a reverse of the scenario that was originally contemplated by Congress, under this "less restrictive alternative," the programming would remain available unless it was blocked.[85]

Dissenting in the case, Justice Stephen Breyer took issue with both parts of the majority's analysis. First, he expressed concern about the number of American children—which he pegged at 22 or 29 million, depending upon one's interpretation of the evidence presented in the case—who might be exposed at one time or another to the pornographic programming.[86] Based upon these statistics, which he accepted in spite of their relatively imprecise nature, Breyer harshly disagreed with the majority's view "that the Government failed to prove the seriousness of the problem—receipt of adult channels by children whose parents did not request their broadcast."[87] (Indeed, he opined that "[t]his claim is flat out wrong.")[88]

Next, Justice Breyer explained the practical need to address the problem in the way that Congress did:

> [the statute] inhibits the transmission of adult cable channels to children whose parents may be unaware of what they are watching, whose parents cannot easily supervise television viewing habits, whose parents do not know of their ... rights [to request blockage], or whose parents are simply unavailable at critical times ... This legislative objective is perfectly legitimate. Where over 28 million school age children have both parents or their only parent in the work force, where at least 5 million children are left alone at home without supervision each week, and where children may spend afternoons and evenings watching television outside of the home with friends, [the provision] offers independent protection for a large number of families.[89]

In contrast with the majority's approach, which can be characterized as ideological, Justice Breyer's was clearly pragmatic. As I will discuss below, the Court's contemporary First Amendment doctrine as applied in this line of cases involving restrictions on speech to protect children relies upon the outdated legal fiction that parents in the United States today continue to be available as they were historically to act as guardians of their children's access to adult speech. In doing so, this doctrine ignores the voluminous facts to the contrary, upon which Breyer based his dissent.

In the end, *Playboy* is most significant for the shifts that it signals away from prior doctrine that had tended to uphold for the benefit of children restrictions on adult speech that involved pornography. Indeed, it is difficult if not impossible to reconcile the case with its precedents, and especially with *Ginsberg, Pacifica Foundation*, and *American Booksellers*. This difficulty stems in no small measure from the fact that these precedents assumed that protecting children from pornography was a sufficiently important interest that adults might properly be inconvenienced—having to walk to a sequestered part of the magazine or video store to purchase pornography, or having to wait until after hours to hear "dirty words" on the radio—to ensure that protection. Moreover, although these "older" cases acknowledged that pornography was protected speech, they did not contemplate, as does the *Playboy* case, that pornography might someday turn out to be a proverbial First Amendment "truth." As a result, they did not imagine that such minor inconveniences for adults, such as having to make a call to get access to pornography on cable television, might be constitutionally barred.[90]

These new obstacles to restrictions on access to pornography are ultimately insignificant, however, in comparison with those that First Amendment doctrine interposes in the separate but related areas of violent and otherwise offensive speech, including so-called "hate speech." Indeed, as I have already noted, the Amendment purposefully protects material that is "vicious, irresponsible, and depraved" because this material is believed to contribute to the free market of ideas, both political and cultural, and because liberal theory rejects a role for the government in sorting out the truth from among competing viewpoints on the subject. The practical application of this theory can be seen in the position typically taken by the federal government that violent speech is not fit for regulation because it is impossible clearly to define the relevant terms and thus to do the objective triage that would be required to make any such regulation constitutional. For example, "[a]s early as 1972, the FCC concluded that it could not prohibit broadcast violence because the subject matter would prove impossible to define."[91] At that time, the FCC is said to have wondered "how to treat *Peter Pan*, where the crocodile eats Captain Hook."[92]

Catherine Ross extends the list of definitional dilemmas in this area to "other children's classics such as *Bambi*, who sees his mother shot by a hunter, or *Babar*, whose mother is similarly dispatched at the beginning of the first volume," and describes "one Congressman [who] recently wondered, does violence mean 'a movie like "*Home Alone*," ... a movie like "*Ben Hur*," ... [or] a movie like "[*Saving*] *Private Ryan*"?'"[93] And, she suggests that other "protected controversial speech"—including hate speech and other antisocial communication—"is even more resistant to precise definition" and thus to regulation that would withstand First Amendment scrutiny.[94]

It is not clear to me that doing triage in these areas is any more complicated than it is along the fuzzy line between pornography and obscenity. Presumably, just as the Court can "know obscenity when it sees it," it could know violence that was over the constitutional edge when it saw that, particularly if the inquiry is made in child development terms.[95] What is clear from its decisions, however, is that the Court (likely reflecting the values of the society as a whole) is willing to engage in the exercise, however futile, to distinguish objectively between pornography and obscenity, but it is not willing to do the same for violence and other forms of controversial but protected speech.[96] This reluctance to add to the categories of unprotected speech even to protect children again is consistent with the general trend of the society and of the Court to protect a highly liberal version of the right to free speech, even in the face of the most significant competing state interests.

The existence of a consistent body of state law decisions prohibiting private lawsuits that seek compensation from producers of violent and otherwise anti-social music, movies, and video games for their role in influencing children to commit acts of violence provides additional evidence that Ross's analysis is correct. An excellent illustration of this point is *James v. Meow Media, Inc.*,[97] which arose out of the 1997 school shooting in Paducah, Kentucky. In *Meow Media*, fourteen year-old Michael Carneal "took six guns, including a pistol, to the Heath High School in McCracken County, Kentucky ... [and] shot Jessica James, Kayce Steger, and Nicole Hadley ... to death ... [and] wounded five others."[98] The victims and their families filed suit in negligence against several defendants, including "the makers and distributors of a movie titled *The Basketball Diaries* ... the creators and distributors of various video games ... [and] various owners of internet websites."[99]

The Basketball Diaries was described in the complaint as "a nihilistic glamorization of irresponsible sex, senseless and gratuitous violence, hatred of religion, disregard of authority, castigation of the family, drug use, and other self-destructive behaviors."[100] The video games were described as "violent" and as "ma[king] the violence pleasurable and attractive, and disconnected ... from [its] natural consequences."[101] And the Internet sites were said to contain "certain pornographic and obscene material" of a particularly violent sort.[102] All three groups of producers were further characterized in the complaint as contributing substantially to Carneal's progressive emotional disintegration, and ultimately to the shootings themselves. For example, the Internet sites were said to have "served to further attenuate actions from consequences in Carneal's mind, made virtual sex pleasurable and attractive, provoked violence in Carneal, and disconnected the violence from the natural consequences thereof, thereby causing Michael Carneal to act out the violence."[103] In the face of these allegations, which had to be taken as true as a procedural matter, the district court granted the defendants' motions to dismiss on the ground that the plaintiffs had failed to state a viable claim.[104]

Specifically, the court found that Carneal's response to the violence in these products was "unforeseeable" and thus that the plaintiffs had failed to establish as a threshold matter that the defendants even owed them a duty of care:[105]

> Simply put, would reasonable people conclude that it was foreseeable to Defendants that as a result of disseminating their products and failing to warn of the materials contained therein, a fourteen-year-old boy who played their video games, watched their violent movie, and viewed their provocative website materials would go to a friend's house, steal guns, take the guns to school the next day, and gun down his classmates during a prayer session?[106]

The court obviously believed that its question was rhetorical, as it quickly concluded "as a matter of law [that] ... it was clearly unreasonable for Defendants to have foreseen Plaintiffs' injuries from Michael Carneal's actions."[107] And thus, "[b]ecause the injuries were unforeseeable, Defendants did not owe a duty of care upon which liability [could] be imposed."[108] In support of its decision, the court cited the strikingly consistent decisions of courts in other jurisdictions that have faced similar complaints.[109]

What is clear from this case (and those decisions that it cites) is that it is not based upon an analysis of the facts about reasonable foreseeability, but rather upon a policy-based or normative view about the kinds of harms that, "as a matter of law," will be considered compensable.[110] In other words, based upon the ample literature that explains the important negative influence that media technologies likely have on some children's emotional development and health, and on previous reported incidents just like this one, it is absolutely plausible that reasonable jurors could conclude that the defendants foresaw or should have foreseen that some children might react to their products just as Carneal did. (In this sense, "reasonable foreseeability" is merely "code" for the society's determination that a particular harm is compensable.)

It is also clear that the policy basis for the courts' analyses of the foreseeability issue was an overriding concern about free speech. Thus, while it expressly declined to decide the case on First Amendment grounds, the *Meow Media* court noted its view that

> [a state] court considering the application of [that state's] common law in this situation would obviously be aware of the constitutional problems looming in the background—and if possible, we believe, such a court would avoid applying the common law in a way that would bring the constitutional problems to the fore. The constitutional problems would be avoided, of course, by holding that the plaintiff failed to show a justiciable issue as to any breach of a recognized legal duty.[111]

The court went on expressly to incorporate free speech doctrine and considerations in its analysis of the foreseeability issue, adopting the view of the California Supreme Court in a related case that "it is simply not acceptable to a free and democratic society to impose a duty upon performing artists to limit and restrict their creativity in order to avoid the dissemination of ideas in artistic speech which may adversely affect emotionally troubled individuals."[112] According to that court, "[s]uch a burden would quickly have the effect of reducing and limiting artistic expression to only the broadest standard of taste and acceptance and the lowest level of offense, provocation and controversy."[113] Because it found that "[n]o case has ever gone so far," it concluded that there was "no basis in law or public policy in doing so here."[114]

Finally, this incorporation of free speech doctrine into the negligence calculus (in the context of foreseeability analysis) appears to have been based upon practical considerations as well. As the court noted in *Zamora v. CBS*,[115] a related case applying Florida law,

> [a] recognition of the 'cause' claimed by the plaintiffs would provide no recognizable standard for the television industry to follow. The impositions pregnant in such a standard are awesome to consider. Here the three major networks are charged with anticipating a minor's alleged voracious intake of violence

on a voluntary basis; his parents' apparent acquiescence in this course, presumably without recognition of any problem and finally that young Zamora would respond with a criminal act of the type in question. Again ... the question is appropriate; how and why should the Court create such a wide expansion in the law of torts in Florida? (Passing for the moment the important considerations presented by the First Amendment.) The clear answer is that such expansion is not warranted. Indeed, this Court lacks the legal and institutional capacity to identify isolated depictions of violence, let alone the ability to set the standard for media dissemination of items containing 'violence' in one form or the other.[116]

It should come as no surprise that the result in *Zamora* and the rationale just quoted have been cited repeatedly by other courts considering similar claims, including by the court in *Meow Media*.[117]

CHAPTER TEN

THE CONSTITUTION'S ROCKWELLIAN IMAGE OF LIFE IN CONTEMPORARY AMERICA

It ought to be clear from the foregoing discussion that the doctrines of parental autonomy and free speech separately establish formidable if not insurmountable barriers to the most immediately obvious, law-based solutions to the Columbine problem.

The Fourteenth Amendment's doctrine of parental autonomy precludes restrictions that limit the ability of parents to choose such things as when they will return to work after the birth of a child, whom they select to supervise and care for their child when they do re-enter the workforce, when they will leave their child completely alone, the sorts of relationships and interactions their child will have with others, and what access their child will have to entertainment and information technology. The right to make these choices is viewed as being the essence of parental autonomy—how the children will be raised, by whom, and in other respects what outside influences will be permitted to exist in the child's environment. Protecting such decisions from government interference ensures that parents retain their fundamental right to determine whether their children become part of or separate from the mainstream.

Similarly, the First Amendment's free speech clause precludes restrictions on the right of producers and distributors of media technologies—including movies, music, video games, television shows, and the Internet—to develop and make generally available material that is violent and antisocial, so long as it is not obscene. As the *Playboy* case suggests, it appears increasingly to be the case that even restrictions on pornography that may be obscene for children are unlikely to withstand constitutional challenge. Thus, restrictions on access to such material would contravene the essential understanding of the First Amendment, namely that the speech reflected in the material appropriately competes for the status of truth in the marketplace of ideas.

The preceding discussion also described the development of law in which the two doctrines operate in tandem, that is, in cases where the government sought specifically to protect children by restricting speech. This is the context in which the true strength of liberal theory as an obstacle to fixing Columbine becomes clear. The overarching theme of these cases, particularly the most recent ones, is that the First Amendment's speech clause is as close to inviolable and intransigent as an intellectual institution might be. More specifically, because it is the paramount business of that doctrine to ensure that protected speech is unfettered so that adults can freely engage the marketplace, it is emphatically not the doctrine's business to take care of (or to accommodate) children who are unprepared developmentally to shop side by side with adults. Rather, raising and protecting children as human activities are viewed in constitutional law as the near exclusive province of parents *whether they actually are engaged in that effort or not*. In this respect, parents are considered to be both the best caretakers of the children and to have the last clear chance to remedy any problems that may arise from inside and outside the home that would detract from that best care. Parents are thus legally also the most important factor in the success and failure of children, no matter how powerful any other influences might be in their development. While courts rarely have occasion to treat this issue formally as one of causation, there is little doubt based on the rationale of cases from *Dyson* to *Zamora*, that the failures of education and parental intervention, rather than any failure of First Amendment doctrine, are the responsible agents when children go awry. Whether or not this is factually true, the law treats it as if it were.

The clearest articulation of this theme is in the *Playboy* case, where the majority rested its interpretation of the First Amendment on the Rockwellian fiction of parents who are present in their children's lives to assist them in their triage through the various sorts of speech present in the marketplace. This case was not aberrational; the precedents upon which it relied also viewed parents as principally responsible for teaching the children how to discern the truth amidst the cacophony of ideas competing for their attention and patronage. Thus, for example, while the state statute restricting the sale of pornography to children was upheld in *Ginsberg*, the Court rationalized its result on the twin grounds that it was assisting parents in their work and that these same parents had the absolute right themselves to provide this literature to their children. On the other hand, the decision in *Playboy* is undoubtedly more liberal than in *Ginsberg* in rejecting a role for the state in assisting parents who cannot continually supervise their children. Finally, while we generally accept the notion that society and the government have a role to play in assisting parents to fulfill their responsibilities to children, or even in caring for the children themselves in some circumstances, this generalization falls apart where the problem for the children is also the subject matter of the First Amendment. Here, unlike in other aspects of the culture, the government is all but categorically prohibited from meddling.

What all of this means in practice is that when parents complain, as one mother did when she told Senator Joseph Lieberman that "I feel as if I'm in a competition with the entertainment industry to raise my children, and I'm not winning,"[1] the response of the law is explicit that "the constitutional remedy is not censorship... [but] education."[2] In other words, the law tells parents that if they really care about victory in this battle, they must see to it themselves that their children are taught to become "mature people ... [capable of tolerating and even of understanding the political and philosophical cultural importance] of four letter words and explicit pictures."[3] Moreover, the law is also clear that it is the job of parents—and not the entertainment industry or the government—to ensure that children do not have access to the influences parents consider corrupting of the values they wish to instill. In this endeavor, the law (of parental autonomy) will protect them; but in their effort to restrict in any meaningful way the products of the entertainment and technology industries that undermine their roles as parents, the law (of free speech) will more than likely be an obstacle.

It is no subtle point that the assumptions embedded in this constitutional scheme largely mirror the developmental research that I discussed in Part I. That is, the courts' application of law based upon the view that parents are the children's first and best caretakers and their last clear chance to avoid the problems posed by negative external influences is consistent with the view of experts in the field of child development. And, the courts' assumption about the relationship children have or should have with their parents also mirrors the reality of an earlier time that saw at least one parent, usually a mother, at home and in the classic parenting role. In other words, the law reflects what the culture historically assumed were the best child care practices, an assumption that has strong proponents within the contemporary child development community.

Having noted this, however, it is impossible not to bemoan the ironic circumstances in which this law has put the children: In its incorporation of the "best parent" model in both First and Fourteenth Amendment doctrine, and in its purposeful ignorance of the reality that large numbers of American parents today are not acting or being permitted by the society to act in a manner consistent with this model, the law has deprived the children and their advocates (including sometimes their parents) of some of the most obvious tools that could help the society to respond to the Columbine epidemic. The fact that this same doctrine has room for abuse and neglect laws that seek to protect children from bad parenting means little to nothing since these laws are themselves defined by its boundaries. At the end of the day, American children are left by and in the law without an individual or institution that is responsible in anything other than a moral sense for much of their developmental well being.

It is impossible in these circumstances not to echo the irreverent lament that "the law is a[n] ass."[4] Americans cannot morally or logically be committed to a jurisprudence that threatens in such a dramatic way the health and welfare of the society. This notion, that a pure version of liberalism will be the undoing of the United States because there can be no long term survival of the community without a real commitment also to social and individual responsibility, is not a new one. I am simply and in my particular factual context re-stating it again here. In any event, it bears repeating the point that has been both noncontroversial and essential certainly in American political history that the children are critical to the future welfare of the society, and thus that their well being is very much the society's business. Given this state of affairs, we must contemplate how the law might be altered to maximize our children's potential for a healthy future. I suggest that we might begin by reconsidering some aspects of both the doctrines of parental autonomy and free speech.

Parental autonomy is obviously the most intransigent of the two because it is at its essence a natural force rather than a political, philosophical, or legal construct. In the jargon of those fields, it predates our entry into the social compact, and it certainly predates the founding of this country. Human parents have taken care of their children as other animals have taken care of theirs since the dawn of time, and this care taking has been largely and throughout history unrestricted by the law. Indeed, the law's entry into this area of human relationships is quite recent as history goes. For example, in the United States, it was not until the early-to-mid nineteenth century that states first began to pass laws restricting the right of parents to kill or to have killed their disobedient children.[5] And certainly, parenting practices short of this often were completely unrestricted. As I have demonstrated, with a few significant exceptions, the jurisprudence has largely gone along with this view of the parental role and thus it is a most cemented aspect of our society. Nevertheless, there are at least two places where it is flexible enough to accommodate changes; changes that are crucial if we want to make progress against the Columbine epidemic.

The first relates to the laws of abuse and neglect, and specifically provisions that address emotional abuse and neglect. These provisions are relatively new in comparison with those that treat physical abuse, and perhaps because of this, but certainly also because the law generally is wary of all sorts of claims based upon emotional injury, they are rarely used.[6] Nevertheless, such laws exist, and to the extent that our understanding of the etiology, nature, and consequences of emotional injuries continues to grow, there is no doubt that the legal notion of emotional abuse and neglect should command increasing attention.

For example, as I described in Part I, developmental experts including researchers in the field of neurobiology understand today what they did not and perhaps could not understand before, that emotional neglect can cause physical alterations in the brain of the young child that are likely irreversible and that have significant implications for that child's chances for future emotional success. Similarly, research has been done which confirms that older children suffer from emotional neglect when their primary caretaker parents are physically absent from their daily lives or do not provide suitable parental substitutes, and that such neglect has equally significant consequences. The evidence in these respects is highly persuasive in much the same way that evidence of non-accidental physical injuries inflicted by a parent is persuasive evidence that a child is sufficiently at risk so that the law might properly intervene into the family to protect the child.

There are, of course, problems attendant upon emotional abuse and neglect cases that do not typically exist in cases of maltreatment with physical consequences. The clearest illustration of this point is the difference between an eight-year-old with a badly broken arm and an eight-year-old who suffers from deep loneliness: The existence of the broken arm is clear where loneliness may not be. And we understand without a doubt that a broken arm is a bad thing where we are likely to minimize the significance of loneliness, or at least to assume gradations of harm and concern that are not at issue with a physical injury. Nevertheless, while a greater effort may be necessary to imagine a charge of emotional abuse or neglect, it is both possible and essential that this effort be undertaken; simultaneously of course, it is critical that the society's resources be marshaled to assist parents to avoid such charges. As I explained in Part I, it is in large measure the tendency to minimize emotional dysfunction (and to view children as resilient despite the absence of support systems to ensure that resilience) that has created the Columbine problem in the first instance.

The second aspect of parental autonomy that ought to be reconsidered involves the sorts of parental conduct that might be said to cause unlawful emotional harm. As I noted above, even where the courts consider (generally as pendant problems) the emotional state of children who are subject to physical abuse or neglect, they tend to shy away from judgments that would treat negligent parenting as a proper subject of an emotional abuse or neglect charge. Thus, for example, the courts are loathe to consider the practice of raising latchkey children as negligent. They might assume that a parent who decides to leave a child at home alone has made a more-or-less conscientious and knowing assessment of his capacities for such independence. Or, they have concluded that the circumstances of the parent are such that she has little choice but to engage in this practice, and that there is little objective evidence that the child otherwise is at risk. Similarly, courts have not entered the discussion about caregiver-to-child ratios in day care centers so that they might opine, for example, that some particularly high ratio subjects the children to emotional abuse or neglect, and therefore that parents who choose those alternative parenting arrangements are guilty of maltreatment. (Obviously, to the extent that an individual parent's choices in this respect are limited by her income, the burden would need to be assumed by the government as it is already for other necessities such as food and shelter.) I suggest that the evidence concerning the negative effects of the latchkey practice and poor day care programs is clear enough or at least discernible in individual instances so that the courts ought to consider engaging these issues.

Free speech doctrine is not nearly so entrenched in our society in a historical sense, and thus should be more malleable in appropriate circumstances. For example, in contrast with the doctrine of parental autonomy, there is a strong sense that free speech is likely a political or philosophical idea rather than a natural one. There is certainly some dispute about this—for example, Rodney Smolla has expressed the view that man's thoughts, being natural, do not become unnatural simply because they are spoken aloud—but my point is simply that the concept is not so inflexible as parental autonomy. The doctrine in its most liberal and contemporary incarnation is also extremely young, dating by some estimates to the early 1960s. Certainly, the law as it applies to children is only that old; and based upon the changes wrought most recently by *ACLU v. Reno* and *Playboy Enterprises*, I would argue that its most problematic features are only in their infancy. Their relative youth cuts both ways, of course, and the most objective interpretation of the dominant cut is that Americans today are especially committed to an increasingly liberal version of rights, including the right to free speech. Indeed, as Mary Ann Glendon explains, the lay person's sense of the scope of that doctrine is likely more absolute even that the most liberal judicial interpretation. Nevertheless, as with the doctrine of parental autonomy, there are at least three aspects of free speech law that should be revisited.

The first is the Court's most recent abandonment in *Playboy* of its traditional practice of accepting the government's argument that it always has a compelling interest in protecting children. As far as I was able to determine, this was the first time in its history that the Court demanded that the government offer substantial proof of its compelling interest in protecting children, beyond its customary invocation of that purpose. In the past, including in its

1997 decision in *ACLU v. Reno*, the Court had consistently accepted the government's compelling interest representations—either without comment, or with a conclusory statement along the lines of, "of course" the government has such an interest—engaging in an evidentiary examination only of the merits of the particular means chosen to meet it.[7] Catherine Ross agrees with the majority of the Court (and presumably the ACLU) that a more searching examination of the government's allegations about its interest was necessary, arguing that "[s]erious consequences flow[ed] from this lack of attention to the nature of the interest served by regulating speech in the name of children."[8] As an academic writing from the perspective of a child's rights advocate, she defends this position on the ground that perfunctory acceptance of the compelling state interest representation "lead[] to the tacit assumption that the government's proclaimed interests are virtually immune from scrutiny,"[9] and because "it suggest[ed] that the boundaries of the speech from which children must be protected are virtually limitless."[10]

Even if this is true in certain respects, however, I suggest that it is equally clear in others that there are serious consequences, both practical and moral, to this assumption that the government is inappropriately involved in the care and welfare of the society's children. (By definition strict scrutiny review incorporates the rebuttable presumption that the government has no legitimate role to play in a particular context.) As I noted earlier, the courts' traditional deference to the government's compelling interest claim was based upon judicial acceptance of the *parens patriae* role of the state, as well as of the state's role under the police power to protect the health and welfare of society more generally, in which the protection of children generally is viewed as paramount. As an initial matter, it can hardly be said that this deference has come without substantial scrutiny. Indeed, political science literature is replete with discussion of the proper (often expansive) role of the state with respect to children, beginning at least with Plato's *Republic*. To the extent courts are seen as "deferring" to the state's claim of compelling interest, therefore, it is not because they have failed to scrutinize it strictly, but rather because they have accepted the analysis of previous generations that the standard is in fact met. Most important, however, where individuals and ultimately courts permit themselves to challenge this premise, either on philosophical grounds or by requiring extraordinary evidence of cause and effect (which may be impossible to produce for reasons having nothing to do with the merits of the claim) children in need often will be left without their traditional alternative guardian, and the society will be left with inadequate means to protect its posterity.

The second aspect of free speech doctrine that ought to be revisited is the reactive harms principle. As it is described in the literature, this principle prohibits restrictions on speech based upon the likelihood that it may cause a harmful emotional or intellectual reaction in others. And it requires victims who can be identified specifically and individually; that is, an assertion such as that which I make in this book, that large numbers of children are being harmed or placed at risk by their emotional reactions to exceedingly violent and antisocial speech is insufficient to justify restrictions. Notwithstanding the principle, however, free speech doctrine has allowed for barriers to obscenity and defamation; both of these categories of speech generally trigger emotional or intellectual reactions, and neither satisfies the imminence or physical harm requirements that underlie other restrictions such as bars against inciting imminent violence. These exceptions have been carved out, as we have seen, on the ground that their subject matters are "of such slight social value as a step to the truth that any benefit that may be derived from [them] is clearly outweighed by the social interest in order and morality."[11]

This same rationale could justify constitutional restrictions on speech that was known to be toxic to children, even though the harm they suffer also may be classified "reactive." That the Supreme Court has not done this reflects on its judgment that this exception should remain very narrow, and that any expansion would constitute a proverbial "slippery slope," to be avoided at all costs. On the other hand, to the extent that the rationale is valid at all, it is doubtful that extraordinarily violent and antisocial material holds "serious social value as a step to the truth," and thus that we would be treading on or jeopardizing the essence of the First Amendment by restricting access to the material to protect children. While I own this doubt, I am willing to gamble that many others—and perhaps even a majority—would claim it as well, including many of its consumers; I also am willing to gamble that even the most faithful adherents to a liberal free speech doctrine do not imagine a day where this material properly wins the marketplace's competition for "best idea" (or even "good idea").[12] Contemplating this possibility as the Court and First Amendment purists do is merely a rhetorical game that has everything to do (yet again) with their concern for the "slippery slope" and nothing to do with an assessment that this material might be even "a [small] step to the truth." Indeed, if it were otherwise, and the day came when the toxic material of which I speak—Nazi propaganda, violent sex, and virtual pedophilia, for example—became the ultimate truth in this country, the United States will have ceased being a liberal democracy, and will have devolved into what Fareed Zakaria has characterized as an "illiberal" one.[13]

In any event, the Court confirmed its fealty to the reactive harms principle in *Playboy*, when it demanded that the government prove that individual children in substantial numbers saw and were harmed by pornographic transmissions. And the lower courts since that case have rejected further government efforts to protect children from child pornography on the Internet (which ordinarily would be unprotected) on the ground that the particular pornography in question was virtual, and thus that no real child was victimized in the making of the material. Consistent with the notion of reactive harms, these courts ignored the indisputable fact that child pornography harms not only children who "act" in the productions, but all children who by virtue of the genre are likely to be objectified by the deviant adults who indulge in them. These cases suggest both that the trend in this area is increasingly liberal, and that this suggestion to revisit the scope of the principle of reactive harms likely already has been rejected. On the other hand, as my discussion in Part I showed, there still is much to be said for yet another visit: Children are most likely being harmed in a wholesale and irreparable manner by violence and antisocial messages. And as I have just argued in the context of changes to the doctrine of parental autonomy, we understand today that emotional harm can be as damaging as physical harm, and thus that protection from such harm is equally deserving of constitutional sanction.

The third aspect of free speech law that bears reconsideration is that which views as untouchable certain violent and antisocial speech. Currently, such speech is not only "protected" but as a practical matter is virtually inviolate because lawmakers and judges view it as impossible to separate good or harmless (and thus constitutional) from bad or harmful (and thus unconstitutional) speech in these areas. No one can dispute that this task would be difficult, but certainly no more so than the task of discerning pornography from obscenity. Justice Potter Stewart's well-worn judicial test for obscenity—"I could never succeed in intelligibly [defining obscenity] [b]ut I know it when I see it"—is equally applicable to speech that is harmfully violent and antisocial.[14] Indeed, we engage in a similar process daily, when we do the voluntary triage between age-appropriate and inappropriate speech. In other words, although it may be messy and "requires ascertainment of [a] dim and uncertain line," it can be done;[15] and *Ginsberg's* "variable obscenity" test provides a roadmap for its implementation, allowing us to keep the offending speech in its current protected category for adults, but to treat it as unprotected for children. The effect would be the same as it is for the speech at issue in *Ginsberg*: Adults would have to jump through a few hoops to speak or to access excessively violent and antisocial material, and children presumably would access it (easily) only through their parents.

As I noted earlier, it is clear from the Court's most recent decisions, especially *Playboy*, that the Court is no longer inclined—as it was, for example, in *Ginsberg, Pacifica Foundation*, and *American Booksellers*—to inconvenience adults in order to protect children, which suggests that it is unlikely to arrive at this different result in the near future. Nevertheless, it behooves us to recall exactly how minimal the inconvenience is: magazines wrapped in brown paper rather than available for all to see; movies on tape and video games in a separate part of the store rather than mixed in with those that are apparently child-appropriate; movies and television shows on adult-only access cable stations or broadcast only late at night rather than at all times of the day without restriction; and legislation that assures that inappropriate media products are not marketed to an under-age audience. Such measures are a small price to pay if they reduce the causes of the Columbine problem. Indeed, it is myopic to consider them in any other light.

I am ultimately a pragmatist. A doctrine that works only in theory, that is, a doctrine that assumes and even promises the "best care" or the "truth" but that utterly fails in practice is unworthy of the careful protection that defines our most basic rights. For that reason, these constitutional critiques are legitimate. Furthermore, the changes they implicate are critical; they would go a long way to allowing for some of the more important law-based solutions to the epidemic of dysfunctional children that currently plagues this nation. Perhaps most importantly, the law itself is flexible enough to accommodate them. Nevertheless, because the trend is obviously in the opposite direction, it is essential to evaluate the feasibility of the more popular extra-legal alternatives.

CHAPTER ELEVEN

THE ROLE AND EFFECTIVENESS OF RELIGION AND COMMUNITARIANISM

Perhaps because they understood (and even endorse) the obstacles that the doctrines of parental autonomy and free speech interpose to any law-based solution to Columbine, politicians across the political spectrum have talked almost exclusively of voluntary solutions to that problem.[1] Specifically, both the events at Columbine and the larger national crisis that it reflects have prompted impassioned calls from individuals as far removed ideologically from one another as former President Clinton and Patrick Buchanan for a new commitment to community, religion, and family values. Each of these suggestions reflects an understanding that, in this area, liberalism has failed our children, or at least that within its boundaries communitarian or group-based philosophies are the most promising antidotes.[2]

As the following discussion reveals, this notion may be correct in theory but it is inherently flawed as a practical matter, because the United States is as committed in its culture as it is in its law to liberal rather than communitarian tenets. This point is obviously redundant of the preceding discussion. What is perhaps not so evident is that this commitment also suggests strongly that Americans are unlikely voluntarily to subscribe to a new course of conduct to protect the children from emotional dysfunction if the cost is relinquishment of the personal freedoms that are at the core of the Columbine problem. The fact that politicians have now joined the chorus begun years ago by the clergy to care daily for the children and for family is likely to have no more impact than the clergy has had acting alone.

President and Hillary Clinton's speeches to the children of Columbine, their parents, and teachers in the aftermath of that tragedy were most extraordinary in this regard, both because the two have in other respects elevated the care and protection of children to an unique level in the history of the nation's politics, and because they are not only convinced of but also committed to the power of the law in general to affect change in society and specifically to protect children.[3] (In other words, their particular choice to join what has most typically been a conservative chorus is more indicative of the measure of liberalism's impact than are similar pronouncements coming from political conservatives.)[4] In those speeches, which in large measure were indistinguishable, the Clintons addressed the causes of Columbine, and suggested strongly that the real solution to the problem was to be found within the community-minded individual who would voluntarily join together with others to build a new American culture where faith, self-awareness, and a new respect for children and individual differences were the predominant personal and cultural values.[5]

For example, Hillary Clinton "imagined" a country where "everyone acted ... as a family ... that was really committed to making sure we helped each other, we cared about each other, we reached out to one another."[6] She emphasized the protection of children, of course, "imagining" again a future where "every adult in America began looking at his or her personal life, professional life and public life with a view toward making sure that whatever we do is good for children."[7] While the President's speech hinted at some related political initiatives—increased risk analysis and security precautions in public schools, for example—his language left no doubt that these would be designed merely to complement the largely voluntary personal and cultural shift that was the principal focus of his remarks.[8] In other words, the Clintons conceived of a society where liberalism continued to prevail in the law, despite their apparent view that at least this social problem cannot be solved unless the people acting as a whole and in the exercise of their rights choose a communitarian path.

In their collective sentiments on the subject of Columbine, the Clintons and their erstwhile conservative opponents are correct. There is little doubt that communitarianism, some religious doctrines, and family values broadly defined are good for children.[9] This is because all of these see the individual as existing within and deriving her self-satisfaction largely from membership in a community, and correspondingly emphasize individual responsibility for the care and protection of others within that community, particularly those who are vulnerable. Thus, children, and some adults who are poor, disabled, and elderly clearly benefit from adherence to their tenets. On the other hand, because liberal theory emphasizes the "centrality of the individual's concerns as opposed to those of the family, community, or state," the vulnerable in our midst, including the children, are less likely to receive the best protection in this tradition.[10]

Thus Adrien Katherine Wing explains that

> individualism undervalues and denigrates the contributions of those in society who are unable to take care of themselves, such as the elderly, children, the disabled and stay-at-home parents. These categories of people need assistance not only on an individual basis, but often also on a group-wide basis. Their very survival depends on the efforts of others and they are unlikely to be able to assert their rights on their own behalf. Yet the theory of individualism does not accommodate their need for assistance.[11]

Mary Ann Glendon concurs, noting that "[i]n its relentless individualism [rights talk] fosters a climate that is inhospitable to society's losers, and that systematically disadvantages caretakers and dependents, young and old."[12] To the extent that constitutional rights doctrine incorporates the notion that even the strongest fundamental rights can be overcome where the government can show that it has a compelling state interest—that is, a very important societal or communal need—it cannot be said to be liberal in its purest sense. Rather, such doctrine can be said to incorporate both liberal and communal interests, however, obviously elevating individual rights over communitarian objectives in its particular formulation.

This academic (or theoretical) view of the impact of liberalism on children is mirrored in related developmental literature as well as in religious and other cultural commentary. Thus, for example, Penelope Leach writes that while "most people [within this society] want to be self-respecting, solvent citizens and good parents," the society's "overall 'social ethos' of individualism and competition" makes it all but impossible to achieve this objective.[13] According to

Leach, "[t]hat ethos is inhospitable to all personal caring roles because caring always demands a sharing, even a subsuming, of
self."[14] And she notes that "[i]t is especially inhospitable to parenting because children's minute-by-minute physical and emotional
dependency may be as great as that of even the most dependent
adults—the acutely sick, the frail aged—and lasts much longer."[15]
Finally, Leach emphasizes the all-important impact of work and
the drive for money on contemporary American parenting practices:

> Social attitudes and institutions reflect individualism and rein-
> force the conflict [that exists for parents as a result.] Individual
> endeavor and achievement, personal fulfillment and self-es-
> teem, social recognition and rewards are all focused on work
> that is both conceptually and actually separated from interper-
> sonal aspects of living and sometimes so salient to individuals
> that it serves as a replacement for those aspects. Work is paid
> with money, of course, but money that is valued for itself as
> well as for what it buys.... Once social status and self image are
> not merely associated with but built through the accumulation
> of wealth itself, personal and pecuniary motives for work be-
> come inextricably entangled, unpaid activities degraded, and
> satisfaction in the actual processes of daily work, or in any-
> thing it produces other than money, a rare privilege. Rarest
> privilege of all—as parents particularly know—is the time and
> energy to enjoy what work and money buy: to have fun with
> the children, use the longed-for products, visit the saved-for
> vacation home ... It may be thought worthy to work at per-
> sonal relationships ... but it will usually be considered more
> interesting to work at professional ones ... and get paid for
> doing so.[16]

The Christian theologian Ted Peters elaborates on these same
themes, explaining that contemporary

> values emphasize self-expression, personal fulfillment, and the
> pursuit of happiness for the individual. What has become mar-
> ginalized and subordinated is loyalty to the family bond—that
> is, a loss of parental fidelity to children who are dependent on
> adults to support and guide their lives.[17]

In the end, Peters focuses his own attentions on the prevailing notion of individual choice as "a symbol of the triumph of the liberal ideals that guide our Enlightenment society."[18] And, he writes that in this scheme—which he clearly sees as pervasive and immutable—the only solution to protect the vulnerable, including the children, is to convince individual adults that it is in their selfish interests to exercise their freedom of choice in a manner that would yield that result: He says that "[t]he trick will be to show how commitment to family life and the loving of children is an expression of, rather than an alternative to, choosing the path of self-fulfillment."[19]

While Peters' own focus is on convincing Christian adults to enter into a "covenant" to protect the children, his suggestions certainly can be divorced from religion and applied more broadly to others who would care to make this same commitment.[20] Despite this appeal, however, and particularly because it continues to be premised on individual choice, this solution is as flawed as the suggestions made by the Clintons and others in the aftermath of the events at Columbine High School. That is, it would solve the Columbine problem only for those children whose parents and supportive adults chose voluntarily to make his covenant.[21] Based upon the discussion in Part I, it is clear that even in the face of dramatic statistics on childhood dysfunction—extraordinary rates of suicide, violent crime, depression, and anxiety disorders primarily—few relevant adults appear willing or even able in many instances to respond positively to that call. Indeed, in spite of the enormity of the problem, parents appear increasingly likely to leave their children alone or with inadequate alternative care givers; at the same time, the children appear to be increasingly likely to encounter an emotionally toxic environment in other respects, including from the media.

What is clear at the end of the day, then, is that in the search for comprehensive solutions to the Columbine epidemic, liberalism leaves us with very little in the way of realistic possibilities: Its embodiment in the relevant constitutional jurisprudence assures that no complete answer that is law-based is likely to survive judicial scrutiny; and its almost complete vanquishment of our cultural norms simultaneously assures that any extra-legal or voluntary solutions also are likely to fail. This is an odd and even frightening predicament for a society like the United States which prides itself on the flexibility of its laws, and more specifically on its conviction that liberalism as a political philosophy and liberal democracy as its institutional incarnation are the best systems that have ever or could ever be conceived.

PART III

A PARTIAL ANSWER IN THE PUBLIC SCHOOLS

In Part I of this book, I described the epidemic of childhood dysfunction that I call the Columbine problem, or Columbine *writ large*. In that context, I explored the ultimate causes of most contemporary childhood dysfunction: inadequate parenting and parent substitutes, unmediated exposure to violent and antisocial media, and a toxic external environment, including in the schools. In Part II, I discussed the fealty of American law and culture to classic liberal principles, focusing particularly on the doctrines of parental autonomy and free speech. And I argued that these doctrines preclude all immediately obvious and comprehensive law-based solutions to Columbine. I concluded that Part with a discussion of the inadequate promise of religion, family values, and related voluntary communitarian initiatives as alternatives to fixing the epidemic.

In this Part of the book, I argue that a viable albeit partial remedy lies in a re-invented curative role for the public schools.[1] I first argue that the public schools provide what is perhaps the only feasible law-based solution that would address the principal causes of Columbine, because they have since their origins been conceived as a special enclave of *mandatory* communitarianism in American law and political philosophy. Because of this, the relevant constitutional doctrine empowers the government to institute a culturally-corrective curriculum despite its tendency to privilege certain values and behaviors. Next, I argue that the curriculum of the public schools should be reformed consistent with this doctrine to assure that American children are provided those prophylactic and curative lessons and protections that are necessary according to the child development model to produce, as the schools were intended to do, "well-developed [wo]men and citizens."[2]

Earlier in the Introduction, I characterized the contents of this reform as a secular "book of virtues." I expand upon this characterization below. In this same discussion, I also argue that the school day and year, as well as the period of public school education, should be lengthened not only to accommodate this curricular reform, but also to provide a safe haven for children who would otherwise be without appropriate supervision and care. Finally, and perhaps most importantly, because Columbine is a public health problem that is national in scope, I conclude this part with the suggestion that a national solution is essential to assure that it is fixed across the board. Specifically, I argue that the reformed curriculum should be federalized so that all children across the United States will have access to its curative properties. I conclude by rejecting the notion that the necessary uniformity can be obtained by the actions of local school boards, and with an explanation of why the seemingly insurmountable obstacle of "local control" of public education is in fact as malleable as we are willing politically to make it.

CHAPTER TWELVE

WHERE LIBERALISM YIELDS TO COMMUNITARIANISM IN THE LAW

In its almost-singular focus on the health and welfare of the community, the doctrine that defines the purposes of the public schools is quite unlike that which governs other mandatory or law-based political institutions in the United States. This communitarian focus has existed since the nation's otherwise liberal founders and their philosophical mentors conceived the idea of universal public education expressly to ensure *both* that the children (as future citizens) would grow to be well-mannered and virtuous *and* that they would be able to read, write, and do arithmetic. In other words, this initial concept was not, as we might imagine today, singularly focused on the acquisition by the children of the classic "three R's." Indeed, quite to the contrary, the assumption was that academic learning needed to be tied together with lessons in "virtue" to ensure the success of the fledgling democracy. The discussion that follows reveals that this original concept is alive and well in the most contemporary American jurisprudence.

As Lawrence Cremin explains, the original concept for the public schools in the United States was premised on "four fundamental beliefs," each of which linked the schools directly and purposefully to these dual communitarian objectives. Those beliefs were

[1] that education was crucial to the vitality of the Republic; [2] that a proper republican education consisted of the diffusion of knowledge, the nurturance of virtue (including patriotic civility), and the cultivation of learning; [3] that schools and colleges were the best agencies for providing a proper republican education on the scale required; and [4] that the most effective means of obtaining the requisite number and kind of schools and colleges was through some system tied to the polity.[3]

This notion of the multiple purposes underlying public education, and in particular the emphasis on "the nurturance of virtue," held a prominent place in the original writings of John Locke, among others. Thus, in *Some Thoughts concerning Education*, Locke emphasized that the "aim of education is to produce a healthy, virtuous person,"[4] and he defined "virtue" specifically to include such character traits as "civility, feeling of humanity, generosity, gracefulness of voice and gestures, honour, humility, industry, kindness, love of God, love of study, modesty, politeness, prudence, reverence, self-control, self-denial, [and] self-restraint."[5] As one scholar explains, "Locke's [educated] person is, in short, a socialized and Christianized individual."[6] Given Locke's status among contemporary Americans who are faithful to the most liberal small government ideology, his position on education for the common good is clearly most significant.

Cremin's "four fundamental beliefs" about public education, including particularly this view of the role of virtue in a good curriculum, were shared by the important intellectuals at the time of the nation's founding. Indeed, "[n]o theme was so universally articulated during the early decades of the Republic as the need of a self-governing people for universal education. The argument pervaded the discourse of the Revolutionary generation ... [so that b]y the 1820s the need of a self-governing people for universal education [incorporating these precepts] had become a familiar part of the litany of American politics."[7] For example, Benjamin Franklin,[8] Benjamin Rush,[9] John Adams,[10] James Madison, Thomas Jefferson, and George Washington[11] all argued that the success of their democratic experiment rested on some version of a universal system of public education that would feature the necessary lessons in knowledge *and* virtue.[12]

Benjamin Franklin's writings on the subject are typical in this respect. For example,

> [i]n 1750, [he] wrote to Samuel Adams of his educational dreams: "I think with you, that nothing is more important for the public weal, than to form and train up youth in wisdom and virtue. Wise and good men, are, in my opinion, the strength of the state; much more so than the riches or arms, which under the management of ignorance and wickedness, often draw on destruction, instead of providing for the safety of the public."[13]

In particular, Franklin suggested the "abandon[ment of] both religious education and traditional education for more enlightened philosophies."[14] (One can imagine that such a suggestion would not sit well with local puritan school boards.[15]) Franklin, described as "[a]n admirer of Lockean social psychology, ... rejected the prevalent belief in innate ideas for the environmentalist's argument that men were molded by their experience and surroundings. Consequently, an enlightened people would institute good political and social systems that in turn would ensure the development of good people."[16]

The curriculum that Franklin conceived to accomplish these ends was described in his *Proposals Relating to the Education of Youth in America*.[17] It included the "abandon[ment of] both religious education and traditional education for more enlightened philosophies."[18] Specifically, Franklin believed that

> [t]o prepare the young for careers in the bustling business civilization of eighteenth-century America, ... they should be encouraged to form useful habits, master business skills, and follow the practical sciences ... [And t]o ensure that the profit-minded youths would not worship Mammon unduly, [he] recommended a sufficient dosage of moral science for each student.[19]

Not surprisingly, his rejection of existing curricula caused substantial consternation among traditionalists who "opposed his plan for the mass education of the young."[20]

Benjamin Rush appeared to hold a similarly national perspective on the education of American youth. For example, he "sought to introduce schools in Pennsylvania that would be modeled after the schools of Scotland," which were organized jointly and with unparalleled success in Europe by the national government of that country and the church.[21] And while Rush clearly disagreed with Franklin on the matter of rejecting traditional religious-based education for a more utilitarian approach, he did share Franklin's concern that education of the young was critical to the success of the new national enterprise. Indeed, "Rush, unlike Franklin, invoked the aid of religion to bolster his educational theories. Religion to him was the moral basis for any republican scheme of education."[22] His views about the purposes of education were much broader than this, however. For example, "[i]n his essay 'Education Agreeable to a Republican Form of Government,' Rush praises education as a purger of prejudice and superstition in religion, a boon to liberty, a promoter of just laws and good government, a teacher of

belief and support of the ideas undergirding the American
founding, spelled out in the Declaration of Independence and
the U.S. Constitution, and further revealed by statesmen like
Washington, Jefferson, and Lincoln; representative democracy;
individual equality under the rule of law; faith in the public
schools as agents of upward mobility; the value of a common
language; and the benefits of capitalism and the rewards of
thrift.[33]

Miller attributes largely benevolent motives to this movement.
Thus, he states that "[t]he Americanizers were motivated partly by
altruism—a sincere desire to help their neighbors make a home in
the United States and become contributing members of society. But
worries also affected them. What would happen if these new immigrants did not assimilate?"[34] Despite Miller's take on the Americanizers, there is a substantial argument that their motivations, or at least
the motivations of some in their midst, were ethnocentric or racist.
Indeed, the very notion that the Anglo-American culture was to be
preserved at the expense of immigrants with different cultural incli-
nations is seen by many critics as unassailable evidence of the ethno-
centrism of the times, and of the paternalism of its proponents who
assumed that there was little to no value to be gotten for the larger
society out of that cultural difference.[35] Notwithstanding this argument and how it might be resolved, there is little doubt that the
Americanization movement helped to solidify in the average person's mind the founders' belief in the significance of the public
schools as the social institution that could best or most effectively inculcate the norms that were necessary to assure a particular version
of success for the broadening American community.
    It was in this context that the United States Supreme Court
rendered its seminal decision on the question of governmental
authority over the schools and their curricula. Decided in 1923,
Meyer v. Nebraska still stands for the narrow proposition that "in
time[s] of peace and domestic tranquility," the state may not prohibit the teaching of modern languages other than English to elementary school students in private schools.[36] More broadly, however, and in the absence of controversy, the case established the
right of the state "to prescribe a curriculum for institutions which
it supports."[37] Similarly, the case established the constitutionality

of government-imposed curricular requirements that were designed to "improve the quality of [the state's] citizens, physically, mentally, and morally" for both public *and* private schools.[38] Thus, the Court in *Meyer* expressly condoned "[t]he desire of the legislature to foster a homogenous people with American ideals, prepared readily to understand current discussions of civil matters."[39] And it condoned the development of a mandatory curriculum designed to assure that American children learn not to exhibit the personal "characteristic[s] of [the nation's] truculent adversaries."[40] Given the date of the decision, the Court here likely was referring to Germans and citizens of the other Central Powers.

Consistent with *Meyer*, and in spite of its evident jingoism, the law remains unequivocal that the government has "absolute discretion" in its regulation of the public schools curriculum.[41] (The principal constitutional exception to this rule is, of course, the bar against the establishment of religion in state-sponsored education.) More specifically, the case law since *Meyer* has been clear that the government may regulate the curriculum expressly to inculcate those values which it believes are "plainly essential to good citizenship."[42] As the Court emphasized in its decision in *Brown v. Board of Education*, the government must be permitted such latitude so that the schools can operate as intended, as "a principal instrument in awakening the child to cultural values, in preparing him for later professional training, and in helping him to adjust normally to his environment."[43]

The Court's 1986 decision in *Bethel School District No. 403 v. Fraser*, which addressed state restrictions on "lewd speech" by children in the schools, emphasized the continuing vitality of this doctrine:

> "[P]ublic education must prepare pupils for citizenship in the Republic.... It must inculcate the habits and manners of civility as values themselves conducive to happiness and as indispensable to the practice of self-government in the community and the nation." ... The process of educating our youth for citizenship in public schools is not confined to books, the curriculum, and the civics class; schools must teach by example the shared values of a civilized social order. The schools, as instruments of the state, may determine that the essential lessons of civil, ma-

ture conduct cannot be conveyed in a school that tolerates lewd, indecent, or offensive speech and conduct.[44]

The Court in *Fraser* held that the state could punish a student for making a "lewd" speech to the student body during a session that was designated as "curricular."[45] In doing so, it noted specifically that "[n]othing in the Constitution prohibits the states from insisting that certain modes of expression are inappropriate and subject to sanctions. The inculcation of these values is truly the 'work of the schools.'"[46]

Relatedly, while the courts have found unconstitutional some curricular measures and compulsory education requirements, all of these decisions continue to emphasize the proper role of the government in assuring that children are educated to become good citizens and otherwise positively functioning members of the society. The best (and most famous) illustration of this point is *Wisconsin v. Yoder*.[47] In *Yoder*, the Supreme Court held that the state of Wisconsin could not punish Amish parents who refused to send their fourteen and fifteen year old children to school despite that this refusal violated the state's compulsory education laws, because it agreed with the parents that the enforcement of this requirement would place an unconstitutional burden on the free exercise of their religion.[48] In so holding, the Court specifically found that requiring Amish students to attend school between the ages of fourteen and sixteen (the last years of compulsory education) would result in their exposure to mainstream values and lifestyles that were contrary to those of the Amish.[49] It further found that such exposure risked diminishing the commitment of the Amish students to their religion and to their insular community and, because of the small numbers of individuals involved, ultimately risked the existence of the community as a whole.[50] Finally, the Court found that while the state had a significant interest in mandating formal education for children through the age of sixteen, this interest was insufficient in the narrow circumstances of the case to outweigh the heavy burden the mandate placed on the parents.[51] That is, it involved only children between the ages of fourteen and sixteen who would, as a result of their parents' preferences, miss at most two years of formal education.

What is significant for my purposes is that even in this case where the Court found in favor of parents who wished to preclude their children's exposure to mainstream values, it continually emphasized the narrowness of its holding. Specifically, the Court noted that its decision was confined to its peculiar factual context, including that the Amish children at issue would not, if their parents had their way, ever participate in mainstream society.[52] It further emphasized that the additional two years of formal mainstream schooling the state wished to impose would not, in any event, have a significant effect one way or the other on the ability of these children to function in mainstream society; after all, the state had been given the opportunity to inculcate its values in those children up until they were fourteen.[53] Finally, the Court emphasized the long history of the Amish people and their positive contributions to the society despite their insularity, but especially "the adequacy of their alternative mode of continuing informal vocational education in terms of precisely those overall interests that the State advances in support of its program of compulsory high school education."[54] In other words, the Amish were already advancing the same interests the state itself sought to pursue in its programs of public and compulsory education. Cases decided since *Yoder* have emphasized these same points in ruling, one way or another, on parental claims that state curricular requirements have impinged on their right to raise their children as they wished.

Ultimately, it is in the context of the so-called "Scopes II" case, *Mozert v. Hawkins County Board of Education*, that this longstanding doctrine has been most recently and completely articulated.[55] In *Mozert*, a decision out of the United States Court of Appeals for the Sixth Circuit, the state's authority to teach majoritarian values to all students in the public schools was directly challenged by parents who described themselves as Fundamentalists or Born-Again Christians.[56] These parents argued that the school board's requirement that students read from a textbook series that incorporated such values as tolerance, gender neutrality, and secular humanism, forced upon them an unconstitutional choice between the government benefit of public education and their right freely to exercise their religion.[57] (The parents' free exercise claim was premised on the view that, because the children involved were of a particularly impressionable age, the lessons risked undermining the contrary religious training they received at home.) Significantly, one parent—Vicki Frost—testified that the school had no need for such values-laden texts, since the purpose of lessons and school was to "learn to read, to have good English and grammar, and to be able to do other subject work."[58]

Calling the lessons "mere exposure and not indoctrination," the Sixth Circuit rejected the parents' position that they imposed an unconstitutional burden on the parents' free exercise of their religion.[59] As a result of this approach and ruling, the court never reached directly the question of the state's interest in those lessons. Despite this, however, and in the related context of its analysis of the constitutionality of the burden the lessons imposed on the parents' rights, the court emphasized the historical acceptance of the state's plan for the "character education" of its students: According to the applicable statute, character education was designed "'to help each student develop positive values and to improve student conduct as students learn to act in harmony with their positive values and learn to become good citizens in their school, community, and society.'"[60] And thus, with respect to the formal "inculcat[ion of] the habits and manners of civility as values," *Mozert* specifically recognized that "character education," including "teaching students the boundaries of socially appropriate behavior," is a "societal interest" of substantial value.[61]

Given this longstanding focus on the needs of the community in the development of the legal doctrine that governs the public schools, it is intriguing that much of the political rhetoric and the assumptions of many ordinary citizens are to the contrary. Here I include the Vicki Frosts of the society, as well as others all across the political and ideological spectrum, who assume as she did that the principal if not singular purpose of public education is to "learn to read, to have good English and grammar, and to be able to do other subject work" for the benefit of the individual parents and children concerned.[62] Indeed, the sense that citizens are consumers of a educational product that is a benefit or entitlement (because someone pays taxes) pervades the modern discourse about the failures of the public schools system, and in large measure drives the discussion about vouchers as an alternative that would assure that consumers get their due.

A good example of this self-centered view of public education can be found on a website devoted to the 1996 presidential election, which provides that,

> with violence, failure, and truancy soaring to record highs, the public school system has proven itself unable to deliver a quality education, or even a safe environment, for our children. We have waited patiently for improvements in public education, while time has been running out for the millions of young people in school today. We have had enough of new programs, pedagogical reforms and superficial experiments; we must act decisively and boldly to change the essential nature of American education.[63]

This characterization of public education as a defective product set the stage for proponents of school vouchers to argue the merits of that alternative:

> Choosing the best school for their children is a critical decision for all parents, regardless of wealth, race, or religious affiliation. American parents must be able to take responsibility for this key decisions in their children's lives. School vouchers offer a remedy for the inefficient schools our present system of public education has taught us to expect. In the voucher program, Americans would vote with their feet, sending their children to the schools that work best, while those schools which fail to provide a quality education would have to improve or close. The best schools will no longer be reserved only for those who can afford to spend thousands of dollars a year on tuition. Americans want less government intervention in their lives and more choices. School vouchers put the power back into the hands of the people.[64]

This discussion is filled with "rights talk" that itself furthers the notion that the public schools system exists to provide the citizenry with opportunities for individual advancement. Nevertheless, while there is little doubt that individuals benefit in many ways and directly from the system, and that equal protection principles assure to some extent their right to those benefits, its history and the cases are clear that this self-centered perspective is an erroneous or at least ancillary one: At its essence, public education exists first and foremost to benefit the American community.[65]

CHAPTER THIRTEEN

CURRICULUM REFORM AS AN ANTIDOTE TO COLUMBINE

In this chapter, I suggest that contemporary progressive approaches to curriculum reform that include character education and civics lessons, pre-school programs, and extensions of the traditional school day and year, are entirely consistent with the historical approaches to curriculum development that I have just described. Specifically, the use of the schools in the curative roles that are contemplated by these programs is consistent with the function they have served as a means to solidify the commitment to democratic government, to assure the existence of a single American community in the midst of extraordinary pluralism, and to guarantee that the members of this community succeed so that the future of the nation in turn can be secured. I agree with some others that because these progressive approaches go to the roots or ultimate causes of the Columbine problem, they stand a good chance of helping significantly to ease that epidemic and to restore some measure of health to the fifteen to twenty-five million American children who suffer its effects.

Thus, for example, educators and policy makers over the past several years, but particularly in the past two-to-three years have been steadily advancing proposals for curriculum reform or at least proposals for the use of the schools to address some of the problems raised by the Columbine epidemic. Perhaps the best and most important example of this phenomenon is the report that was recently issued by the Bipartisan Working Group on Youth Violence, constituted by republican and democratic members of the United States House of Representatives, which called for the "nation's young people [to] be given moral education, safer schools and more access to mental health services."[1] Responding specifically to the rise in youth violence and to the sensational recent examples of this problem, including specifically to the Columbine case, this legislative group noted that "[t]he most important contributing factor to youth violence is the absence of a nurturing and supportive home environment," and in particular the prevalence of what it termed "negative parenting."[2] The legislators concluded that "[t]he prevalence of parental disengagement is 25–30 percent, and [that] a quarter of American adolescents are not sure that their parents love them."[3] The group advocated the inclusion of moral education in the curriculum of the schools as a counterweight to this deprivation, and in the process "endorsed [Representative Bob] Etheridge's proposal that the federal government provide money to school districts to include moral education in their curriculum."[4] Etheridge himself noted that "[t]he U.S. Department of Education could help school systems get started teaching character, integrity, respect and honesty."[5] The report concluded that "prevention and early intervention programs are essential to reducing youth violence."[6]

While I endorse both the positions outlined in this report and Representative Etheridge's separate suggestions—they are as I said, emblematic of the general discussion on this matter—I depart from most in my assessment, based upon the child development literature I set out in Part I and the related legal analysis I engaged in Part II, that these programs will succeed only if they are implemented nationally, in combination, integrated throughout the curriculum, and fully funded. I also disagree with the exclusive "responsibilities" orientation of most contemporary political proposals for character education, and thus with the omission from those proposals of a dual orientation that also would include components designed to build self-esteem and a general sense of self worth.[7]

The omission of this dual orientation in many if not all contemporary proposals may be explained, at least superficially, by the fact that they have tended to be reactions to violent events like those that took place at Columbine High School. These events involved (most immediately) child perpetrators rather than apparent victims, whose sense of social responsibility was severely diminished or entirely absent. At the same time, this approach is naive at best because those perpetrators were in fact victims in a child development sense; there was no need even to scratch the surface of their stories to see this. It is also naive because the Columbine epidemic is vastly larger and more complicated than these measures would indicate. As the data on contemporary childhood dysfunction shows, many more children are inwardly ill than are outwardly destructive; remedies designed only to address the tip of the iceberg are thus illusory in the broadest sense.

In any event, the developmental literature is clear that this dual orientation is necessary: As I explained in Part I, the ultimate causes of Columbine are a lack of adequate childcare from the beginning of a child's life through adolescence, including in particular an absence of parental love, nurturing, and supervision; and an otherwise socially toxic environment, both within and outside of the home, including extraordinary access to real and virtual violence and other anti-social messages. Because these fundamental factors all implicate the absence of consistently caring adults teaching the lessons that are essential for healthy emotional development, a reform that assures their influence throughout most all of the children's day is necessary to inoculate them from at least some of the dysfunction that otherwise results from that absence.

As a threshold matter, I want to make plain the purpose and inherent limits of my suggestions, and indeed, of all contemporary progressive approaches to public school curriculum reform intended to ameliorate the emotionally difficult circumstances of American children. Schools and schoolteachers, even the best of them, cannot replace the gifts (including the lessons and the protections) that good parents can give to their children. And thus, while the public schools in particular have long had as a fundamental objective the inculcation of "virtue"—this being defined to include such life lessons as "generosity ... honour ... kindness ... [and] self-control"—there is no doubt that these same lessons learned at home are of incomparable value. Thus, I do not intend to suggest, nor should anyone, that the schools are a complete or even adequate replacement for good parenting. On the other hand, *in the absence of such parenting*, and particularly in contemporary circumstances where the world, real and virtual, is often quite unfriendly to children's emotional needs, good schools and good teachers can make the difference between outright personal failure and some measure of resilience (and hopefully even success) if they teach the lessons and provide the protections that are otherwise missing. As James Garbarino has emphasized, that which distinguishes children who do and do not become emotionally dysfunctional in abusive or neglectful situations "seems clearly linked to a compensatory relationship."[8] These relationships typically involve

cultural" curriculum—have largely failed because these ground rules were neither established at the outset nor were they followed throughout the discussion.[17] And thus, the participants have tended to advance their own often anti-majoritarian or anti-communitarian agendas, with the alleged hope of capturing the particular iteration of virtue that finds its way into the curriculum.

I say "alleged" hope in this context, because I believe that those who follow this course know that it is unlikely in the end to result in any real consensus on the terms of a comprehensive program in character education for the public schools. For example, contemporary liberals have tended to advocate programs that would be imbued with notions of absolute cultural relativism or unbounded tolerance for individual difference, and conservatives have tended to advocate programs that would be imbued with a particular religious bent. Others—for example, Representative and current republican House Majority Leader Tom Delay—have disallowed the possibility that there might be any discussion of the subject at all, on the ground that the schools' only mission should be academic. Although they clearly are a force in the political landscape, their categorical stand is so clearly at odds with both the longstanding purposes of the public schools and the contemporary sense that they are critical to the children's and the society's success that they must ultimately be discounted, or else persuaded in some manner also to come to table. Ultimately, however, this partisan approach has and will continue to doom otherwise legitimate efforts at consensus.

By way of illustration, the contemporary American community will never agree on posting or incorporating the Ten Commandments as such into the curriculum of the public schools; that at least the first three Commandments relate directly and originally to the Lord God of Israel makes this a foregone conclusion.[18] And even if we did agree, the First Amendment's establishment clause properly would preclude this posting or incorporation in any event. Proponents of such a goal know this, and thus are disingenuous when they claim to seek a real solution and agreement on the merits of their larger proposal for a values-driven curriculum. In the same vein, it is useless in a pluralistic and liberal democracy such as ours to suggest—as some opponents of "multiculturalism" do—that tolerance of individual and cultural differences within the bounds of ordered liberty ought not to be a focus of the children's training in civic virtues. Indeed, given that the schools have always had an assimilationist mission, a mission to make "one of many" at least in the respects that matter to the development and success of the democracy, and that they have a mandate to teach especially to older children the rules for operating within a democracy, it would be illogical if not self-defeating to design and implement a curriculum that excluded such lessons. Vicki Frost lost her case in *Mozert* for several reasons; but chief among them, and correctly so, was the fact that she sought to force the Hawkins County School Board to inculcate her own values especially with respect to religion and (in)tolerance, in all of the county's children. Because her values are squarely in conflict with those of the majority, and to some extent with constitutional doctrine, they could not be made part of the curriculum. Of course, in the same scheme, Frost's values are entirely legitimate—they are within the bounds of ordered liberty—and thus the county's children, as part of the indoctrination in tolerance that she fought so valiantly, were taught that while they do not have to subscribe to those values, they do have to tolerate their existence within the society.

At the same time, those who suggest that children in the public schools ought to be taught absolute (rather than bounded) tolerance for pluralism are equally disingenuous; or at least, they also are not playing by the rules. Just as Americans are not likely to tolerate the public schools teaching our children the Ten Commandments, they also are unlikely to tolerate their teaching that all values are equivalently worthy. (The debate on this particular point focuses on the concepts of moral relativism, and the belief in secular humanism, both of which emphasize the contextual propriety of conflicting value systems).[19] As but one example of this point, I suggest that the contemporary majority, which is committed to treating little girls and boys alike in the educational environment, is unlikely to allow the public schools to give these children an unfettered choice between the values of patriarchy and gender neutrality. Indeed, the public schools in this country (and elsewhere) are precisely about inculcating particular values and discouraging others that are contrary; thus, the values that these schools must teach, the values that they were designed to teach, are those that reflect the laws and majority perspectives in *this* democracy and in *this* culture.* This is particularly true of children in elementary school who need as a developmental matter to firm up their own values before they can begin to understand the context in which others might arise. Ultimately, whatever one's *personal* views on the merits of cultural relativism or of particular values that would fall outside of the majority's boundaries, the discussion is inherently delimited by the "client" that is the public schools and its uniquely mainstreaming and assimilative mission.† And so, Vicki Frost may have been right that the Hawkins County School Board went too far when it selected a textbook series for that county's elementary schools that adopted a "full tolerance" or secular humanist approach to many critical subjects.[20]

On the other hand, there are many critical values and lessons upon which the American majority (as diversely constituted ideologically, religiously and otherwise as it is) can and must agree. The best and most ubiquitous illustration of this point is the so-called "Golden Rule" that tells us, in some form or another, that as "you wish that men would do to you, do so to them."[21] Although Christians likely own this particular formulation, the underlying notion

---

* The assumption that underlies this position, that American culture itself is distinct and worthy of primacy at least on United States soil, is often challenged by these same groups; however, at least in the context of public education, this challenge has never been viable.

† Those in the society who hold extra-majoritarian values and engage in extra-majoritarian practices are obviously offended and even handicapped by this approach if they wish to enroll their children in the schools. This is because their children will necessarily be subjected to indoctrination in two conflicting value systems even in the particularly formative early-to-middle childhood period. But as the history of the public schools shows, there is no logical or doctrinally permissible solution that can satisfy their legitimate concerns given the purposes and mission of the public schools. In other words, the public schools' mainstreaming, assimilative mission is opposed by definition to a value system that is anti-majoritarian. The court in *Mozert* noted this point expressly, suggesting that the plaintiffs there could not require the public schools to accommodate them, and suggested alternatives that would preserve intact their ability to inculcate only their own values in the children, including home and private schooling. 827 F.2d at 1067. Of course, many in the society who stand in the *Mozert* plaintiffs' shoes do not have these options as a practical matter, and thus, for them, there is no viable alternative.

itself is very much in the public domain. At my own children's politically correct Montessori school, for example, the same principle is "secularized" and taught this way: "Treat other people how you want to be treated." And every member of that community—which includes practicing Christians, Jews, Muslims, as well as the non-religious—is quite happy, because whatever the precise words, the phrase translates directly into the *universally-held* values of kindness, courtesy, respect, empathy, loyalty, and inclusion.[22] The same is true of other presumptively Christian principles, including, for example, the contents of the Fifth, Seventh, and Eighth Commandments, which tell us that killing, stealing, and lying are wrong.[23] Clearly, we all can agree in principle on these concepts, regardless of whether we are or are not affiliated with the religious denominations that subscribe to the Ten Commandments. And, apart from these lessons in social responsibility, there is also little doubt that most would value educational care and exercises that lead to children's enhanced self-esteem. The message "every child is special and worthy," like the Golden Rule, pervades or should transcend, all American cultural and ideological boundaries.

William Bennett obviously has seen the value of "secularizing" virtues so that they may be appropriate moral compasses for everyone: His *Book of Virtues* emphasizes the value of courage and perseverance; responsibility, work, and self-discipline; compassion and faith; and honesty, loyalty, and friendship.[24] And he uses non-Christian tales including *Aesop's Fables* to bring these virtues to life for children.[25] As his inclusion of "faith" amongst the virtues indicates, however, he is inconsistent about this, and many of his stories intentionally include or feature the Christian God.[26] In this respect, his otherwise inclusive approach is flawed, at least as a useful blueprint for the teaching of virtues in the public schools.[27] (For the same reason, it also is unattractive to parents who are not Christian who nevertheless wish to teach their children the bulk of the values he emphasizes.)

In the end, my objective is not to provide a complete alternative curriculum. There are ample existing sources that likely would suffice, at least as a starting place. As but one example which I know personally and well, my children are enrolled in their traditional (ideologically strict) Montessori "children's house" specifically because the education, care, and nurturing are comprehensive of academics and virtues, including *both* those that enhance the child's sense of self and self-worth *and* those that focus upon his or her relationships with others.[28] Again, as the child development literature shows, the former is as critical as the latter to better the chances that the child can avoid the debilitating emotional dysfunction that can come from *either* a lack of self-esteem and self-worth *or* a lack of appropriate socialization. Given this, I emphasize only that it is possible to achieve consensus about such a curriculum, once anti-majoritarian obstacles are eliminated from the conversation, and thus that the phrase "character education" and its derivatives need not trigger an immediately partisan reaction: We *all* want our children to have character of the sort that will ensure their emotional and social success.

THE COMPONENTS OF SUCCESSFUL CURRICULUM REFORM

The inculcation of the necessary virtues by consistently caring teachers acting in *loco parentis*, in combination with an extension of the relevant periods of public education to accommodate this inculcation and to provide the children otherwise with a safe harbor, offer the best available approach for fixing Columbine. This is because the absence of such adults teaching these lessons lies at the core of the Columbine epidemic. While teachers cannot be expected entirely to replace the children's absent parents, their "responsive and emotionally available" presence in the child's day can provide the care-giving relationship that the experts agree is essential to "[c]hildren's successful adaptation, and perhaps their very survival."[29] Indeed, following the blueprint provided by the experts in child development, and considering the historic exodus of parents from the family home, we can imagine that teachers can help in quite significant ways.

Teachers and schools can help the pre-school child to understand by their attention that she is special and worthy; they also can help her to "manage [his or her] feelings, emotions, and relationships."[30] And they can help that child to gain "self-consciousness and ... the beginnings of shame and pride, the capacity for empathy and the potential, at least, for altruism."[31] Values such as the "Golden Rule," the principle of non-exclusion during play, and early lessons in mediation as the solution to disputes in the classroom and on the playground, are appropriate fodder for curriculum building in this period. And certainly, the school environment provides, by definition, the much-needed opportunity for "richly varied and largely social play" which is necessary to the development of appropriate and successful peer relationships.[32] Teachers can help the child in middle-childhood to "mesh ... into his society," by providing a beneficial "social value system" that can, if necessary, counter negative influences and values that are otherwise present in their environment.[33] As Penelope Leach emphasized, "[c]hildren's identification with parents *or parent figures* is the basis of all social bonds ... The relationship that was the basis for the child's development of socialized behavior now becomes the basis for her dawning social morality."[34] And teachers and schools can help the adolescent by reinforcing the social utility of these early lessons. Thus, the pre-school mantra "everyone can play" becomes "no exclusive cliques" in high school, and so on.

Teachers and schools also can mediate the effects of internal biological and emotional influences as well as external peer and media influences, by providing a *safe* "social laboratory where rules and roles can be practiced, evaluated, and incorporated."[35] Finally, as a practical matter, the schools as a physical presence in the lives of adolescents can combat the toxicity of the real and virtual outside worlds by providing the opportunity for alternative activities. Adolescents and other children who are engaged in school-sponsored work and activities are less likely to be left alone or engaged inappropriately with media technologies and life on the streets than are their counterparts who are not afforded this alternative.

Time is clearly integral to the development of a curriculum that would meet all of these ends. Thus, an expanded period of public education throughout the calendar year—or year-round school—is critical, as well as the extension of the day through the afternoons, at least beginning in elementary school.* This is necessary

---

* The adoption of a longer school day is critical especially to the elementary school child because the data show that this is when children most typically begin to be left alone, as so-called "latch-key kids," by their par-

as a practical matter to assure the full integration of character education into the curriculum, as well as to the notion of schools as a consistently available safe harbor. Importantly, support for these measures appears to be building rapidly for reasons that are related both to the "safe harbor" basis for my own suggestions, as well as to the need for additional time to ensure full coverage of the academic components of existing curricula. Thus, for example, during his campaign, President G.W. Bush repeatedly emphasized his moral commitment to such after-school programs. His apparent refusal at the time to tie a financial package to that commitment made it cynical, of course, but at least he and his advisors recognize this essential need.[36] More importantly (given that it holds the government's purse strings) the congressional Bipartisan Working Group on Youth Violence urged the development of after-school programs, noting in its final report that, "statistically speaking, schools are among the safest places for children to be."

Support for such measures is, of course, not guaranteed. Leaving aside for a moment the looming economics, many Americans today may be reluctant to commit to the suggested evolution away from long free summers and relatively short school days. For example, we are variously committed to the memories of the carefree times we had as children ourselves during summer vacations, the convenience that this block of time affords for long family vacations, and for some the relief from oppression that is pervasive in the often negative ecologies of the schools.[37] The first two of these concerns are most easily dismissed as anachronistic. "Summer vacation" was instituted so that the children could help their parents on the family farm.[38] This rationale is no longer viable, if it ever was, for most American children. Thus, it appears to have been replaced by the fact of tradition—it has always been this way—which also must be rejected because today, and in most cases, neither parent is there to assure that the benefits of the tradition are obtained; indeed, the fact that they are absent assures the contrary,

---

ents. Before then, parents in all economic categories tend to make arrangements for some adult supervision for the child. Of course, these arrangements, for example, day care, often are also detrimental emotionally for the children. The answer to the latter problem likely does not lie in the public schools, however, and thus it is beyond the scope of this book.

that children most often will be left alone. And with respect to the long family vacation of yesteryear, it is now one or two weeks at the most, and year-round schools do and can accommodate this.[39] Most importantly, however, the fealty to tradition also flies in the face of the fact that American children are in school for fewer days each year and fewer hours each day than children in most if not all other industrialized societies, and thus that it is possible and even useful in an academic and competitive sense to imagine such extensions. The third concern is more substantial, and thus I describe it further below.

It is also essential that the period of public education be extended back to include the pre-school or pre-kindergarten period. There is already ample public discussion of the merits of this proposal, which include the enhanced likelihood of academic preparedness and success, as well as the potentially curative nurture and care that (emotionally) deprived children might be afforded in that context.[40] I have only one important critique of that discussion: While many educators, policy-makers, and citizens are convinced about the value of programs such as "Smart-Start" that most typically are offered to lower-income families with pre-school aged children who are deemed to be "at risk" of academic failure, these groups are less committed (and certainly the society as a whole has yet to commit) to the notion that all American children are potentially "at risk" in the essential developmental sense.[41] As I have made clear, however, such a commitment is absolutely necessary. Indeed, what Columbine demonstrates is that emotional development is as crucial to eventual success as academic development, and that "risk" in the broader sense that would encompass emotional development knows few if any class or ethnicity-based limits. In other words, the fact that Eric Harris and Dylan Klebold lived in the suburbs, were white, drove legally-purchased expensive cars, and were able accurately to quote and understand Shakespeare, did absolutely nothing (or so it appears) to mediate their extraordinary emotional dysfunction. In fact, as I described in Chapter One, Harris and Klebold themselves allowed that their emotional dysfunction existed in spite of these traditionally insulating factors, and because, beginning in early childhood, they *felt* alone, unloved, abused by their peers, and otherwise unable to adjust socially.

Finally, it is critical to the success of any effort to use the schools to fix Columbine that the inculcation of the necessary virtues, and the positive personal and emotional reinforcement that is part and parcel of that project, not be relegated to the "after-school" component of the school day, or, indeed, to any individual component of the day or week. Just as the "Sunday School" approach to character building is generally insufficient to the successful inculcation of values unless it is also reinforced throughout each and every day, so too an academic hour of character building is likely to fail to achieve its ultimate ends. This is because children, particularly before adolescence, need developmentally to have their lessons modeled and repeated by adults when the circumstances make them relevant.

For example, the lessons in inclusion, empathy, and mediation that may be provided in a special session in the form of role-plays can have a real impact on children only if they are used to set the stage for a future reinforcement of their substance. The same is true of lessons that are designed to teach the inherent value of each child. Teachers have to have the time, the training, and the curricular imperative to engage those lessons not only formally, but informally and repeatedly as they are needed. In very practical terms, children need to be taught—demonstratively—that they are special whenever they do something that merits such recognition, or whenever they are made to feel by their circumstances that they are not. They need to be taught that this is true until it is internalized. Similarly, children who demonstrate a tendency to exclude others during play, a practice that signals the beginnings of clique behavior, need to be stopped in their tracks and taught—unequivocally—that this tendency is unacceptable, because it is hurtful and because it deprives the group of the special contributions that each child could bring to the enterprise. "Everyone can play" must be the only moral option whenever the choice to exclude arises. Finally, children who are prone to react aggressively to conflict must be taught the value of a peaceable solution, as well as the mediation process that would enable it, each and every time their antisocial instinct threatens other children. Importantly, those children who would be their victims also must be taught the value of participating in that process.

The most obvious reactions to any comprehensive proposals for curriculum reform along these lines are likely to come from those who are concerned about expanding and thus paying for public school programs; teachers and school administrators who already feel oppressed by their existing academic mission; parents and related advocacy groups who are concerned about their degree of control over the development of any reforms; others who, by virtue of their own experiences with the public schools and school reform, simply do not believe that this institution is capable of such positive change; and children, including both those who have bought into the erroneous notion that the schools exist solely to serve them as individual consumers of an educational product and thus who would be concerned about a perceived shift in the mission of the schools, as well as those who are subjected to ostracism and even brutality in the schools and thus who are concerned about the additional time the reforms would add to that experience. Without denigrating the importance any of these concerns—indeed, I believe they all are legitimate or at least understandable—I suggest that each triggers a relatively simple response.

For example, to those who have given up on the public schools for various reasons, or who just do not want any of their dollars spent funding them, I suggest that they review the relative economics of fixing and not fixing Columbine. If the data provided by the Centers for Disease Control, the National Institutes of Health, and others, are correct—and there is no reason to believe they are not—funding a curricular reform however much that may cost in financial terms as well as in related institutional investment is likely to pale in comparison and in the long run with the costs of doing nothing to help the generations of dysfunctional children that mark the epidemic. Moreover, to the extent that the current deficiencies in the schools that have prompted these reactions are remedied by the curative curriculum, that is, if the reformation is compelling, the reactions themselves are likely to dissipate. While there is a small swell of childless individuals who most recently have begun to complain that forcing them to contribute to subsidies for children and families is discriminatory, most in the society who are concerned about funding the public schools hold this view because they believe that the effort is a waste, that they are putting good money after bad.[42]

I have heard from several quite knowledgeable people that my suggestions are impossibly optimistic. In their view, the schools are

Ultimately, many of these ideas have already been discussed in policy circles and even implemented in model private school curricula. What is clearly missing from this contemporary discussion, however, is the sense that it has historical and doctrinal context and legitimacy; that even in this age of extraordinary pluralism—religious, ideological, political, ethnic, and racial—we can devise an approach and adopt correct ground rules that will allow us to reach consensus on the contents of a curative curriculum; and that the driving force for that consensus today is or should be the extraordinarily compelling nature of the Columbine epidemic. Most importantly, and in light of Columbine, the contemporary debate is missing the necessary integration of all of these ideas. It is missing a clear vision of the whole, beyond the details that have independently captured the attentions of one or another educator or politician. I suggest, as I have throughout this book, that this vision can be had only by examining the problem through the prism that is provided by research in child development, which establishes the blueprint for (and serves to remind us about) how the children must be cared for and raised if they are to be healthy.

CHAPTER FOURTEEN

FEDERALIZING THE SOLUTION TO A NATIONAL EPIDEMIC

To begin to counter the Columbine problem, I have suggested in the previous discussion that a new curriculum for the public schools ought to be adopted that assures to the extent possible that children are provided with the environment that is necessary to the development of socially-beneficial values and skills. I have also argued that it is within the constitutional authority of the public schools to establish such a curriculum. Because I am concerned that the cultural and financial politics of "local control" of the public schools—defined by Attorney General John Ashcroft as "power [in] the hands of parents, teachers, and school boards"—would preclude its uniform or even substantial implementation, in this chapter I conclude that the federal government should assume control of those aspects of the curriculum that are implicated by these reforms.*

I recognize, of course, that this argument will face substantial—some might suggest insurmountable—obstacles for the simple reason that the politics of "local control" are so firmly entrenched in the society. Indeed, the statute that authorized the United States Department of Education expressly conditions its existence on the assurance that it will stay out of curricular matters, the exclusive responsibility for which Congress reserved for the states.[1] Never-

---

* I make no attempt in this book to provide a detailed blueprint for how federalization might be accomplished. Rather, my aim is more general, namely to suggest that it makes sense to do this, and that it would not run afoul of the Constitution in the ways that other efforts to fix Columbine would. Having said this, in this chapter, I do discuss the traditional spending power basis for federal involvement in public education, and this certainly would provide the most obvious constitutional authority for federalization. I also suggest that the statistics on the national fiscal impact of the epidemic of childhood disaffection which I explore in Part I would support an argument that the federal government might legislate directly in this area, using its commerce authority.

theless, as I explain in the remainder of this book, I think that the federal government should and can take the action I propose for two reasons. First, there is no effective alternative to fix Columbine; to abandon this option is to abandon the children to the increasingly harsh results of our deep seeded commitment to liberalism. Second, despite the rhetoric to the contrary, there really is no strong or immutable case for "local control" of public education.

THE NEED FOR UNIFORMITY AND THE POLITICS OF THE SCHOOL BOARDS

Many schools and school systems, both public and private, have either adopted or are considering the adoption of curricula that contain at least some of the progressive measures that I and others have identified as necessary to fix Columbine. For example, much of what is today described as curative has been integral to the private traditional Montessori schools' curriculum since its conception by Maria Montessori in the late nineteenth and early twentieth centuries. And some of these progressive measures—including especially character education—have been incorporated into the programs of schools like that which was most recently described by Dary Matera in his book *A Cry for Character: How a Group of Students Cleaned up Their Rowdy School and Spawned a Wildfire Antidote to the Columbine Effect*.[2] Finally, as I also have described, politicians across the political spectrum today are touting the benefits of a character-based education, and appropriate after-school programs. These are encouraging developments, and if nothing more were done, they certainly would at least to begin help to repair the disturbed emotions of many children, and prevent other children from ever succumbing to those same dysfunctions. Unfortunately, though, however wonderful those programs are, they reach only a small percentage of the total number of American children who are afflicted by the Columbine epidemic, so long as we defer to local control of the development and implementation of the curricula for the public schools.

There are two reasons for this. First, many local school districts are relatively poor, and thus will never be able to fund the necessary reforms. Second, many of the local school boards, whose members are elected from among the community's population, are certain to have difficulty reaching consensus on a subject so apparently controversial as character education, and thus, in these districts, children also will be left without a cure. As the Supreme Court recently remarked in *Plyler v. Doe*, "we cannot ignore the significant social costs borne by our Nation when select groups are denied the means to absorb the values and skills upon which our social order rests."[3] Because the Columbine epidemic is a national heath problem, unbounded by special local or even regional issues, it is critical that the matter of a cure not be left in the hands of the localities. At best, local school boards could achieve no more than a patchwork of partial remedies. At worst, they would make of the children for whom they were responsible the "select groups [that would be] denied the means" to achieve the general emotional health "upon which our social order rests." In this respect, Columbine is just like other such epidemics that have plagued this country in the past: It makes no more sense to adopt a regional strategy to fight this epidemic than it would have to adopt such a localized approach to fight polio.

The contemporary practice and politics of funding the public schools is the first and foremost obstacle to national implementation of the necessary curricular reforms. While the states and the federal government contribute substantially to the budgets of the schools nationwide, a significant portion of their operating expenses still are raised (or not) locally through the collection of property taxes.[4] As a result, schools in relatively prosperous areas are fully funded and can afford quality programs of all sorts, while schools in relatively poor areas operate on austerity budgets at best. These facts are well known. For example, in Ohio,

> [t]he system's dependence on local property taxes has resulted in vast disparities among Ohio's six hundred eleven public school districts due to the differences in revenue generated by each. For instance, according to a memorandum prepared by Mike Sobul at the Ohio Department of Taxation for the 1995 fiscal year, a one-mill property tax on Class I real property produced $272.90 per student in the district with the highest property tax base and $13.34 per student in the district with the lowest. A system that places too much reliance on local property taxes puts property-

poor districts at a disadvantage, because "'they must tax at significantly higher rates in order to meet minimum requirements for accreditation; yet their educational programs are typically inferior.'"[5]

The Ohio Supreme Court ultimately based its decision to order the state's legislature to abandon it reliance on local property taxes as the primary source of funding public education on this extraordinary disparity, emphasizing in *DeRolph v. State* that

[t]he inherent inequities of [such] funding systems ... not only are extremely difficult to rectify, but also run counter to our Constitution's explicit requirement for a statewide system of public schools. The valuation of local property has no connection whatsoever to the actual education needs of the locality, with the result that a system overreliant on local property taxes is by its very nature an arbitrary system that can never be totally thorough or efficient. In a very real sense, this problem underlies most of the other deficiencies in Ohio's school system, and is either the direct or indirect cause of them.[6]

Children in other states have not been so lucky. For example, in North Carolina, the courts have found that while all children have a right to *an* education in the public schools, they have no right *either* to parity of programs and facilities *or* even to an adequate education.[7] As that state's Supreme Court concluded in a case addressing the same issue of disparate funding, "provisions of the current state system for funding schools which require or allow counties to help finance their school systems and result in unequal funding among the school districts of the state do not violate constitutional principles."[8] In reaching this conclusion, the court read the state's constitution to permit relatively wealthy localities to supplement the state's own authorizations—which are designed to provide some basic education to all—thus allowing for enriched opportunities for children in those localities.[9] As a result of this reading, legislation in North Carolina typically provides—as does this most recent bill or curricular reform—that

[l]ocal boards of education shall develop character instruction ... beginning with the 2002–2003 school year. If a local board determines that it would be an economic hardship to begin to imple-

ment character instruction by the beginning of the 2002–2003 school year, the board may request an extension of time from the State Board of Education.[10]*

Separately, and independent of a particular locality's ability to fund good schools, there is the problem that many in the society today are unwilling further to support the public schools. The result of this reluctance or refusal has been a prominent series of failed bond issues, which have left children to be housed in decrepit and hazardous old buildings or trailers, and taught from shared and outdated textbooks, among other things. The two reasons most frequently given by the voters for rejecting further funding for education include the sense that they are not responsible to educate their neighbors' children, and that the public schools are not responsive to their concerns—a more specific version of the argument that the public schools are just not doing a good job—and thus are not worth any further investment. I have already discussed these arguments at some length in Chapter Thirteen.

These attitudes are deeply ingrained, and thus require a significant national strategy to overcome. Before they will invest in the schools, the citizenry has to be convinced that schools are being managed by qualified individuals who are responsive to children, to parents, and to the society's needs. Of course, in the first instance, the skeptical citizenry has to be convinced that using experts is essential as a developmental matter. This is no small thing given the belief of some that any call for expert governance of the schools is political code for stealing the minds of the children away from their parents. Nevertheless, I believe that this can be done successfully, using data and information about child development such as that which I provided in Part I of this book. Finally, those who do not understand that the health of the nation is intimately tied to the health of its children must be convinced of the depth of

---

* While this bill requires that hardship petitions be submitted to the State Board "on or before April 1, 2002," it does not provide any final deadline for the implementation of the program in those localities that would receive the extension. In other words, apparently, the extension might well persist forever. See also General Assembly of North Carolina, Session 2001, House Bill 195, N.C. History Taught/Student Citizen Act of 2001, at Section 4(2) (providing for the same exception for poorer localities).

the epidemic, and the reality that its ramifications threaten also
their personal and individual well being. Local school boards simply do not have the moral or practical account that is necessary
successfully to accomplish these twin objectives.

Related to the funding question is the matter of reaching consensus about the elements of a curative curriculum. I harbor significant doubt that the process local school boards use to reach
consensus about such things is capable of achieving the ends that I
believe are essential, namely the development of a national or at
least a uniform strategy to combat the Columbine epidemic. This
critique in general is not new. Indeed, Thomas Jefferson supported
the notion of a local school board in part because it would "g[i]ve
adult citizens a chance to exercise self-rule," an admittedly useful
project in what was then a novel experiment in democracy.[11] And
once universal public education became a reality for most of the
country, by the 1890s, the citizenry heeded this call in vast numbers, as "American school board members constituted the largest
group of public officials in the world" in that era.[12]

At the same time, and perhaps especially because of this goal
and the widespread public participation in its pursuit,

> achieving a sense of common purpose has never been easy. For
> two centuries, public school districts have been political arenas
> in which citizens have contended with one another. In a society
> as socially diverse as the United States, controversies about pur-
> poses and practices in public schooling are hardly surprising.[13]

What is also hardly surprising is that these controversies often are
left unresolved or, when they are resolved, the result tends to be a
compromise that fails to focus on the interests of the children themselves. The most recent battle in the Kansas schools system concerning a ban on the teaching of evolution in that state's curriculum is
but one particularly egregious example of this phenomenon.[14]

As I argued in Chapter Thirteen, reaching consensus on the
components of character education as part of this ameliorative
curriculum need not be a partisan battle. However, my sense in
this respect is conditioned, as I explained there, on the participants' understanding and acceptance of the ground rules for the
conversation; that is, that the agenda for the public schools is both
majoritarian and assimilative. Without impugning anyone's good

motives, where the battle is literally for "the public culture," it is difficult if not impossible to imagine that a majority among the thousands of school board members across the country would agree to subscribe to these rules.[15] On the other hand, it is entirely likely that one "national school board" could be created whose members could be relied upon (in part because that is the basis on which they were selected) to engage the process appropriately.

OVERCOMING THE OBSTACLE OF "LOCAL CONTROL"

Even if Americans are prepared to discuss the matter of federal control of the curriculum for the public schools, as I suggest that they should, there remains the question whether the institution of local control stands as an invincible obstacle to such apparent innovation. The mantra of "local control" of the schools is an old one, based in a firmly-established order that is accepted as immutable even by those policymakers and politicians who would prefer that it were otherwise.[16] Consistent with this entrenched perspective, the federal enabling legislation that established the Department of Education contains a provision that explicitly prohibits the Department from meddling in curricular matters. And yet when one examines the traditional rationales for this order in the context of contemporary American life, it becomes clear that "local control" is no longer a viable principle; indeed, in many if not most instances, it already is empty rhetoric. As I explain below, those rationales are the long history of local control of public education, which some argue warrants its protection under the Tenth Amendment to the United States Constitution, and the notion that parental and (local) community control of the curriculum results in more successful students and communities.

THE ARGUMENT ACCORDING TO HISTORY
AND THE TENTH AMENDMENT

The basic argument according to history was once articulated by then Missouri Senator John Ashcroft. In an academic debate on the subject, Ashcroft—a staunch supporter of local control—posited simply that this institution has been a "cornerstone of education since our country's inception," and that "our nation's founders intended for education to be a local, rather than federal responsibility."[17] For Ashcroft and his ideological colleagues, the fact that American schools have been governed in many respects by local school boards since *their* inception is merely proof of this point. As I will explain, however, the facts are quite a bit fuzzier than this blanket position reveals. Indeed, there are two equally plausible and quite divergent ways to look at the history of the policy choices that were made about how public education would be governed, including about the intent of "our nation's founders" with respect to this issue of governance.

For some in the society, local control was always central to the entire enterprise, which was and still is primarily a vehicle for individual self-fulfillment. For others, local control was simply a temporary means to accomplish a higher goal, which was and still is (as Benjamin Rush described it) the "homogenizing"of individuals within the society to the extent necessary to assure the success of the nation. Ultimately, as I will describe, this divergence (however it is resolved) itself suggests that there is no historical imperative for a locally controlled system of public education in the United States, particularly where the exigencies of the present render such control ineffective and even damaging.

The best argument for local control based on history goes like this:

First, it is the case that public education has its origins in the United States in the seventeenth and eighteenth centuries in the New England colonies, and these schools were plainly controlled by parents and localities.[18] As James Conant explained, the "Puritan founders of the Massachusetts Bay Colony" already had established a system of compulsory elementary education in the period 1645–1647.[19] It is this system that is "often referred to as the basis for our present system of local control."[20] Thus, "[t]own meetings often voted to provide elementary schooling for ten or twelve weeks a year. They often favored boys over girls and charged parental fees to supplement the town's support."[21] Parents themselves (probably fathers) voted in these town meetings, assuring that they would retain as much control over their children's education as they would have in a more conventional church-based or private secular school.[22] And while universal public education across the nation did not emerge until the mid-to-late nineteenth century, whenever children elsewhere were educated prior to that, parents retained absolute control of their education, using tutors or private schools that were in every way responsive to parents.[23] In fact, this premise of parental control was so ingrained that even the locally controlled "quasi-public schools in the New England colonies [were viewed as] a notable exception to the common practice."[24]

Second, it may be argued that the "nation's founders" and other important policy makers in the period of the Constitutional Convention understood this history and incorporated it, at least implicitly, in their own thinking on the subject of public education. Thus, for example, James Madison is said to have believed that "national education systems would present constitutional difficulties," and thus to have "preferred to leave school planning to local authorities."[25] And Thomas Jefferson is said to have "argued that locally controlled public schools were key democratic institutions in two ways. By teaching correct political principles to the young, they could nurture virtuous citizens. Equally important, local control gave adult citizens a chance to exercise self-rule."[26] Finally, according to Conant, prominent New England-based educators of the nineteenth century, including Horace Mann and Henry Barnard, "stood firmly for local schools, locally managed and largely locally financed."[27] The fact that the records of the Constitutional Convention and the Constitution itself fail to mention the subject of public education—apart from a brief and positive reference to the notion of a national university in the Convention records—is taken by proponents of local control as support for the general premise that leaders at the time shared these views or at least understood that the education of children was in fact the exclusive business of parents and localities. Indeed, according to Ellwood Cubberley, this constitutional silence meant that "[b]y the tenth amendment to the Constitution ... the control of schools and education passed, as one of the unmentioned powers thus reserved, to the people of the different States to handle in any manner which they saw fit."[28]

Third, the original system of public education which began in earnest in the mid-to-late nineteenth century undoubtedly also was controlled by parents and local school boards. Thus, "[b]y 1890, public schools became dominant and enrolled about nine in ten pupils.... In doing so, they stayed close to their roots and formed the most decentralized system of school governance in the world. They controlled and financed schools locally."[29] According to David Tyack, "[p]ublic education would not have thrived without this self-rule" because "[i]t enabled citizens to keep a close eye on their schools and to resolve issues by local majority rule."[30] And keep an eye on the schools they did. As I previously noted, in the formative period of universal public education, "American school board members constituted the largest group of public officials in the world.... They outnumbered teachers in a number of rural states."[31] And while the authority of the local school board has been stripped to some extent in many places across the country, replaced by more centralized county or state-based authorities, proponents of local control still suggest that the school board today retains much of its original vitality. That is, to the extent that the debate about "local control" today can be said primarily to pit proponents of a national authority against those who advocate state or more local authority, there is little doubt that the curriculum of the public schools is still very much in "local" hands. Viewed this way, from its origins in the New England Colony schools of the seventeenth and eighteenth centuries to the present, there is a seamless web of commitment to the policy of local and parental control of public education.

There is no such seamless web for opponents of local control. Indeed, the best argument against local control (or at least against the notion of its immutability as a doctrinal matter) focuses precisely upon the conflict between the forces that would continue to place parents in positions of authority over the curriculum and those who would use the schools to mainstream children in ways that were important to the success of the democratic enterprise:

First, while some communities in the original New England colonies did develop quasi-public schools in the seventeenth and eighteenth centuries which could be said to be "some partial precursor to the [universal system of] public schools" that developed later on, these early institutions were quite distinct in substance and mission from those that were later designed for the purpose of mainstreaming children to assure the success of the fledgling democracy, independently of the wishes of parents.[32] Specifically, it would be difficult to describe the early New England colony schools as anything other than parent-driven efforts to educate their own children according to their own values, albeit that those values were in part also collective ones. The fact that these original schools were established by parents at town meetings with the participation of others in the community, and partially paid for by parents when local funding was inadequate, makes this proposition clear. Add to this the fact that the communities existed as such precisely because of a homogeneity of values—religious values in particular—and it becomes almost impossible in relevant ways to distinguish these early institutions from the private schools (including the explicitly church-based schools) that also existed at that time and that continue to exist today in communities across the country. Indeed, the similarities in curricular content and mission between the New England colony schools and private ecclesiastical institutions of that period caused at least a few of the nation's most prominent founders, including Benjamin Franklin and George Washington, to reject them as the model for a universal system of public education.

Second, however equivocal the history of public education is in other respects, it is quite clear that apart from the New England colony schools, and before the mid-eighteenth century, there was no such thing as public education in the United States. As I have already noted, Jefferson believed that requiring parents to relinquish control of their children to the government for this purpose was a notion "far too radical" for the citizenry of that time to accept.[33] Thus,

> [a]cross all the colonies—French and Spanish colonies as well as in British America—schooling was less important in the education process than it was in the later industrial world. These societies were largely agricultural. Work was learned on farms and plantations. Families carried most of the responsibility for children's learning, along with churches, neighbors, and peers. Not only was schooling less important and thus not very extensive, but in general it was not free, not governmental, and not secular.[34]

Most importantly, as Jefferson's views suggest, parents ultimately determined whether their children were schooled or not, to the extent such opportunities existed.[35] If the citizenry could not even imagine true public education—which by definition diminishes parental authority—it certainly did not imagine how and by whom that education might be controlled.[36] The "deal" that ulti-

mately resulted in the first real public schools in the mid-to-late
nineteenth century and that provided for indirect parental control
of education through the local school boards had yet to be crafted.
Thus, it is misleading at best to suggest, as Ashcroft did, that local
control was even in that earlier period a "cornerstone in education"
in America.

Third, it is against this landscape that we must derive the significance of the relative dearth of real evidence about the intent of the
nation's founders with respect to the *governance* of any system of
universal public education. That is, while "the papers of Franklin,
Washington, Jefferson, Madison, Rush, John Adams, Samuel
Adams, Alexander Hamilton, and Patrick Henry would disclose
their educational thinking," we know very little about how most of
them would have distributed authority over any universal and
mandatory system of public education that eventually would be
developed.[37] As I discussed in Chapter Twelve, however, we do
know that several of the most important men of that time, both
philosophers and politicians, believed strongly that a system of
universal public education was essential to secure the success of the
democratic experiment. We also know that at least some of these
men believed that the existing institutional and curricular models,
steeped as they were in provincial and ecclesiastical concerns, were
not up to that task. While this does not directly show a preference
for regional or national control of the public schools, and against
local control, it is some good circumstantial evidence in support of
that proposition.

Thus, for example, while Benjamin Rush insisted on the significance of religion to a republican education, he also imagined a national curriculum that would be "a purger of prejudice and superstition in religion, a boon to liberty, a promoter of just laws and
good government, a teacher of manners and the art of conversation, and a stimulater of agriculture and of manufactures."[38] In
fact, he went so far as to "call for a 'general and uniform system of
education' that would 'render the mass of the people more homogeneous and thereby fit them more easily for uniform and peaceable government.'"[39]

And Benjamin Franklin championed a "utilitarian curriculum"
for the schools that would "make respectable those educational values consistent with the needs of a flexible, changing society."[40] Sig-

nificantly, Franklin disagreed with Rush on the necessity of including religion in a model curriculum and even suggested "abandoning both religious education and traditional education for more enlightened philosophies."[41] Such a position likely would not have sat well with local puritan school boards and the parents who controlled them; and thus, one could suggest that neither of these two men likely were wedded to the notion of such a board.

While Jefferson is said to have elaborated on the potential for a dual role for the local school board in educating the children and training the adult members of the board in participatory democracy, he clearly also believed in schools with a bent toward teaching those lessons that were essential to the survival and success of the national government. He believed this so strongly, in fact, that even while he was "an avowed states' rights advocate," he also "recommended the application of federal funds" to this among other "great purposes" which included also "'roads, rivers, canals, and other objects of public improvement.'"[42] And the curriculum he developed for the schools in Virginia was designed to achieve these ends.[43] The fact that he understood that his ideas were radical for that time did not mean that he agreed personally with his would-be opponents' views on absolute parental control of education.[44]

Finally, given Madison's belief in the significance of education to secure the American enterprise, and his certain understanding of the revolutionary nature of this proposition, the same might be implied from his concern that "national systems of education would present constitutional difficulties" and thus that "school planning" should be left to "local authorities."

Viewed in this light, the almost total absence of the subject of public education from the records of the Constitutional Convention, and the literal silence of the Constitution itself on the subject, takes on a new or at least a different meaning from that which is suggested by proponents of local control.[45] For example, rather than signifying the framers' assumption that local control of public education was a good idea—as Ashcroft's comments would suggest—one might well imagine that this relative silence meant only that the issue could not be broached if it would threaten the fragile compromises upon which the establishment of the nation depended. Again, the fact that universal public education was at the time merely a glimmer in a few of the framers' eyes, and thus was

The fourth and final historical argument against local control is based upon the development of the public schools after the Constitutional Convention, beginning in earnest in the mid-to-late nineteenth century. As I described in Chapter Twelve, this history is clear that the leaders of that movement were motivated by larger societal ends, rather than merely the ends of individual parents interested in educating their children. Thus, for example, the New York public schools system began in mid-century with the mission to ensure "the permanency of our free institutions" and specifically "to qualify [the children] for usefulness, and render them safe and consistent members of the political body."[53] In the course of New York's development of its schools, its leaders expressly acknowledged that this mission would "alienat[e]" some of parents' "natural right of controlling their children."[54] That this alienation was not only permissible but also a fundamental aspect of the mission of the schools became clear in the Americanization period which yielded, among other things, the seminal Supreme Court case in this area, *Meyer v. Nebraska*.[55] As I already have described, *Meyer* stands in principal part for the still vital proposition that the government may control absolutely the curriculum of the public schools even at the cost of abrogating the parents' own interests in how their children are raised. *Meyer* has since spawned an unbroken line of cases that reinforce this principle.

Of course, in the late nineteenth century through the mid-to-late twentieth century, and notwithstanding this strong language, authority over the curriculum of the public schools was very much in the hands of the local school board. And so to the extent that government in this form "alienated" children from their parents, the alienation was not that great or threatening, especially for those parents who were in the cultural mainstream. That is, both as a matter of geography and ideological compatibility, parents were not for the most part upset by these circumstances. At least this was the case after a time, when the notion of universal public education had become less radical and was otherwise largely accepted by most in the society. And thus, over the course of the twentieth century, parents like those in *Meyer* and its progeny, including those in *Mozert*, came to represent a distinct minority. In the vein of those recalcitrant parents described by Jefferson in the late eighteenth century, this minority rejected the doctrine that in the context of public education, the government might properly determine and uniformly impose the entire content of the curriculum.

The isolation of these parents increased significantly from the mid-to-late twentieth century, when the initial experiment with the local school board was rejected in substantial ways by state governments that began, jurisdiction by jurisdiction, to seize control of the curriculum of the schools for themselves and their *state* boards of education. Some states opted for an intermediate solution and a regional or county authority, but the point in all instances was the same: Such centralized control was necessary "to bring uniformity to the system" and thus to assure its deliberate growth and success.[56] Today, in most states, local school boards continue to operate with important authority over certain aspects of school policy, including the funding of "extra" programs, but the curriculum and the textbooks that define it are in the hands of regional or state-wide authorities.[57]*

Indeed, because the majority of textbooks available for selection and use by the public schools across the country are developed and produced by a very few publishers, most of whom are located in the state of California, it is accurate to say that the curriculum in any given jurisdiction (even in state-wide jurisdictions) is already far from malleable.† The state or regional authorities that are re-

---

* In North Carolina, certain legislators—responding, presumably, to their constituents—have been so consternated by this state of affairs that they have even most recently tried to legislate to change things back to the way they used to be. Thus, in April 2001, four representatives to the state assembly developed "[a] bill to be entitled 'An Act to Make Textbook Selection a Local Decision.'" General Assembly of North Carolina, Session 2001, House Bill 1199, Textbook Selection at Local Level, April 12, 2001. Among other things, the bill specifically contemplates that "[l]ocal boards of education shall ... have sole authority to select and procure textbooks, supplemental textbooks, library books, periodicals, audiovisual materials, and other supplementary instructional materials needed for instructional purposes in the public schools of their units." Id. at Section 3(b). The bill is clear that this authority would be wrested away from its current holder, the State Board of Education.

† For example, the "multicultural" textbook series at issue in the *Mozert* case was developed and published by Holt, Rinehart and Winston out of California for use throughout the curriculum of grades one through eight.

sponsible for selecting among these textbook series in the main are administered by educational policy experts, with some continuing input from parent representatives.[58] In this respect, the situation largely mirrors that which appears to have been intended by at least some of the nation's founders, as well as by those responsible for the first real systems of universal public education. The fact that it was apparently necessary in the transition between that early period and the mid-to-late twentieth century to give parents more authority in the form of the local school board should come as no surprise: What better way to convince the skeptical and even recalcitrant public of the value of universal public education than to give local institutions the reins (at least partly) in the formative period? If this was intended, as seems possible, it was truly an extraordinary deal.

All of this begs the obvious question, what do parent groups and conservative policy makers (and especially conservative candidates for political office) mean today when they talk about "local control" of the public schools? I wondered this when I began writing this book, and, because we were in an election cycle, I called the offices of several regional candidates who had made the issue of "local control" their principal theme. Not one of them had a substantive answer to the question "what is it that you mean by 'local control'"? At most, their answers reflected the theme that "[a]ny movement toward national control of education savages principles that we as Americans hold dear: parental authority and control, teachers who are free to teach core subject matter and school boards that are responsive to their communities, not held captive by distant bureaucrats."[59] But, that battle already has been lost; the

---

See *Mozert*, 827 F.2d at 1059. Holt, Rinehart is one of several book publishers that form the California-based textbook industry. See Charles Mantesian, "The Schoolbook Bonanza," Governing Magazine, Nov. 1999, at 46. Not only does California have a large market, but is also serves as an "adoption state": The California State Education Department reviews and chooses textbooks from the publishing companies; and California's approval process, as well as that of Florida and Texas—the other two "adoption states"—affects the textbooks schools use nationwide. Id. See also Neil R. Pierce, "California Leading Fight for Better Textbooks," The National Journal, October 26, 1985, at 2441; Mary Bruno, "A Dunce Cap for Textbooks," Newsweek, Sept. 30, 1985, at 78.

contest now is between the states and the federal government. Embedded in political campaign commercial after commercial, their chant was thus largely empty rhetoric.

In the end, there are two divergent views about local control of public education that are supported by history. One, the proponents' argument, posits a logical and unbroken chain of events and objectives from the early New England colony schools through the present. This unbroken chain is said to include "the founders of the nation" who might have believed that parents, perhaps through local schools boards, ought to control their children's education. This argument further assumes that local control has remained constant in this form. The second argument posits precisely the opposite, an unbroken commitment to a form of public education that, with or without the parents' ultimate approval and control, would serve first and foremost the interests of the larger society and ultimately of democratic government. This argument highlights the important and essential distinctions between the New England colony schools and the system of universal public education that came later; it suggests that some of the most prominent of the nation's founders conceived of this system in certain respects that were quite incompatible with the notion of local control; and it is supported by evidence that the schools in many ways were intended to "alienate" children from their parents, either because the parents did not wish their children to be educated at all (at least not outside of their control) or because the parents were not part of the mainstream that the schools were intended to promote.

In describing these two readings of history, I do not intend to make the claim that the framers secretly supported the federalization of elementary education. Indeed, since they did not expound on the subject, and since the foundation for such a debate did not even exist during their time, it is impossible for me or anyone else to know definitively what they thought about it. Rather, I suggest that if we are to play the game "find the framers' intent" as some contemporary proponents of local control imply that we should, there is certainly an argument that the framers' writings on the subject of education lend themselves to an argument for central control.

Ultimately, it is my view that the second of these two readings of history is the better analysis, simply because the historical case for local control ignores too many essential facts. Most notable among these is the traditional purpose of and jurisprudential doctrine that attaches to the schools, and the shift of curricular authority from the localities to the states beginning in the middle part of the twentieth century. Nevertheless, my purpose in this book is not so much to convince the reader that my view of history is correct, but rather to emphasize that the history of the public schools and of local control is equivocal and thus cannot be the basis for any sort of imperative to continue the practice "as we always have" and "as it was intended to be."

THE ARGUMENT ACCORDING TO THE NEEDS AND SUCCESSES OF THE CHILDREN AND THEIR COMMUNITIES

The second argument in favor of local control was perhaps best articulated by former Iowa Governor Terry E. Branstad, who explained his view that

> [s]tate governments, and ultimately, local school boards are in the best position to know the needs of the children. Our education systems must reflect the social, cultural and economic values of our communities. Those local values are best determined by the people who are most accountable in that area; parents, local administrators, teachers and school board members. The well-financed public interest advocacy groups in Washington D.C. are too far removed to know these local values.[60]

Branstad's position is closely related to the theme that local control of curricular matters is especially important to "improv[e] children's academic achievement."[61] (Presumably, this latter argument is merely a twist on the notion that children are best off when their parents, teachers, and school boards are "in charge" of curricular decisions.) As I argue below, this "needs and successes" argument for community and parental direction of local public education is flawed for three reasons.

First, the argument is almost completely anachronistic. Contrary to Branstad's suggestion, there is today no such thing in most places in the United States as an immutable link between the children's needs and the "social, cultural and economic values" unique to any particular community. Few individuals in the contemporary society live in such geographically or ideologically isolated communities. Even then, while there continue to be some regional differences with respect to their political, religious, economic, and ethnic composition, those differences do not translate into different curricular needs in the way they may have a century or more ago. This is because the children of these communities will be, and in many instances already are, part of the national and even international communities as a result of their exposure to and relationships with others who are not like them, and because of the essentially mobile nature of contemporary adult society.

Children today are exposed to heterogeneity as a result of changing demographics, work-related dislocations, and national and international media, including the Internet. As a result, there are simply too few instances in which children can be expected to benefit from presumptions of intellectual and spiritual isolationism on the part of their parents and local school boards. In this context, parental or local school board decisions that would shield children from curricula that reflect that broader culture are not likely to be positive in assisting the children to grow to become successful individuals and useful citizens of the society. Indeed, this is precisely why the courts frequently sustain the authority of the states to impose certain curricular requirements even on private schools that purport to prepare students for an adult life in the majority society. Charles Faber made this point as early as 1991, when he wrote that the "Gemeinschaft societies" of the eighteenth and nineteenth centuries that spawned the local school board, and which are characterized by a heterogeneity of culture, self-sufficiency, and "a strong sense of community identity," soon would "will cease to exist."[62]

In the modern or post-Gemeinschaft context, an educational organization that operates at the national level can both know and understand local values since these are in the main national values. Because of this and the greater ability of national authorities to commission relevant research, the allocation of decisional authority on the national level has the potential to result in schools that are more successful than those in which decision-making is allocated to local school boards.[63] Such national schools, because they would be created in concept by national representatives, likely also would enhance the general sense of the public that the curriculum was designed to permit children an opportunity for success in the national and international communities and economies, where increasingly our destiny is shaped. Of course, there are those for whom this result is precisely the problem with any discussion of national involvement in education. However, as the Fourth Circuit explained in *Mozert*, and as I have discussed above, it is the function of the public schools to prepare students for life in the national community; if parents do not care for that objective, they have the option at least to some extent of choosing alternative schooling.[64]

In this regard, it is relevant that the United States is almost alone among industrialized nations in its decentralized governance of public education; in other such societies, public education has long been conceived as a national or federal interest, and there is significant *de facto* if not *de jure* curricular uniformity in their schools. Moreover, studies consistently demonstrate that children in these other countries are generally as (if not more) successful than American children academically, and the comparative data on the Columbine epidemic shows that the same is certainly true in terms of their emotional and social success.

Second, the argument according to the needs and successes of the students and their communities is flawed because it rests upon the similarly erroneous assumption that parents and localities are both more knowledgeable about what children need, and more interested in and active about assuring that their needs are met. I have just discussed the flaw in the argument that local communities around the country are still distinctive in their ideological and economic profiles, and thus in their judgment about the children's need for a curriculum that reflects those distinctions. The other flaw in this argument is that it ignores entirely the fact that children "need" more than just an education that will allow them to compete in the local marketplace for employment, and that communities "need" more than citizens who are qualified primarily to work in local or even state specific employment. As Part I of this book described, both children and communities, including the larger society, need institutions that will secure their emotional health as well as the fulfillment of their academic or economic potential. Thus, they need institutions that will nurture them as individuals, and that will teach them self-esteem and appropriate social behavior. They need physical spaces that will protect them from the loneliness and toxicity of the outside world. And they need these spaces to be free of individuals and forces that would alienate them and render them anti-social. Unless children are afforded these things, they will continue to be at substantial risk of personal and social dysfunctional. And this will happen as it is happening today, regardless of how well suited the academic component of the curriculum is for the children's intellectual development. Eric Harris and Dylan Klebold became murderers and killed themselves because they were ill; the relatively excellent quality of their school's academic offerings was obviously irrelevant in the calculus of their dysfunction.

Furthermore, the evidence is far from clear that parents and local school boards continue to be captivated by such weighty matters as the substance of the curriculum; indeed, the reason there is an epidemic of emotionally disturbed children is that those closest to and accountable for the children's welfare are no longer paying sufficient attention to their needs to enable them to succeed emotionally. That the national press periodically reports on the curricular shenanigans of some school board that would, for example, ban the teaching of evolution in that community's classrooms, is only evidence that in a few jurisdictions with particular homogeneous demographics, it is still possible to change the curriculum on the local level. But, such stories are not evidence of a general activist tendency on the part of parents and school boards around the country. Indeed, the contrary is true. As I already have described, curricular decisions today are largely made at the state and not the local level. And, as Faber has explained,

> [i]n all states, the local district must offer a curriculum approved by the state. States differ in the degree of control exercised, but even in states where local districts retain some discretion, course offerings must meet state guidelines. Most states permit local school districts to select their own textbooks, but these districts usually must choose books from state-approved lists.[65]

Nor do parents today widely feel that they are in control of their children's education. In fact, if the debate about education around the 2000 presidential election was any indication, they feel quite the opposite and are anxious for a reform of the system that would ensure that the children's needs both emotionally and academically were met. While this fact might mitigate at least theoretically in favor of local rather than regional or national control, the evidence is otherwise. Parents seem in many cases to have abandoned any reliance they previously had placed on local authorities for a solution to their problems with the schools, and instead now look to state and even national governments that command the money and broad perspective necessary to the development and implementation of successful responses.[66]

Third, the argument that the children's and the community's success depends upon local control fails because it erroneously suggests that parental and school board involvement in curricular decisions produces students who are more successful and happier than those who are subject to centralized programs. As far as I have found, there is no good evidence to support this proposition. Indeed, the only strong evidence on the subject suggests that children succeed in the important intellectual and emotional respects when they attend good schools staffed by good teachers, and when they perceive that their parents care about and participate in their experiences in such schools.[67] As studies have shown, "the most tangible and indispensable characteristics of effective schools are strong administrative leadership, expectation of high achievement by all students, a positive school climate, an emphasis on basic skills, devotion of school energy and resources to fundamental objectives, and frequent monitoring of pupil progress."[68] Whether this is the result of local or central control is largely irrelevant to the ultimate outcome. This much is clearly demonstrated by the categorical success of isolated domestic and international efforts at centralized curriculum development. These efforts have involved both public and private institutions. In other words, good schools, good teachers, and good parents clearly can and do exist where there is local decision-making. My point is simply that this is not the requisite characteristic of a successful program.

It bears emphasis that parental involvement in a child's education is clearly beneficial to the child's successful engagement of that process and environment. This is both intuitive and empirically supported. However, contrary to the arguments made by advocates of local control, the involvement that is dispositive is not political participation in school board matters, but rather personal participation in the school life of individual children within a family. When the child sees and feels on a day-to-day basis that her parent(s) care about her experience and success in school, for example by inquiring in person and with real interest about the child's day, and assisting with homework and other school projects, the child is motivated to do her best.[69] The fact that an otherwise disengaged parent regularly attends school board meetings and advocates a particular curriculum simply cannot have the same (if any) impact. Indeed, the contrary suggestion fails for the same reason that working parents are wrong when they claim that their children are fine despite their absence because their work is socially important, individually rewarding, or even personally necessary. In general, children, and particularly young children, cannot truly understand this for a long time (if they ever do) because what they need and want as a developmental matter is a nurturing parental presence in their day-to-day lives. Without it, as the evidence about the Columbine epidemic shows, they risk immeasurable failure.

The most illustrative vignette I have heard on this point was written most recently by John Hartmire, whose father was Executive Director of the National Farmworker Ministry in the period when that Ministry was led by Cesar Chavez. Hartmire noted that for the thirty years following his father's appointment to that position, "our lives were defined by Cesar and the United Farm Workers."[70] And he described the effect his father's political commitment to this cause had on his childhood:

> [d]uring those years my father was gone a lot, traveling with, or for, Cesar. I "understood" because the struggle to organize farmworkers into a viable union was the work of a lifetime, and people would constantly tell me how much they admired what Dad was doing. Hearing it made me proud. It also made me lonely. He organized the clergy to stand up for the union, went to jail defying court injunctions and was gone from our house for days on end, coming home, my mother likes to say, only for clean underwear. It was my father who fed the small piece of bread to Cesar ending his historic 25-day fast in 1968. It's no wonder Dad missed my first Little League home run.... I try to remember Cesar Chavez for what he was ... and not what he took from my childhood. Namely, my father. I still wrestle with the cost of my father's commitment, understanding that social change does not

come without sacrifice. I just wonder if the price has to be so damn high.[71]

Given the equivocal nature of the historical argument in favor of local control, and the clear failure of the more contemporary arguments according to the needs and successes of the children and the local communities, it seems that there must be a better but more complicated argument in favor of local control lurking somewhere behind the rhetoric. In the end, I believe that argument is probably the same one that retarded the original birth of mandatory public education, and that assured—at least for a time—that once this institution was finally established it was controlled locally.

Universal mandatory public education uniquely excludes otherwise autonomous parents from a critical aspect of the child-rearing process. In a culture and legal system that continues in other ways to view children as the property of their parents, and parents as bearers of unique and corresponding rights with respect to the upbringing of their children, the intrusion that is public education continues to be as radical today as it was in Jefferson's era. Parents went kicking and screaming into public education in the first instance, and a significant minority still wage the fight. And thus, to the extent there is any seamless web in the history of public education, and as cases from *Meyer* to *Mozert* reveal, this is it.

In addition, there also is the profound sense among many in this country, a sense that transcends history, that those who have the power to raise the children also have the power to influence the future. Plato explored this theme in his *Republic*, and since then the struggle for the minds of the children in the West has continued to be central to the relationship between individuals and their governments. Assuring through the doctrine of local control that what is taken away with one hand is returned (at least partially) with the other for some is the only practical way to make the intrusion of public education a palatable one, and thus the relationship between parents and the government continually viable. For these citizens—President G.W. Bush and Attorney General John Ashcroft among them—it is likely that this was the tacit deal that was struck long ago and that remains critical today.

On the one hand, there is no doubt that such a deal is inconsistent with the public education jurisprudence. As Justice Byron White explained in the Supreme Court's 1985 decision in *New Jersey v. T.L.O.*,

> the Court has recognized that 'the concept of parental delegation' as a source of school authority is not entirely 'consonant with compulsory education laws.' Today's public school officials do not merely exercise authority voluntarily conferred on them by individual parents; rather, they act in furtherance of publicly mandated educational and disciplinary policies.[72]

On the other hand, whatever the jurisprudence says, suppositions about this tacit deal are significant because they imply that parents as voters ultimately hold the key to the question whether local control in its current stripped-down version will survive as an institution in this democracy, or whether it will be replaced by an integrated program that better serves the needs of the children, the general public, and the future of the nation.

CONCLUSION

As we come together as a society in the aftermath of the recent terrorism, and as we begin to contemplate the ways in which we might become better citizens of the world, we must not forget that this new community we are forming offers previously unimaginable possibilities not only for our adult souls and bipartisanship in government. It also offers the possibility to revisit how we raise our children. This, in turn, provides the opportunity for us to cure the Columbine epidemic and truly to secure the nation's future.[1]

In March 2001, Representative Patsy Mink (D-Hawaii) introduced H.R. 1118, a bill in the United States House of Representatives "to establish comprehensive early childhood education, staff development programs, model Federal Government early childhood education programs, and for other purposes."[2] Among other things, and as its title suggests, the bill addresses the impact on young children of working mothers, and provides that "no mother should be forced to work outside the home as a condition for availing her children of early childhood education programs."[3] It proposes to authorize four billion dollars annually for programs that are developed under its auspices.[4] And it provides for the creation of universal early childhood education programs that include "comprehensive physical and mental health, social, and cognitive development services;"[5] a "full-day, year-round program of daily activities;"[6] teacher training and evaluation;[7] and the "promulgat[ion of] a common set of program standards" by the United States Secretary of Education.[8]

In its sheer breadth, and especially in its implicit premise that schools can be effective only if their programs are defined by and serve the needs of the children, Representative Mink's bill lies in stark contrast with those others that seek merely to provide small grants to random organizations to study over a period of years the matter of character education. In these ways, her proposed legislation is also extraordinarily idealistic; some would say naively so.

After all, why would the American public ever agree—particularly in the midst of an expensive war on global terrorism and a domestic recession—to the immense allocations of funds or to the delicate intrusions on parental primacy that are contemplated by this bill? This question is especially salient in this time also of increasing individualism, commitment to tax reductions, and diminishing faith and interest in the public schools.

My own proposal to begin to fix Columbine by revolutionizing and federalizing the public schools is quite like the Mink bill in many respects, including that it is certain to be viewed (in the best light) as overly idealistic and even naive.[9] Indeed, both are likely to be perceived as the pipe dreams of mothers who do not quite understand political realities, or at least who have not allowed themselves to see these realities clearly through the veil of their overriding concern for the children. My response (at least to any critique of my own proposal) is this: It is my love and concern for the children that has allowed me a perspective from the trenches, and this perspective has compelled me to appreciate the true dimensions of the children's contemporary dysfunction. As a result, I have no doubt whatever that I am seeing quite clearly, and that, as I have said in another context, "[i]t is negligent for the society to disregard the ultimate causes of [the children's] dysfunction, and only to seek to avert the effects when children finally go over the edge."[10]

The data that I have marshaled to support this allegation are compelling: A large percentage of American children in all income brackets and at all ages are no longer being "mothered" by anyone. At the same time, they are surrounded by both real and virtual influences that are emotionally toxic in many important respects. The unsurprising result is that they are suffering egregiously from depression, anxiety, and related anti-social disorders. In the society more generally, meanwhile, adults have demonstrated an ever-increasing fealty to individualism, and a commensurate decrease in any real commitment to communitarian or even family ideals. The almost-perfect reflection of these cultural trends in the constitutional jurisprudence has all but sealed the children's fate: Children need their parents—and perhaps in some stages, particularly their mothers—not only to nurture them but also to shield them from harm. And they need the society generally to protect them from developmentally inappropriate influences. These are the very needs that are ignored or at least substantially marginalized by the adult world's ever-growing demand for more liberty.

The reason that my proposal and legislative measures such as H.R. 1118 must be taken seriously despite the war on terrorism, the recession, and whatever else may occupy our front-burners on any given day, is that without the changes they contemplate, only the bigger and even more idealistic cultural revolution that these trends suggest can fix Columbine. For example, any other alternative would require working mothers and fathers to sacrifice lifestyle and a certain sort of self-fulfillment to return to the hearth, and producers of toxic virtual realities to give up on that market in favor of more healthful but likely less lucrative options. My working assumption is that these alternatives are even less viable as solutions than is my own, because they are even more idealistic: Practically speaking, and on balance, the steep cost of fixing Columbine in the manner that I propose is still less expensive than is either alternative of leaving the children in their current deplorable state, or of sacrificing the liberties of parental autonomy and free speech that are primarily implicated in this context.

Ultimately, given the developmental facts and the legal landscape, the failure to act pragmatically to find a remedy for the Columbine epidemic risks the health not only of millions of innocent children but also of the nation's future. I am by no means the only one to recognize this stark reality. Most prominently, Marian Wright Edelman has admonished that "[t]he mounting crisis of our children and families is a rebuke to everything America professes to be. While the cost of repairing our crumbling foundation will be expensive in more ways than one, the cost of not repairing it, or of patching cosmetically, may be fatal."[11] And, as yet others also have noted before me, the failure more generally to recognize that liberty has its price is likely also to be increasingly detrimental to the success of the society. Here I have in mind specifically the freedoms to be left alone to raise our individual children as we would like or be best able to do, and to speak whatever thoughts and thus to create whatever derivative products we individually might conjure up. Mary Ann Glendon, for example, has urged that "[a]n intemperate rhetoric of personal liberty ... corrodes the social foundations on which individual freedom and security ultimately rests."[12]

This point may appear at first blush to be internally inconsistent: How can freedom depend upon its even partial abdication? In the end, however, it brings us full circle to the nation's founders, those who originally conceived the notion of a liberal democratic state governed by the rule of law, who imagined it to be self-evident that liberty had to be bounded in order to ensure the survival and success of the larger community. In the words of Benjamin Cardozo, "[l]iberty in the literal sense is impossible for anyone except the anarchist, and anarchy is not law, but its negation and destruction."[13] Most specifically, the point brings us back to the founders' generally strong commitment to mandatory universal public education, which they saw as a necessary institution to secure the survival and success of the otherwise liberal enterprise. They taught—and they were right—that unless the citizenry as a whole understands and respects that enterprise, *including its collective aspects and needs*, there is little real hope of a viable future for the society.

One final note. Throughout this book, I have emphasized that it is impossible to imagine a complete cure for the Columbine epidemic without first, recognizing its existence, and second, acknowledging that "good parenting" is necessary to a child's most successful development. Action by individuals and relevant institutions within the society consistent with this recognition and acknowledgment obviously also is essential. I also have argued that the law alone cannot make this happen, and indeed, that in important respects the law is even an obstacle to that end. Nevertheless, and while this has not been my mission here, there is no doubt that it is in our collective interest to facilitate the cultural compromises that eventually would bring children and their parents closer together. For example, as Europeans have already done, we must develop strategies that recognize and reflect women's value *both* to the economy *and* to the children. Stated slightly differently, we must develop strategies that honor many women's desires or needs to contribute *both* to the economy *and* to the children. It is also critical that such strategies include men, so that the "quality of life" their employment affords does not preclude their real participation in the family. While these things would be true anywhere in the world, they are perhaps especially important in the United States, which has long acted upon the theoretical assumption (at least) that the family and parents are the child's first and best caretakers,

and which has—despite the Columbine epidemic and related social upheaval—steadfastly refused to acknowledge that anything
has changed.

NOTES

NOTES FOR
INTRODUCTION

1. David Rinker, Letter to the Editor New York Times Magazine, Nov. 26, 1999, at 26 (regarding article by Lisa Belkin, "Parents Blaming Parents" New York Times Magazine, Oct. 31, 1999, at 61).

2. Andrew Ferguson, "What Politicians Can't Do," Time, May 3, 1999, at 52.

3. Id.

4. Id.

5. Laura F. Rothstein, "Genetic Information in Schools," Genetic Secrets: Protecting Privacy and Confidentiality in the Genetic Era, at 317, 319 (Mark A. Rothstein ed., Yale Univ. Press 1997).

6. Id.

7. While no one at least in the legal literature has made this argument, the role of the federal government in education in general has certainly received attention. See, e.g., Charles F. Faber, "Is Local Control of the Schools Still a Viable Option?" 14 Harv. J.L. & Pub. Pol'y 447 (describing the tradition of local control and suggesting that it will always be a part of the American educational paradigm); Richard Briffault, "The Role of Local Control in School Finance Reform," 24 Conn. L. Rev. 773, (discussing the traditional and contemporary meanings of the concept of "local control" and its viability in the current political and economic landscape, particularly as it pertains to financing of public education).

NOTES FOR CHAPTER ONE
COLUMBINE HIGH SCHOOL, APRIL 20, 1999

1. Matt Bai, "Anatomy of a Massacre," Newsweek, May 3, 1999, at 25, 29.

2. See id. (several students were critically injured).

3. David Olinger, "2 Gunmen Planned 500 Deaths," Denver Post, Apr. 26, 1999, at AA-01.

4. See id.

5. Nancy Gibbs and Timothy Roche, "The Columbine Tapes," Time, Dec. 20, 1999, at 20 (quoting from tapes made by Harris and Klebold).

6. Id. at 18–19.

7. Id. at 20–21.

8. Id. at 26–27.

9. Bai at 25–26.

10. Id. at 25; Nancy Gibbs, "The Littleton Massacre," Time, May 3, 1999, at 26.

11. Gibbs, "The Littleton Massacre," at 27.

12. See Bai at 31; Gibbs, "The Littleton Massacre," at 29 (describing the graffiti omen written in the boys' bathroom, "Columbine will explode one day. Kill all athletes. All jocks must die.").

13. Bai at 31.

14. Gibbs, "The Littleton Massacre," at 36.

15. Id.

16. See id. at 26–27.

17. Id.

18. Gibbs and Roche, "The Columbine Tapes," at 20.

19. Gibbs, "The Littleton Massacre," at 26–27; see also id. at 36 (describing the "year's worth of meticulous planing for the attack on Hitler's 110th birthday.").

20. See Lisa Belkin, "Parents Blaming Parents," New York Times Magazine, Oct. 31, 1999, at 61.

21. Gibbs and Roche, "The Columbine Tapes," at 22 (quoting videotapes made by Harris and Klebold about their plans and their motivations).

22. Id.

23. Gibbs, "The Littleton Massacre," at 34.

24. Id.

25. Id.

26. Id. at 36.

27. See Belkin at 61 (describing law suit filed by some victims and their families); and Amended Complaint (on file with author).

28. Belkin at 62.

29. Gibbs and Roche, "The Columbine Tapes," at 28.

30. Id. at 29.

31. Id.

32. Scott Johnson, "One Father's Unique Perspective," Newsweek, May 3, 1999, at 38 (Johnson was the father of Mitchell Johnson, who was responsible for the school shootings in Jonesboro, Arkansas, the year before Columbine); see also, Remarks by President W.J. Clinton and First Lady H.R. Clinton to the Columbine High School Community, May 20, 1999, http://www.pub.white-house.gov/urires/I . . . di://oma.eop.gov.us/1999/5/21/22.text.1, at 5 ("What happened at Columbine has pierced the soul of America.").

33. The presidential impeachment was ranked number one among news stories in 1999 in the "annual Associated Press poll of American newspaper editors and broadcast executives." Arlene Levinson, "A President's Acquittal, and a Horrific School Massacre," Austin American-Statesman, Dec. 31, 1999, at A2. That same poll ranked the Columbine story #2. Id. However, "[i]n a year of big TV news stories that included the impeachment and Monica Lewinsky interview as well as the wall-to-wall, round-the-clock coverage accorded the death of JFK Jr., this is the one we can't get out of our heads." Phil Rosenthal, "Compelling Images: What We Just Had to Watch," Chicago Sun-Times, Dec. 26, 1999, at 22.

34. Most of the 800 or so stories about impeachment involved the Clinton impeachment, but many related to other impeachments around the world. Westlaw "Allnews" (last visited Apr. 30, 2001). According to Westlaw, in 1999, there were 37,464 news stories about the Columbine tragedy. Westlaw "Allnews" (last visited Apr. 30, 2001). Since 1999, and again according to Westlaw, there have been approximately 22,000 stories that mentioned Columbine. Id.

35. Gibbs, "The Littleton Massacre," at 25.

36. Id. at 26; see also, Belkin at 94, 100 (describing this same epiphany).

37. See James Garbarino, Lost Boys: Why Our Sons Turn Violent and How We Can Save Them (The Free Press 1999) at 2–3 (summarizing these prior events and noting that they signaled that "no one is immune.")

NOTES FOR CHAPTER TWO
COLUMBINE *WRIT LARGE*: AN AMERICAN EPIDEMIC

1. See U.S. Census Bureau, "Resident Population Estimates of the United States by Age and Sex: April 1, 1990 to July 1, 1999, with Short-Term Projections to November 1, 2000," available at http://www.census.gov/population/estimates/nation/intfile2-1.txt (last visited May 26, 2000).

2. Id.

3. Garbarino at 8. Garbarino is an expert in child development and youth violence at Cornell University.

4. Id. at 7.

5. Id. at 8.

6. Id. at 9.

7. Centers for Disease Control, "1997 Youth Risk Behavior Surveillance System," available at http://www.cdc.gov/nccdphp/dash/yrbs/natsum97/suin97.htm (last visited May 9, 2001).

8. See id., available at http://www.cdc.gov/nccdphp/dash/yrbs/natsum97/susc.htm (last visited May 9, 2001).

9. Philip J. Cook and John H. Laub, "The Unprecedented Epidemic in Youth Violence," in Youth Violence, Crime and Justice: A Review of Research, Vol. 24 (The University of Chicago, 1998) at 27–28.

10. Id.

11. Id.

12. Garbarino at 8 (commenting on the "drop of 17 percent between 1994 and 1995").

13. See Bart Jansen, "Mother Testifies about Teen-Age Son's Suicide," Portland Press Herald, Sept. 8, 2001, at 1B (discussing testimony on childhood suicide before Senate Health, Education, Labor and Pensions' Subcommittee on Children and Families).

14. Id.

15. Nevada is reported to lead the nation in teen suicides, at 14 per 100,000. Id.

16. Garbarino at 9.

17. See Eric J. Mash and David A. Wolfe, Abnormal Child Psychology (Wadsworth Publishing Co. 1999) at 289 (based upon the publication date of their book, the decade to which the authors refer is 1990–1999); Ted Peters, For the Love of Children: Genetic Technology and the Future of the Family (Westminster John Knox Press 1996) at 2. The National Institute of Mental Health indicates that "[s]ince 1964, the suicide rate among adolescents and young adults has doubled." National Institute of Mental Health, "Brief Notes on the Mental Health of Children and Adolescents," available at http://www.nimh.nih.gov/publicat/childnotes.cfm (last visited May 9, 2001). The Centers for Disease Control provide the following, quite similar data: "From 1952–1995, the incidence of suicide among adolescents and young adults nearly tripled." Centers for Disease Control, "Suicide in the United States," available at http://www.cdc.gov/ncipc/factsheets/suifacts .htm (last visited May 9, 2001). It also suggests that "[f]rom 1980–1997, the rate of suicide among persons aged 15–19 years increased by 11% and among persons aged 10–14 years by 109%." Id. And, it notes that "[f]rom 1980–1996, the rate increased 105% for African-American males aged 15–19." Id.

18. See Susan Roth, "Senate hears testimony on teen suicide problem in Guam," Gannett News Service, Sept. 8, 2001 (describing same Senate hearing).

19. Garbarino at 9 (noting rate of 15%); CDC, "Suicide in the United States," (noting 1997 survey demonstrating rate of 20.5%).

20. Garbarino at 9 (giving lower figure); CDC, "Suicide in the United States," (giving higher figure).

21. Centers for Disease Control, "Assessing Health Risk Behaviors Among Young People: Youth Risk Behavior Surveillance System," available at http://www.cdc.gov/nccdphp/dash/yrbs/yrbsaag.htm (last visited Sept. 24, 2000.) The Centers for Disease Control also note the following facts: Suicide is the "third leading cause of death for young people aged 15–24." Id. "Persons under age 25 accounted for 15% of all suicides in 1997," CDC, "Suicide in the United States"; "In 1997, more teenagers and young adults died from suicide than from cancer, heart disease, AIDS, birth defects, stroke, pneumonia and influenza, and chronic lung disease combined," id.; "among persons aged 15–19 years, firearm-related suicides accounted for 62% of the increase in the overall rate of suicide from 1980–1997," id.; "the risk for suicide among young people is greatest among young white males; however, from 1980 through 1995, suicide rates increased most rapidly among young black males," id. The National Institute of Mental Health also notes that "[i]n 1996, suicide was the 3rd leading cause of death in 15 to 24 year olds—12.2 of every 100,000 persons—following unintentional injuries

and homicide." National Institute of Mental Health, "In Harm's Way: Suicide in America," available at http://www.nimh.nih.gov/publicat/harm-away.cfm (last visited Sept. 24, 2000); "[s]uicide was the 4th leading cause in 10 to 14 year olds, with 298 deaths among 18,949,000 children in this age group," id.; "[f]or adolescents aged 15 to 19, there were 1,817 deaths among 18,644,000 adolescents. The gender ratio in this age group was 5:1 (males: females)," id.; "in 1996, the age-specific mortality rate from suicide was 1.6 per 100,000 for 10- to 14-year-olds, 9.5 per 100,000 for 15- to 19-year-olds ... ('in this age group, boys are about four times as likely to commit suicide than girls are, while girls are twice as likely to attempt suicide.')" "Mental Health: A Report of the Surgeon General," Chapter 3, "Children and Mental Health," available at http://www.surgeongeneral.gov/library/mentalhealth/chapter3/sec5.html (last visited Sept. 24, 2000); "[S]ince the early 1960s, the reported suicide rate among 15- to 19-year-old males increased threefold but remained stable among females in that age group and among 10- to 14-year-olds." Id. It is no surprise that research (conducted by the National Institutes of Health) "has shown that 90 percent of people who kill themselves have depression or another diagnosable mental or substance abuse disorder," NIMH, "In Harm's Way: Suicide in America." For example, "research has shown that alterations in neurotransmitters such as serotonin are associated with the risk for suicide." Id.

22. Peters at 2. Peters is an academic theologian who studies the effects of culture on children. While "[r]ecent evidence compiled by the World Health Organization indicates that by the year 2020, childhood neuropsychiatric disorders will rise proportionately by over 50 percent, internationally, to become one of the five most common causes of morbidity, mortality, and disability among children," id., the U.S. is clearly off of even this chart. NIMH, "Brief Notes on the Mental Health of Children and Adolescents."

23. "Mental Health: A Report of the Surgeon General," Chapter 2, "Epidemiology of Mental Illness," available at http://www.surgeongeneral.gov/Library/MentalHealth/chapter2/sec2_1.html (last visited May 9, 2001).

24. For example, one study cited by the Surgeon General

estimated that almost 21 percent of U.S. children ages 9 to 17 had a diagnosable mental or addictive disorder associated with at least minimum impairment. When diagnostic criteria required the presence of significant functional impairment, estimates dropped to 11 percent. This estimate translates into a total of 4 million youth who suffer from a major mental illness that results in significant impairments at home, at school, and with peers. Finally, when extreme functional impairment is the criterion, the estimates dropped to 5 percent.

"Mental Health: A Report of the Surgeon General," Chapter 3, "Children and Mental Health" (describing the "MECA Study," also known as the

"Methodology for Epidemiology of Mental Disorders in Children and Adolescents.") The National Institute of Mental Health (NIMH) gives somewhat lower figures, but even these are astounding. For example, a recent paper from that organization notes that "[i]n the U.S., 1 in 10 children and adolescents [approximately 7,840,100 children] suffer from mental illness severe enough to cause some level of impairment," NIMH, "Brief Notes on the Mental Health of Children and Adolescents."

25. NIMH, "Brief Notes on the Mental Health of Children and Adolescents."

26. Mash and Wolfe at 289. Mash and Wolfe are child psychologists.

27. Id.

28. Garbarino at 41.

29. Id. at 42.

30. Mash and Wolfe at 289. These data are supplemented by those from the National Institute of Mental Health which explain that "[l]arge-scale research studies have reported that up to 3 percent of children and up to 8 percent of adolescents in the U.S. suffer from depression." NIMH, "Brief Notes on the Mental Health of Children and Adolescents. In addition, "[a] number of epidemiological studies have reported that up to 2.5 percent of children and up to 8.3 percent of adolescents in the U.S. suffer from depression," NIMH, "Depression in Children and Adolescents," available at http://www.nimh.nih.gov/publicat/depchildresfact.cfm (last visited May 9, 2001); "[a]n NIMH-sponsored study of 9- to 17-year-olds estimates that the prevalence of any depression is more than 6 percent in a 6-month period, with 4.9 percent having major depression. In addition, research indicates that depression onset is occurring earlier in life today than in past decades," id.; "[i]n childhood, boys and girls appear to be at equal risk for depressive disorders; but during adolescence, girls are twice as likely as boys to develop depression," id.; and that "[d]epression is the leading cause of disability worldwide among persons age five and older," NIMH, "The Impact of Mental Illness on Society," available at http://www.nimh.nih.gov/publicat/burden.cfm (last visited Sept. 24, 2000). According to the Surgeon General,

> [p]opulation studies show that at any one time between 10 and 15 percent of the child and adolescent population has some symptoms of depression. The prevalence of the full-fledged diagnosis of major depression among all children ages 9 to 17 has been estimated at 5 percent. Estimates of 1-year prevalence in children range from 0.4 and 2.5 percent and in adolescents, considerably higher (in some studies, as high as 8.3 percent). For purposes of comparison, 1-year prevalence in adults is about 5.3 percent.

"Mental Health: A Report of the Surgeon General," Chapter 3, "Children and Mental Health."

31. NIMH defines "Generalized Anxiety Disorder" as including symp-

toms of "exaggerated worry and tension over everyday events." NIMH, "Brief Notes on the Mental Health of Children and Adolescents."

32. Obsessive Compulsive Disorder is "characterized by intrusive, unwanted, repetitive thoughts and rituals performed out of a feeling of urgent need; at least one-third of adult cases begins in childhood." Id.

33. NIMH defines "Panic Disorder" as "feelings of extreme fear and dread that strike unexpectedly and repeatedly for no apparent reason, often accompanied by intense physical symptoms, such as chest pain, pounding heart, shortness of breath, dizziness, or abdominal distress." Id.

34. "Post Traumatic Stress Disorder" is defined as "a condition that can occur after exposure to a terrifying event, most often characterized by the repeated re-experience of the ordeal in the form of frightening, intrusive memories, and brings on hypervigilance and deadening of normal emotions." Id.

35. According to the NIMH, phobias include "social phobia, extreme fear of embarrassment or being scrutinized; specific phobia, excessive fear of an object or situation, such as dogs, heights, loud sounds, flying, costumed characters, enclosed spaces, etc." Id.

36. "Separation anxiety" is defined as "excessive anxiety concerning separation from the home or from those to whom the person is most attached." Id. "About 4 percent of children and young adolescents suffer from separation anxiety disorder." "Mental Health: A Report of the Surgeon General," Chapter 3, "Children and Mental Health."

37. NIMH, "Brief Notes on the Mental Health of Children and Adolescents."

38. Id. The National Institute of Mental Health notes specifically that "[a]nxiety disorders are the most common mental health problems that occur in children and adolescents. According to one large-scale study of 9 to 17 year olds, entitled 'Methods for the Epidemiology of Child and Adolescent Mental Disorders' (MECA), as many as 13 percent of young people had an anxiety disorder in a year." Id. "The combined prevalence of the group of disorders known as anxiety disorders is higher than that of virtually all other mental disorders of childhood and adolescence. The 1-year prevalence in children ages 9 to 17 is 13 percent." "Mental Health: A Report of the Surgeon General," Chapter 3, "Children and Mental Health."

39. According to the Centers for Disease Control, ADHD "is one of the most common childhood behavioral disorders and may affect more than two million children and adolescents in the United States." CDC, "Attention Deficit/Hyperactivity Disorder," available at http://www.cdc.gov/nceh/cddh/ADHD/default.htm (last visited Sept. 24, 2000). The Surgeon General suggests more strongly that "ADHD ... is the most commonly diagnosed behavioral disorder of childhood, [and that it] occurs in 3 to 5 percent of school-aged children in a 6-month period. Pediatricians report that approximately 4 percent of their patients have ADHD. Boys are four times more likely to have the illness than girls are." "Mental Health: A Report of

the Surgeon General," Chapter 3, "Children and Mental Health." The National Institute of Mental Health notes that the "core symptoms" of ADHD "include developmentally inappropriate levels of attention, concentration, activity, distractibility, and impulsivity." NIMH, "Brief Notes on the Mental Health of Children and Adolescents." "ADHD has also been shown to have long-term adverse effects on academic performance, vocational success, and social-emotional development." Id.

40. Id.

41. Anorexia Nervosa "leads to a state of starvation and emaciation, [with patients] losing at least 15% to as much as 60% of their normal body weight." "Eating Disorders: Anorexia and Bulimia," WebMDHealth, http://my.webmd.com/content/dmk/dmk_book_40031 (last visited May 9, 2001). It is one of two identified "eating disorders" the other being bulimia nervosa. Id. According to one definition, "[e]ating disorders are devastating behavioral maladies brought on by a complex interplay of factors, which may include emotional and personality disorders, family pressures, a possible genetic or biologic susceptibility, and a culture in which there is an overabundance of food and an obsession with thinness." Id.

42. Bulimia Nervosa is

more common than anorexia, [and] is characterized by cycles of bingeing and purging. Bulimia nervosa usually begins early in adolescence when young women attempt restrictive diets, fail, and react by binge eating. In response to the binges, patients purge by vomiting or by taking laxatives, diet pills, or drugs to reduce fluids. Patients may also revert to severe dieting, which cycles back to bingeing if the patient does not go on to become anorexic.

Id.

43. See generally, Geoffrey Cowley, "Generation XXL," Newsweek, July 3, 2000, at 40–44 (explaining that "[c]hildhood obesity now threatens one in three kids with long-term health problems, and the crisis is growing"); "Bigger Meals, Bigger Kids," Newsweek, July 3, 2000, at 43 (documenting shifts in eating patterns from 1963 to 1994, and among boys and girls in that same period); Claudia Kalb, "When Weight Loss Goes Awry," Newsweek, July 3, 2000 (describing the pattern of eating disorders that has emerged from the "pressure to be thin.").

44. NIMH, "Brief Notes on the Mental Health of Children and Adolescents"(discussing ADHD).

45. Id. (discussing eating disorders).

46. Patricia Hersch, A Tribe Apart: A Journey into the Heart of American Adolescence (Ballentine Books, New York, 1998) at 12 (emphasis added).

47. Id. at 13.

48. See, e.g., CDC, "Assessing Health Risk Behaviors Among Young

People: Youth Risk Behavior Surveillance System," available at http://www.cdc.gov/nccdphp/dash/yrbs/yrbsaag.htm (last visited May 11, 2001) (describing trends in a variety of high risk behaviors among children); CDC, "Fact Sheet: Youth Risk Behavior Trends," available at http://www.cdc.gov/nccdphp/dash/yrbs/trend/htm (last visited May 11, 2001) (same); Garbarino at 8 (noting same with respect to violence in particular).

49. Mash and Wolfe at 13 (noting that "[t]his pattern has been well-documented by research").

50. Id.

51. Id.

52. Mary Pipher, Reviving Ophelia: Saving the Lives of Adolescent Girls (1994) at 11. Pipher is a clinical psychologist.

53. Id. at 28.

54. Id. at 146–231 (describing these phenomena).

55. Henry Holt and Company, Inc., New York, 1999, at xxi. Pollack is a psychologist who specializes in the treatment of boys and men with various emotional disorders.

56. Id. at xxiii.

57. Id.

58. See generally Garbarino, Lost Boys: Why Our Sons Turn Violent and How We Can Save Them; Dan Kindlon & Michael Thompson, Raising Cain: Protecting the Emotional Life of Boys (1999).

59. See NIMH, "Brief Notes on the Mental Health of Children and Adolescents" (describing "[r]ecent evidence compiled by the World Heath Organization [which] indicates that by the year 2020, childhood neuropsychiatric disorders will rise proportionately by over 50 percent, internationally, to become one of the five most common causes of morbidity, mortality, and disability among children.").

60. CDC, "Rates of Homicide, Suicide, and Firearm-Related Death Among Children—26 Industrialized Countries," MMWR Weekly, available at http://www.cdc.gov/epo/mmwr/preview/mmwrhtml1/00046149.htm (last visited Mar. 8, 2001).

61. According to the Centers for Disease Control,

[i]n the 1994 World Development Report, 208 nations were classified by gross national product; from that list, the United States and all 26 of the other countries in the high-income group and with populations of greater than or equal to 1 million were selected because of their economic comparability and the likelihood that those countries maintained vital records most accurately.

Id. Data were collected concerning "suicides," "homicides," "suicides by firearm," "homicides by firearm," "unintentional deaths caused by firearm," and "firearm-related deaths for which intention was undetermined." Id.

71. NIMH, "The Impact of Mental Illness on Society."

72. Id.

73. Hersch at 12–13 (describing this trend).

74. See Garbarino at 5.

75. "The High Costs of Gun Violence," CBS.com, available at http://www.kcncnews4.... ow/story/0,1597,53728-326,00.shtml (last visited Apr. 30, 2001). This same report notes that "[h]ospitals absorb 80 percent of their gun-trauma costs, and sooner or later, that means we all do." Id.

76. Fox Butterfield, "2 Economists Give Far Higher Cost of Gun Violence," FreeRepublic.com, available at http://www.freerepublic.com/ forum/a39c25ele0277.htm (last visited Apr. 30, 2001). Cook is an economist at Duke University, and Ludwig is an economist at Georgetown University. They published their estimate in their book, Gun Violence: The Real Costs (2000).

77. Inter-American Development Bank, "The cost of domestic violence," available at http://www.iadb.org/exr/IDB/stories/1997/eng/XV2e.htm (last visited Apr. 30, 2001). It is unclear what data are and are not included in this broad range cited by the Inter-American Development Bank. However, the report does note that the "most immediate" impact on victims are "health care costs, absenteeism from work, reduced income for the family." Id. And it notes that further (indirect) costs to the society include "the resources of health care systems, law enforcement and the courts" as well as "serious impact on the health of the pregnant woman and their unborn babies." Id. It is thus likely that the range reflects estimates that are more and less inclusive of these downstream or indirect costs.

78. "How Much Does Sexual Violence Cost?" available at http://www.health.state.mn.us/svp/bas05.html (last visited Apr. 30, 2001). The figure of $71 billion is for "[s]exually violent acts against children (ages 0–14). Id. "Sexual violence against adolescents (ages 15–24) costs $45 billion per year...." Id. All of the figures reported by the Minnesota Department of Health are direct costs; they do not include the costs of incarcerating the perpetrators, nor do they include downstream costs such as emotional distress, disability, and the like. Id.

79. "Mental Health: A Report of the Surgeon General," Chapter 2, "Epidemiology of Mental Illness." The Report elaborates that "[w]hile some disorders do continue into adulthood, a substantial fraction of children and adolescents recover or "grow out of" a disorder, whereas, a substantial fraction of adults develops mental disorders in adulthood." Id.

80. Santosky v. Kramer, 455 U.S. 745, 790 (1982), J. Rehnquist dissenting, and quoting Prince v. Massachusetts, 321 U.S. 158, 168, 165 (1944) (finding constitutional the application of the state's child labor laws to a Jehovah's Witness who wished to allow her nine-year old ward to sell religious literature on the street in the evenings).

81. Id. at 789–90. Rehnquist also noted that "[t]he same can be said of children who, though not physically or emotionally abused, are passed from one foster home to another with no constancy of love, trust, or discipline." Id. at 789.

82. Hersch at 12; see also Santosky, 455 U.S. at 789 (J. Rehnquist noting that "children who are abused in their youth generally face extraordinary problems developing into responsible, productive citizens.").

83. Hersch at 12.

84. Bellotti v. Baird, 443 U.S. 622, 633 (1979), quoting Moore v. East Cleveland, 431 U.S. 494, 503–04 (1977) (plurality opinion).

85. Small v. Morrison, 185 N.C. 577, 118 S.E. 12 (1923) (recognizing for the first time the doctrine of parent-child immunity in a negligence context).

86. Bellotti, 443 U.S. at 633.

87. Small, 118 S.E. at 15.

88. Marian Wright Edelman, The Measure of Our Success: A Letter to My Children and Yours (1992).

89. Id. at 79, quoting G. Campbell Morgan, The Children's Playground in the City of God, The Westminster Pulpit (circa 1908).

90. Id.

91. Id. at 86, 89. Edelman is the Director of the Children's Defense Fund.

92. Dan Luzadder and Kevin Vaughan, "Biggest Question of All: Detectives Still Can't Fathom Teen-Age Killers' Hatred," Denver Rocky Mountain News, Dec. 14, 1999, at 7A.

NOTES FOR CHAPTER THREE

THE GENETICS OF VIOLENCE AND DEPRESSION

1. Michael Rutter, "Introduction: concepts of antisocial behaviour, of cause, and of genetic influences," Genetics of Criminal and Antisocial Behaviour (John Wiley & Sons, Chichester, England, 1996) at 1; see also Thomas G. O'Connor and Robert Plomin, "Developmental Behavioral Genetics," Handbook of Developmental Psychopathology, 2d. Ed., edited by Arnold J. Sameroff, Michael Lewis, and Suzanne M. Miller (Klewer Academic/Plenum Publishers, New York, 2000) at 218–19 (noting that "[t]here is no single best design to estimate genetic or environmental influences, or the effects of genotype-environment interactions or correlations," and suggesting that result can vary quite widely depending upon the research methodology.).

2. As one researcher has noted, "[t]here are now well-documented genetic influences on a wide range of major mental disorders using a variety of twin, adoption, family history, and, more recently, molecular genetic approaches." O'Connor & Plomin at 219, citing Plomin et al., 1997. See id.

("Nevertheless, there is now a growing body of empirical evidence on the contribution of genetic factors to individual differences in antisocial behaviour.")

3. Mash & Wolfe at 41; see also O'Connor & Plumin at 230 (describing studies in which a genetic link to various psychopathologies have been identified, including among others neuroticism, schizophrenia, bi-polar disorder, ADHD, reading disability, autism, internalizing disorders including generalized anxiety and social phobia, and obsessive-compulsive disorder.); Sharon Begley, "Why the Young Kill," Newsweek, May 3, 1999, at 34 (quoting Garbarino as having found that "'irritability, impulsivity, hyperactivity and a low sensitivity to emotions in others are all biologically based.'") Many if not all of the relevant studies in this area have pointed to genes that in some manner affect neurotransmitter release, absorption, or transport, including especially those systems that involve serotonin and dopamine. O'Connor & Plumin at 230 (describing a series of studies that implicate dopamine systems, as well as the consistency of these results "with previously reported neurotransmitter evidence."

4. Id. Thus, for example, through traditional inter-generational family studies, it has been shown that a propensity for certain kinds of depression and other psychoses can "run in the family." Depending upon the genes they inherit, the members of such families will be at an increased risk for suffering related symptoms.

5. See Michael Bohman, "Predisposition to criminality: Swedish adoption studies in retrospect," in Genetics of Criminal and Antisocial Behavior at 99.

6. See generally, Genetics of Criminal and Antisocial Behavior, passim.

7. Begley at 32.

8. Rutter at 6.

9. Id.

10. Thomas and Plomin at 229; see also Mash and Wolfe at 40 ("To address the important role of genetic influences [in the development of psychopathology in children], we first need to understand the nature of genes, bearing in mind that virtually any trait a child possesses results from the interaction of environmental and genetic factors") (emphasis in original); Begley at 32 (explaining that "the picture is much more nuanced, based as it is on the discovery that experience rewires the brain"); id. at 33 ("Are certain young brains predisposed to violence? Maybe—but how these kids are raised can either save them or push them over the brink.").

11. Begley at 32.

12. Id. at 34.

13. O'Connor & Plomin at 228. These authors describe a series of studies that confirm this point, including a study that "reported that adversity in the adoptive home environment was associated with adoptee antisocial outcome only in the presence of genetic risks for antisocial behavior"; another study that "found that the likelihood of experiencing depressive symptoms

was especially pronounced in those [women] at genetic risk who recently experienced stressful, severe life events"; another study that "reported that the rate of antisocial behavior among adoptees was considerably greater (40%) in those with both genetic and environmental risks (i.e., in the adoptive home) than in those with only environmental (approximately 6%) or only genetic (approximately 12%) sources of risk"; and another study that "found substantial genetic influence on conduct disorder in males based on retrospective reports in adulthood, but only if the twins had the same friends as children." Id.

14. Begley at 32.

15. Mash & Wolfe at 41.

16. Exceptions to this "rule" have been known to exist in circumstances where populations are particularly isolated, and thus where there is relatively little if any infiltration of new or different genetic characteristics in the population. This isolation assures that the studied group has a relatively stable genetic characteristics, which will often correspond to a particular political boundary. Iceland is a particularly good example of such a circumstance, and indeed, geneticists interested in developing effective pharmaceuticals currently are studying its population for precisely this reason. See Hrobjartur Jonatansso, "Iceland's Health Sector Database: A Significant Head Start in the Search for the Biological Grail or an Irreversible Error?" 26 Am. J.L. & Med. 31 (2000) (describing this genetic landscape). There is also some indication that over (quite long periods of) time, culture—which is not always coterminous with political boundaries—may have an effect on a group's genetic characteristics, either because the group isolates in terms of reproduction, or because it preferences certain behavioral traits over others. See id.

17. Rutter at 6.

18. Id. at 7.

19. Begley at 35. Begley goes on to suggest that "what has changed is the ubiquity of violence, the easy access to guns and the glorification of revenge in real life and in entertainment." Id. While I certainly agree with her that these are factors in the etiology of the larger Columbine epidemic, based upon her own analysis and mine, I would suggest that she is excluding the most significant factor in the analysis, namely the fact of inadequate parenting.

NOTES TO CHAPTER FOUR

The Developmental Role of Parenting
and Parent-Substitutes

1. The mantra that a parent need not "worry about doing 'irreparable damage' to children" in the course of making parenting decisions because "[t]he human spirit is quite remarkable" and "[c]hildren have come out

of the most difficult circumstances with great resilience and strength," is a common but misleading one. See Gracie Bonds Staples, "Dancing a mombo; 'Mother Dance' allows for missteps," Houston Chronicle, Apr. 29, 2001, at 11. As I discuss throughout Part I, the matter of children's resilience is intimately tied to their environment: If the environment is nurturing and secure, children will be resilient. If it is not, they may survive, but the suggestion that they survive intact is undoubtedly wrong. See, e.g., Robert Brooks and Sam Goldstein, Raising Resilient Children (2001) (providing that children must be nurtured and taught to be resilient in a world of stress); Barrie Ann Mason, "Let the Public Speak," The Press Democrat, Apr. 28, 2001, at B6 (noting that "[a] child who is treated with love and respect at home has the resilience to withstand being bullied at school. A teenager who has endured years of belittling at home has no inner strength to contain his rage when he is treated badly by peers.").

2. See, e.g., Mash and Wolfe at 34 (describing "the influence of multiple causes" on the genesis of childhood psychopathology and the "multidimensional" nature of childhood development, and contrasting the efficacy of treatments that assume this approach with those that incorporate a "one-dimensional causal model" of childhood dysfunction.) For example, depression is believed to be the product of "interactions among vulnerability, risk, and protective factors" including most significantly, "family factors, a lack of rewarding experiences, negative thinking, poor self-regulatory skills, genetic factors, neurobiological deficits, and stressful life events." Id. at 306. As I will explain below, among these several factors, parental influence apart from genetics clearly has the potential to be central to a child's emotional and social profile.

3. Rutter at 5.

4. See, e.g., Margaret Talbot, "The Disconnected; Attachment Theory: The Ultimate Experiment," The New York Times Magazine, May 24, 1998, at 24.

5. Id.

6. See id., ("Feminists have long criticized attachment theory as a sentimental scheme for shooing mothers back home.").

7. Mash and Wolfe at 31.

8. Begley at 32.

9. Mash and Wolfe at 31.

10. Talbot at 24.

11. Begley at 33.

12. Id. at 34; see also Charles H. Zeanah, Neil W. Boris, and Alicia F. Lieberman, "Attachment Disorders of Infancy," in Handbook of Developmental Psychopathology at 297 (describing studies that show that "long-term hospitalization, multiple or changing caregivers, or parents who are depressed or afflicted with substance abuse" can "'prevent stable attachments' at least under certain circumstances.").

13. Begley at 34.

14. Id. At 32–33.

15. Id.

16. Zenah, Boris, and Lieberman at 295.

17. See id. (citing the APA's Diagnostic and Statistical Manual of Mental Disorders [DSM-IV], and noting, inter alia, that the disorder has been observed in "institution-reared children" and in "children in foster care.")

18. Id. at 295, 296, 297 (discussing criteria and etiology established by "Zero to Three" for its diagnostic classification); id. (discussing criteria and etiology established by the World Health Organization that includes some form of "abuse or neglect.").

19. Joseph Goldstein, Anna Freud, & Albert J. Solnit, Beyond the Best Interests of the Child, in The Best Interests of the Child: The Least Detrimental Alternative (1996). At the time that they wrote this book, Goldstein, Freud, and Solnit were child development specialists based at Yale University.

20. Id. at 41.

21. Id. at 19.

22. Id.

23. Mash and Wolfe at 306–07. This analysis is widely believed to be accurate among experts in child development. For example, based upon a survey and review of the literature on early childhood depression, others have explained that "depression seem[s] to occur following the prolonged separation of an infant from his or her primary caregiver and was most severe if the infant was old enough to have already developed a preference for that caregiver." Zeanah, Boris, and Lieberman at 294 (describing the phenomenon known as "anaclictic depression" that was found to exist in children who had been institutionalized and who suffered from "maternal deprivation.") This depression, re-characterized in some diagnostic texts as "reactive attachment disorder of infancy and early childhood," is apparently a problem both for the children who would suffer its symptoms, and also a harbinger of future emotional dysfunction. Id. at 295 (noting the use of this term in the 1994 DSM-IV published by the American Psychiatric Association, as well as the problem that "an infant's attachment disturbances [may] constitute a clinical disorder [or] ... a risk for subsequent disorder.). Whatever the state of this scientific literature, adults who have had children of their own that they have chosen or been forced to place with alternative caregivers who are not already attached to the children have likely all experienced this scenario, whether that placement is for a long period of time or merely for a business day.

24. Goldstein, Freud, and Solnit at 19.

25. Mash and Wolfe at 306; see also Zeanah, Boris, and Lieberman at 293–307 (describing attachment theory in general, and its relationship to maternal deprivation in particular).

26. Mash and Wolfe at 307.

27. Talbot at 24. Eyer is a psychologist.

28. Id.

29. See Scott at 615.

30. Penelope Leach, Children First: What Our Society Must Do—And Is Not Doing—For Our Children Today (Alfred A. Knopf, New York, 1994) at 131. Leach is a child psychologist.

31. Id.

32. Id. at 132.

33. Id.

34. Id. at 135.

35. Id. at 136.

36. Id. at 136–140.

37. Id.

38. Id. at 146.

39. Id.

40. Id.

41. Id. at 147.

42. Id.

43. Id.

44. Id.

45. Id. at 149 (emphasis in original) (describing unintended influences as those that result from the unexplained parental behaviors, behaviors that the children might observe and might assume—without contrary indication—reflect "good" values and social practices.)

46. John Rosemond, Parent Power! A Common-Sense Approach to Parenting in the '90s and Beyond (1990) at 163.

47. Id. at 162.

48. Id. at 162.

49. Id. at 163.

50. Id at 180.

51. Id.

52. Id. at 163–64.

53. Id. at 164.

54. Id.

55. Garbarino at 47–55 (discussing the problems that arise for children, particularly boys, who have been abandoned and rejected by their parents.)

56. Id. at 48.

57. Id. at at 50, citing the cross-cultural work of anthropologist Ronald Rohner. Rohner "calls rejection 'a psychological malignancy' that spreads throughout a child's emotional system wreaking havoc." Id.

58. Id. at 47–48 (giving as examples the boys who were involved in some of the school shootings that preceded Columbine).

59. Id. at 49.

60. Walter Kirn, "Should You Stay Together For The Kids," Time, Sept. 25, 2000, at 75–76.

61. Id. at 76.

62. Scott at 630.

63. Kirn at 74–82 (providing up-to-date statistics on the practice and arguing that the issue is still very much debated.)

64. See, e.g., id. at 77 (establishing the issue as whether "children [are] better off in: An unhappy marriage in which parents stay together mainly for the kids" or "A divorce in which the parents are more happy.")

65. Sandra L. Hofferth, "Child Care, Maternal Employment, and Public Policy, in "The Silent Crisis in U.S. Childcare, The Annals of the American Academy of Political and Social Sciences, Vol. 563, May 1999 at 21 (Suzanne W. Helbrun, Special Editor).

66. Id.

67. Helbrun at 8.

68. Id.

69. Id.

70. Peters at 15.

71. Helbrun at 8.

72. Kirn at 76; see also Peters at 2–7. Peters argues that this decline in the traditional family has resulted in a culture of child neglect. Thus, for example, he notes that today sixty percent of American children are born out of wedlock, half of American marriages end in divorce, and "[m]ore than one-fourth of all [American] households are now headed by a single parent." Id. at 7. The result is that twenty percent of American children now live in poverty (compared with fifteen percent in 1970). Id. at 2. Despite these statistics, however, Kirn's article provides that "[t]he U.S. is certainly not the divorce capital of the world." Kirn at 76. It cites Russia at 65%, Sweden at 64%, Finland at 56%, and Britain at 53%, as leading the U.S. at 49% in the international rankings. Id. Canada, France, and Germany follow close behind, at 45%, 43%, and 41%, respectively. Id.

73. Peters at 7, 16.

74. Melissa B. Jacoby, Teresa A. Sulllivan, Elizabeth Warren, "Rethinking the Debates over Health Care Financing: Evidence from the Bankruptcy Courts," 76 N.Y.U. L. Rev. 375 (May, 2001) (citing figures from U.S. Census Bureau data at 475 tbl. 83).

75. Edelman at 44.

76. Laura W. Morgan, "Family Law at 2000: Private and Public Support of the Family: From Welfare State to Poor Law," 33 Family Law Quarterly 705, 710 (Fall 1999).

77. Barbara Bennett Woodhouse, "Child Custody in the Age of Children's Rights: The Search for a Just and Workable Standard," 33 Family Law Quarterly 815, 824 (Fall, 1999).

78. Norma Levine Trusch, "Relocation of Children after Divorce: The Winds of Change," 18 No. 4 Fair$hare 2 (April, 1998).

79. Peters at 14 (emphasis added).

80. Id. at 15.

81. Helbrun at 9.

82. Peters at 10; see also id. at 5, 8.

83. Id.

84. Id.

85. Harry Bernstein, "Europeans put America's child-care law to shame," The News & Observer, Nov. 16, 1990, at A13.

86. Id.

87. Id.

88. Greenberg and Springen at 61 (describing day care programs as "organized care facilities.")

89. Greenberg and Springen at 62; see also Sean Martin, Too Much Day Care May Hurt Parent-Child Relationship, WebMD, available at http://www.webmd.com (last visited Mar. 15, 2000) (quoting a researcher that "the nation's standard of child care quality is only 'fair to mediocre.'")

90. "Behind the Push for Day Care," available at http://www.frc.org (last visited Mar. 15, 2000.)

91. Id. In addition to this broad general concern about children's emotional development in day care programs, there is apparently also "little question that day care before the age of two predisposes children to illnesses of the upper and lower respiratory tract." Lynda Liu, "Keeping kids in day care healthy," available at http://www.cnn.com (last visited Mar. 15, 2000.) While we do not yet know the full nature and extent of the long-term ramifications of such illnesses, medical researchers have urged that special care be taken "to protect young children—whose immune systems are still developing—from dangerous illnesses." Id.

92. Martin, "Too Much Day Care May Hurt Parent-Child Relationship."

93. Andrew P. Thomas, "Day Care—A Dangerous Experiment in Child-Rearing?" Wall Street Journal Europe, 14 Jan. 1988.

94. Id.

95. Martin, "Too Much Day Care May Hurt Parent-Child Relationship."

96. See James Collins, "The Day-Care Dilemma," Time.com, available at http://www.time.com/time/magazine/1997/dom/970203/special.day-care.html (last visited May 2, 2001) (describing caregiver:child ratio in day care as essential to its viability as a healthy parenting alternative, and issues surrounding day care in general.)

97. Greenberg and Springen at 62.

98. See Talbot at 24 (making this controversial yet, in my view, clearly apposite analogy).

99. Martin, "Too Much Day Care May Hurt Parent-Child Relationship."

100. Id.

101. Id.

102. Helbrun at 8.

103. Id.

104. See Transcript, "Talk of the Nation," National Public Radio, May 14, 2001, at 1–7, on file with author.

105. Id.

106. See Mash and Wolfe at 306–310 (summarizing these theories).

107. See id. (describing psychodynamic theory as holding that depression "results from the loss of a love object that is loved ambivalently"; behavioral theories as holding that depression results from deficiencies in "learning, environmental consequences, and skills and deficits in the onset and maintenance of depression"; cognitive theories as holding that depression results from "the relation between negative thinking and mood … [t]he underlying assumption [being] that how young people view themselves and their world will influence their mood and behavior"; interpersonal theories as holding that depression is caused by "disruptions in interpersonal relationships, especially within the family"; and socioenvironmental theories as holding that depression results from "stressful life events.").

108. Talbot at 24.

NOTES FOR CHAPTER FIVE

CHILDREN'S VIRTUAL REALITY AND
THE ECOLOGY OF THE SCHOOLS

1. Postman at 77–79.

2. John K. Rosemond, John Rosemond's Six-Point Plan for Raising Happy, Healthy Children (1989) at 168–169.

3. Rosemond, John Rosemond's Six Point Plan for Raising Happy, Healthy Children at 180.

4. Daniel Okrent, "Raising Kids Online, What Can Parents Do?" Time, May 10, 1999, at 42–43. Walsh is also founder of the National Institute on Media and the Family.

5. Id.

6. Katy Kelly, "False Promise," U.S. News & World Report, Sept. 25, 2000, at 48, 50.

7. Id. at 50.

8. See id., passim.

9. Id. at 50.

10. Barbara Jamison, "Obsessive Internet use poses risk of isolation, depression, researchers say," CNN.com, available at http://www.cnn.com/2000/HEALTH/06/13/internet.addiction.wmd/ (last visited May 2, 2001) (describing this literature) (emphasis added); see also "Internet Isolation?" ABCnews.com, available at www.abcnews.go.com/sections/liv…News/internet_isolation000216.html (last visited May 2, 2001) (describing Stanford University study with similar results.).

11. See id. (describing obsessive use of the Internet as an addiction, and explaining its effects, and its treatment as such).

12. "Study suggests Net does not create isolation," USAToday.com, available at http://www.usatoday.com/life/cyber/tech/cti715.htm (Last visited May 2, 2001.)

13. "Internet Isolation?" (explaining that this use is analogous to drinking alcohol); see also, "Study offers early look at how Internet is changing daily life," Stanford University Press Release, Feb. 16, 2000, available on http://www.sanford.edu/group/siqss/Press_Release/press_release.html (last visited May 2, 2001) (explaining that whatever its ramifications on particular individuals, "[a]s Internet use grows, Americans report they spend less time with friends and family, shopping in stores or watching television, and more time working for their employers at home—without cutting back their hours in the office."). Other studies have reported that hour-for-hour, as Internet use grows, television use diminishes. See, e.g., "Internet Isolation," (noting that "every hour spent online typically reduced television viewing by the same amount, and people who were new to the Internet started watching less television almost immediately.") Of course, whether this is a good or bad thing depends upon the individual and how she or he is using the Internet. In other words, based upon what we know about the detrimental impacts of television, this switch might be beneficial, but only if use of the Internet does not become negatively addictive. For a more thorough discussion of these issues, see "Internet Paradox," 53:9 American Psychologist 1017–1031, Sept. 1998, available at http://www.apa.org/journals/amp/amp5391017.html (last visited May 2, 2001).

14. See, e.g., Richard Rhodes, "Hollow Claims About Fantasy Violence," The New York Times, Sept. 17, 2000, at 19 (arguing that "[r]eal mayhem, not TV and movies, makes kids brutal"); L. Rowell Huesmann and Leonard D. Eron, "The Development of Aggression in Children of Different Cultures: Psychological Processes and Exposure to Violence," in Television and the Aggressive Child: A Cross-National Comparison, L. Rowell Huesmann and Leonard D. Eron, editors (1986) at 6–7 (describing one longitudinal study that "concluded that exposure to television violence does not affect aggressive behavior," and criticizing that conclusion on the ground that the data from which it was derived were similar to those used in the studies that had concluded otherwise, and that the conclusion denying a connection between television violence and real world aggression was likely the result of an inappropriate analytical methodology.) The most important and recurring critique of the notion that there is a causal link (as opposed to a correlation) between television viewing and violence is based upon the fact that the studies conducted to date have not managed to eliminate confounding variables such as individual predisposition, family circumstances, and other related environmental influences. As a practical matter, it is likely impossible adequately to eliminate these in any research design, and thus, while

there may well be a causal connection between the two, it is likely never to be proved.

15. Postman at 81–97.

16. Id. at 95.

17. "Psychologists come down hard on television," Cox News (describing report, "Big World, Small Screen: The Role of Television in American Society.") The report, compiled by the APA's Task Force on Television and Society, indicated that "television programs don't accurately portray women, minorities, and the elderly who have perpetuated negative stereotypes. Family relationships can also suffer when real folks compare themselves to their television counterparts." Id. The report also concluded that "'[c]hildren and parents alike may use television as a source for norms for family interaction.... Families may feel inadequate when comparing themselves to the competent, affluent and successful families that predominate in prime-time programs.'" Id.

18. Id.

19. Huesmann and Eron at 4.

20. Id. at 5.

21. Rosemond, John Rosemond's Six-Point Plan for Raising Happy, Healthy Children at 179–180.

22. Television and the Aggressive Child: A Cross-National Comparison, L. Rowell Huesmann and Leonard D. Eron, editors (1986).

23. Id. at 6, internal citations omitted.

24. L. Rowell Huesmann, "Cross-National Communalities in the Learning of Aggression from Media Violence," in id. at 240.

25. Id. at 242.

26. L. Rowell Huesmann and Leonard D. Eron, "The Development of Aggression in American Children as a Consequence of Television Violence Viewing," in id. at 47 (1986).

27. "The Secret Life of Teens," Newsweek, May 10, 1999, at 46 (quoting Chris Haley, who at the time was a 17 year-old high school junior).

28. Id.

29. L. Rowell Huesmann and Leonard D. Eron, "The Development of Aggression in American Children as a Consequence of Television Violence Viewing," at 48.

30. Id. at 48–49.

31. See Rhodes at 19 (acknowledging these endorsements, but claiming that the studies upon which they are based have been "sharply criticized and disputed within the social science profession).

32. See John Horn, "Hollywood Lands in the Hot Seat," Newsweek, Sept. 25, 2000, at 68 (describing report of Federal Trade Commission that found that "R" rated movies were purposefully marketed to 12–18 year olds, and that similarly violent music and video games also were purposefully marketed to an under-aged audience); Transcript, "All Things Considered," National Public Radio News, Sept. 11, 2000, on file with author (describing

FTC report, commissioned by President Clinton following the events at Columbine High School, which concluded that children were part of the target audience for the adult products distributed by the music, videogames, and film industry).

33. Aline D. Wolf, "Advertising and Children," America, Aug. 1, 1998, at 14.

34. Id.

35. Jim Rutenberg, "A wave of violence surges through children's cartoon programs," The News & Observer, Jan. 29, 2001, at 5B.

36. Id.

37. Id.

38. Id.

39. Amy Dickinson, "Where Were the Parents?" Time, May 3, 1999, at 40 (noting that this was a favorite of Harris and Klebold.)

40. See Richard Corliss, "Bang, You're Dead," Time, May 3, 1999, at 49 (noting this phenomenon, describing these movies in particular, and setting out the debate about the effects of this violence on children.)

41. Joshua Quittner, "Are Video Games Really So Bad?" Time, May 10, 1999, at 50.

42. Chris Taylor, "Digital Dungeons," Time, May 3, 1999, at 50.

43. Quittner at 54.

44. Id. at 50. Greenfield is a child psychologist.

45. Okrent at 41.

46. Id. at 40.

47. Id.

48. Id.

49. Id.

50. Id. at 38, 40.

51. Id. at 38.

52. Id. at 40. Thompson is a clinical psychologist and, together with Dan Kindlon, author of the book Raising Cain: Protecting the Emotional Life of Boys (1999).

53. Donald F. Roberts, Ulla G. Foehr, Victoria J. Rideout, and Mollyann Brodie, "Kids & Media @ The New Millennium: A Comprehensive National Analysis of Children's Media Use," A Kaiser Family Foundation Report, Nov. 1999.

54. Id. at 20.

55. Id. at 12.

56. John K. Rosemond, John Rosemond's Six Steps to Raising Happy, Healthy Children at 165.

57. Id.

58. Kids & Media @ the Millennium. The study concluded that "[w]hen used to excess, some media, including television and computers, can lead to intellectual passivity and in some cases may even contribute to health problems."

59. Kids & Media @ the Millennium at 77.

60. Quittner at 50.

61. Kids & Media @ the Millennium at 9.

62. Okrent at 41.

63. Kids & Media @ the Millennium at 20.

64. Okrent at 41. Interestingly, a different poll addressed to parents revealed that approximately 70% of them believed they had established guidelines. Id. at 42.

65. Peters at 1. Peters elaborates, citing "sexual abuse, abduction, television, accidents, neglect, violence, drugs, vulgarity, and alienation," as the principal issues confronting American children today. Id. at 2.

66. See generally Jonathan Kozol, Amazing Grace (1995) passim (describing the effects of inner city violence and drugs on children's emotional development through the stories of several children who lived in these neighborhoods.)

67. See Garbarino at ix and passim (discussing the endemic problem of the inner-cities and relating it to the toxicity for children of contemporary suburban life.)

68. See Susan Gilbert, "No One Left to Hate: Averting Columbines," New York Times, March 27, 2001 (noting this and exploring "jigsaw classrooms" as a means to solve the problem).

69. Id. Aronson is a social psychologist.

70. Nadya Labi, "Let Bullies Beware," Time, April 2, 2001, at 46.

71. Jeff Kass, "Witnesses Tell of Columbine Bullying," Denver Rocky Mountain News, Oct. 3, 2000, at 5A.

72. Nancy Gibbs, "It's Only Me," Time, March 19, 2001, at 12. Andrew Williams's background is described in Terry McCarthy, "Warning: Andy Williams Here," Time, March 19, 2001.

73. Id.

74. Gilbert, "No One Left to Hate: Averting Columbines."

75. Adam Cohen, "A Curse of Cliques," Time, May 3, 1999, at 44–45.

76. Id.

77. McCarthy at 14–16.

78. Hersch at 11, 13.

79. Id. at 18.

80. Id. at ix.

NOTES FOR CHAPTER SIX

Conclusions about the Ultimate
Causes of Columbine

1. Postman at 151.

2. Peters at 10.

3. Id.

An Introduction to American Liberalism

1. "Liberal democracy" has been defined as "a political system marked not only by free and fair elections, but also by the rule of law, a separation of powers, and the protection of basic liberties of speech, assembly, religion, and property." Fareed Zakaria, "The Rise of Illiberal Democracy," Foreign Affairs, November/December 1997, at 22, 26. This idea is prominent in the Declaration of Independence, among other documents in the canon of American political philosophy. For example, according to the Declaration, "... all [men] are endowed by their Creator with certain inalienable rights ... to secure these rights Governments are instituted among men, deriving their just power from the consent of the governed...." The Declaration of Independence, National Archives and Records Administration, available at http://www.nara.gov/exhall/charters/declaration/declaration.html (last visited May 22, 2001). Paul D. Carrington and Laura Kelley explain that these words, included in the second and third sentences of the Declaration, are "pure Quaker doctrine" rather than Lockean orthodoxy. "A Mother's Day Eulogy for Margaret Wythe," 3 Green Bag 2d 255, 256 (Spring 2000). Specifically, these authors note that "by the standards of most religions, [these words] were fiercely heretical." Id. And "[w]hile the liberalism of John Locke can be seen in the phrase 'Life, Liberty, and the Pursuit of Happiness,' an important editorial change was made, reflecting Quaker influence. Locke's liberalism favored the rights to life, liberty, and property. The substitution by the draftsmen of the phrase "Pursuit of Happiness" was an important qualification of Locke's ideology." Id. at 256–257.

2. See, e.g., U.S. Const., Art. I (enumerating powers of legislative branch); id. at Art. II (enumerating powers of executive); id. at Art. III (enumerating powers of judicial branch).

3. Freedom of speech, association, and religion are the province of the First Amendment. Property is the province of the Fifth and Fourteenth Amendments. And privacy, including parental autonomy, is the province of the Fourteenth Amendment.

4. See, e.g., United States v. Playboy Entertainment Group, Inc., 529 U.S. 803, 120 S. Ct. 1878 (2000) (setting out this "strict scrutiny test that applies to governmental acts that interfere with fundamental rights, in this case the right of free speech).

5. John Stuart Mill, On Liberty (reprinted in part in Michael Curtis Ed., The Great Political Theories, Vol. 2 (Avon Books, New York, 1981) at 186).

6. Doriane Lambelet Coleman, Individualizing Justice Through Multiculturalism: The Liberals' Dilemma, 96 Col. L. Rev. 1093, 1127 (1996). Curtis at 182.

7. Jean Hampton, Political Philosophy (Westview Press, Boulder, Colorado, 1997) at 171 (describing Lockean liberalism).

8. See, e.g., Clark v. Jeter, 486 U.S. 456, 460 (1988).

9. Hampton at 171.

10. Id.

11. Id. at 172.

12. Id.

13. Coleman, The Seattle Compromise 47 Duke L. J. at 717, 718–19 (1998). See also, Doriane Lambelet, The Contradiction Between Soviet and American Human Rights Doctrine: Reconciliation Through Perestroika and Pragmatism, 7 B.U. Int'l L. J. 61, 81 ("The purist notions of Lockean natural law have been tempered by two other philosophical ideas extant in the marketplace: utilitarianism and legal positivism," both of which permit the government to balance the interests of society against the right of individuals to exercise their liberties.).

14. Mary Ann Glendon, Rights Talk: The Impoverishment of Political Discourse (The Free Press, New York, 1991) at x.

15. Id. at 20. Glendon uses England and Canada as points of comparison because of our shared jurisprudential history and political philosophy. She notes specifically that property is "historically the paradigmatic right for England and the United States." Id.

16. Id.

17. See, e.g., Greg Zeigerson, "Fleeing a Dictatorship," New York Times, Apr. 28, 2000 at A22.

18. See id.

19. See, e.g., Laurence H. Tribe, "Justice Taken Too Far," New York Times, Apr. 25, 2000 at A23 (commenting on then Attorney General Janet Reno's decision to use force to remove Elian from his uncle's home in Florida); "Remarks of Senator Connie Mack," New York Times, Apr. 24, 2000 at A1 (describing Reno's decision as an "over-reaching of the power of government"); "Remarks of Governor George Pataki," New York Times, Apr. 23, 2000 at §1, 23 (noting that the break-in of a home to take custody of a child by individuals wearing fatigues and strapped with machine guns is "something that would happen in the Soviet Union, not the United States").

20. Tribe at 23. Tribe apparently was under the mistaken impression when he wrote his opinion editorial that the government did not have a proper search warrant to justify its entry into the home of Elian's Miami relatives. Specifically, he acknowledged in his piece that the government did have a search warrant, but he wrote erroneously that "it was not a warrant to seize the child." Id.

21. See Doriane Lambelet Coleman, Guest Essayist, "Ask the Expert About ... The Elian Gonzales Case," Duke University Alumni Magazine, May–June 2000.

22. Zakaria at 25–26. Zakaria notes that the "canonical figures" of constitutional liberalism include "the poet John Milton, the jurist William

Blackstone, statesmen such as Thomas Jefferson and James Madison, and philosophers such as Thomas Hobbes, John Locke, Adam Smith, Baron de Montesquieu, John Stuart Mill, and Isaiah Berlin." Id. at 26.

23. Glendon at 5. Glendon, is concerned both with what she calls the "rights talk" of contemporary adherents to traditional liberal principles, as well as that of modern-day political liberals or democrats who care more about equal protection and due process rights (i.e., distributive justice) than they do about property rights, for example. See generally, id., passim. Nevertheless, she writes that

> At least until the 1950s, the principal focus of constitutional law was not on personal liberty as such, but on the division of authority between the states and the federal government, and the allocation of powers among the branches of the central government ... the theory was that individual freedom was protected mainly through these structural features in our political regime ... Gradually, however, the Supreme Court developed its "incorporation" doctrine, through which more and more of the rights guaranteed by the first eight amendments to the Federal Constitution were declared to have been made binding on the states (incorporated) by the Fourteenth Amendment. This process accelerated in the 1960s when the Warren Court vigorously began to exercise the power of judicial review as a means of protecting individual rights from interference by state as well as federal governments. Today the bulk of the Court's constitutional work involves claims that individual rights have been violated.

Id. at 4–5.

Glendon's interpretation of the contemporary rights jurisprudence is shared by other legal scholars. For example, Jeffrey Rosen announced recently that the Court has "rediscover[ed] the right to privacy." Jeffrey Rosen, The News & Observer, June 8, 2000, at 21A . In support of this proposition, Rosen describes amongst others the Court's decisions in United States v. Webster L. Hubbell, 530 U.S. 27, 120 S. Ct. 2037 (2000) (upholding the privacy of certain personal documents); Troxel v. Granville, 530 U.S. 57, 120 S. Ct. 2054 (upholding the right of parental autonomy as against grandparents' interests in visitation); Reno v. Condon, 528 U.S.141, 120 S. Ct. 666 (2000) (upholding right of privacy as to personal information and as against state departments of motor vehicles that would seek to collect and then to sell such information). And Laura Underkuffler suggests that the Court's recent case law considering the Establishment Clause has "generally signaled a more permissive attitude toward the provision of state-aid" at least to religious schools; this, among other things and in turn, signals a more permissive attitude toward religious freedom or free expression. Laura S. Underkuffler, "Vouchers and Beyond: The Individual as Causative Agent in Establishment Clause Jurisprudence," 75 Ind. L.J. 167, 167 (2000).

Of course, there are those (generally Christian conservatives) who argue the opposite, i.e., the "demise" of the right of free exercise under the Court's contemporary jurisprudence. See, e.g., Scott E. Thompson, "The Demise of Free Exercise: A Historical Analysis of Where We Are, and How We Got There," 11 Regent U. L. Rev. 169 (1998–1999); R. Collin Mangrum, "The Falling Star of Free Exercise: Free Exercise and Substantive Due Process Entitlement Claims in City of Boerne v. Flores," 31 Creighton L. Rev. 693 (May 1998); John W. Whitehead, "The Conservative Supreme Court and the Demise of the Free Exercise of Religion," 7 Temp. Pol. & Civ. Rts. L. Rev. 1 (Fall 1997); James D. Gordon III, "The New Free Exercise Clause," 26 Cap. U. L. Rev. 65 (1997). I will discuss this opposition further in the context of my analysis of the doctrine of parental autonomy. In any event, Martha Minow agrees with Underkuffler, and on this basis predicts that the Court will validate under that clause certain controversial school voucher programs, in which state monies are directed to religious schools; many believe that such a diversion would not have survived constitutional scrutiny in previous eras. Martha Minow, "Choice or Commonality: Welfare and Schooling after the End of Welfare as We Knew It," 49 Duke L.J. 493 (1999).

24. Accordingly, one of the strategies the Court has used to deny claims under that doctrine—perhaps beginning with its decision in Brown v. Board of Education, 347 U.S. 483 (1954)—has been to emphasize the primacy of the individual (as opposed to the group) in the constitutional scheme. See, e.g., City of Richmond v. Croson Co., 488 U.S. 469, 474–5 (1989) (holding that the 14th Amendment permits attempts to undo the effects of past discrimination which accord a contracting preference to "actual victims of discrimination who can be identified," but that it prohibits discrimination on the basis of race when such attempts have the more abstract, over-arching goal of rectifying the broad societal effects of past discrimination); Adarand Constructors Inc., v. Pena, 515 U.S. 200, 202 (1995) (finding that "government can never have a 'compelling interest' in discriminating on the basis of race in order to make up for past [broader, societal] racial discrimination," since "we are just one race in the eyes of government," and since offering a person preferential treatment because he or she was personally the subject of discrimination would not be a classification based on race, but rather one based on a personal and particular history of negative treatment).

NOTES FOR CHAPTER EIGHT

THE CONSTITUTIONAL DOCTRINE OF PARENTAL AUTONOMY

1. Lacher v. Venus, 188 N.W. 613, 617 (Wis. 1922).

2. Id.

3. Parham v. J.R., 442 U.S. 584, 602 (alteration in original) (quoting Pierce v. Society of Sisters, 268 U.S. 510, 535 (1925)).

tion of "tender years" is merely "one of many factors to be considered in determining custody, not an unyielding rule of law"). The principal remaining exception to this gender neutralization in child custody law is where a dispute concerns a child in or nearing adolescence. In this circumstance, some states permit judges to preference that child's same-sex parent (all else being equal) on the ground that as a developmental matter, such a pairing is beneficial for the child. Finally, there is also an exception which preferences biological mothers in matters of parental rights and custody in circumstances where that mother was not married to the child's biological father at the time of the child's birth. In this case, there is a formal presumption in favor of the mother who has invested at least nine months (during pregnancy) in the child, and a formal presumption against the father who (at that point) has merely a biological, but not a relational, tie to the child. See Stanley v. Illinois, 405 U.S. 645 (1972); Lehr v. Robertson, 463 U.S. 248 (1983).

16. It is rare in modern cases to see the courts justifying this doctrine on religious grounds. That is, courts today will talk about the "natural" and "inalienable" and "fundamental" right of parents to raise their children, rather than about their analogous "God-given" right to do so. See Frances Olsen, "The Family and the Market: A Study of Ideology and Political Reform," 96 Harv. L. Rev. 1497 (1983).

17. U.S. v. Darby, 312 U.S. 100 (1941) (discussing scope of state's authority to regulate child labor); Prince v. Massachusetts, 321 U.S. 158 (1944) (discussing scope of state's authority to regulate child labor and relationship between child labor laws and laws making mandatory school attendance); Meyer v. Nebraska, 262 U.S. 390 (1923) (discussing scope of state's authority to make mandatory school attendance and to develop the curriculum of the schools); Pierce v. Society of Sisters, 268 U.S. 510 (1925) (same); Wisconsin v. Yoder, 406 U.S. 205 (1972) (discussing scope of states' authority to make mandatory school attendance); Jacobson v. Massachusetts, 197 U.S. 11 (1905) (discussing scope of state's authority to vaccinate children); Zucht v. King, 260 U.S. 174 (1922) (same).

18. The states have all enacted abuse and neglect laws in response to this principle. While the statutes do not generally speak of "extreme" abuse and neglect specifically, their application and interpretation is consistent with this principle. The laws themselves vary in their specificity, but in general they all provide that non-accidental injury to a child is abuse, and that the failure to provide a child with necessaries is neglect. While quite a lot of parental action and non-action technically will fit within these terms, they are in fact designed to be interpreted, usually by accompanying regulations, only to allow a child to be brought within the jurisdiction of the child protection umbrella in circumstances that the culture considers extreme. Thus, for example, "reasonable parental discipline" is specifically excepted from the definition of abuse, and the government never penalizes such tradi-

tional American practices as ear piercing and male circumcision, despite that they clearly come within the black letter of the law. The same is true of neglect, where courts will only approve the supervision or removal of a child from her home in relatively egregious cases. On the other hand, the courts are quick to place children under state protection where their lives are potentially in jeopardy.

19. Abuse and neglect laws are enacted by the states pursuant to state law. Their validity for federal constitutional purposes, i.e., under the doctrine of parental autonomy, depends upon whether they are consistent or inconsistent with the terms of that doctrine.

20. See Pierce, 268 U.S. 510 (establishing as a constitutional matter that while states may mandate school attendance, they may not mandate attendance only in public institutions).

21. See, e.g., Minnesota v. Newstrom, 371 N.W.2d 525 (Minn. 1985) (holding that there are no formal requirements for home schooling teachers, despite laws which require essential equivalence); see also, Jeffrey v. O'Donnell, 702 F.Supp. 513 (D. Pa. 1987); Wisconsin v. Popanz, 112 Wis.2d 166, 332 N.W.2d 750 (1983); but see Roemhild v. Georgia, 308 S.E.2d 154 (Ga. 1983); Battles v. Anne Arundel Co. Board of Ed., 904 F.Supp.471 (D. Md. 1995).

22. See Yoder, 406 U.S. at 224–225, 235.

23. Id. at 205.

24. Of course, a parent who wishes to exercise this right and thereby assure this almost absolute degree of autonomy over her children must act to do so, by finding a private school that conforms with her beliefs, by home schooling the child or children, or, along the lines of the *Yoder* decision, by convincing the government that further education for the particular child in the particular circumstances is not necessary. If the parent does not wish or is unable to do this, it is clear that the right of parental autonomy in this regard is fettered in significant ways. For example, when a parent despite these option chooses to send her children to public school she foregoes to a significant extent the right to control the education of her child. See Mozert v. Hawkins County School Board, 827 F.2d 1058 (1987) (noting that in these circumstances, a parent cannot in general restrict the ideas to which the child is exposed); see also Meyer v. Nebraska, 262 U.S. 390, 43 S.Ct. 625 (1923) (noting that the state retains absolute control over the curriculum of the public schools).

25. See, e.g., New York v. Ginsberg, 390 U.S. 629, 629 (1968) (state statute designed to protect children from pornography); H.R. 3783, 105th Cong. (1998) (COPA) (protecting minors by providing new prohibitions for the distribution of pornography on the web); S. 1482, 105th Cong. 1997 (requiring ISP's to provide filtering software and providing enhanced penalty for releasing obscene materials to minors).

26. See, e.g., Ginsberg, 390 U.S. at 639; New York v. Ferber, 458 U.S.

747 (1982) (statute prohibiting persons from knowingly promoting sexual performance by a child by distributing obscene matter to the child withstood a First Amendment challenge); City of Dallas v. Stanglin, 490 U.S. 19 (1989) (city ordinance limiting the use of dance halls to persons between the age of fourteen and eighteen did not violate those persons' First Amendment associational rights).

27. Ginsberg v. New York, 390 U.S. 629 (1968).

28. Christian Scientists, for example, are exempted from the abuse and neglect laws of many states when they choose to use "Practitioners" in an attempt to heal their children. See, e.g. Newmark v. Williams, 588 A.2d 1108 (Del. S.Ct.1990) (describing exemption in Delaware and providing list of similar exemptions in other states); Hermanson v. State, 604 So.2d 775 (Fl. S.Ct. 1992) (setting out Florida exemption and listing spiritual exemption laws in other states). Christian Scientists consider physical disease to be merely a symptom of spiritual ailments, and thus they seek to treat only the spirit; the expectation is that if the spirit can be healed, the physical symptoms also will disappear. See Jennifer L. Hartsell, "Mother May I ... Live? Parental Refusal of Life Sustaining Medical Treatment for Children Based on Religious Objections," 66 Tenn. L. Rev. 499, 503–04 (Winter 1999); Jennifer Stanfield, "Faith Healing and Religious Treatment Exemptions to Child Endangerment Laws," 22 Hamline J. Pub. L. & Policy 45, 48–50 (Fall 2000). Despite that this practice does not actually work in many cases, and that the child sometimes dies as a result in circumstances where orthodox medicine would easily have cured her illness, the courts have consistently upheld the legitimacy of state laws that insulate Christian Scientists from otherwise applicable abuse and neglect law. Simultaneously, the courts reaffirm the authority of parents' on religious grounds in particular to make the determination whether a child is ill in the first instance, and then the manner in which a sick child should be treated.

29. See id.; contrast Hewlett v. George, 68 Miss. 703, 9 So. 885 (1891) (dismissing on grounds of parental immunity a child's suit against her mother for malicious and wrongful imprisonment in an insane asylum, on the ground that "[t]he peace of society ... and a sound public policy designed to subserve the repose of families and the best interests of society, forbid to the minor child a right to appear in court in the assertion of a claim to civil redress for personal injuries suffered at the hands of the parent").

30. Matter of Sherol A.S., 581 P.2d 884 (Okla. 1978); U.S. v. Quarles, 25 M.J. 761 (N-M.C.M.R. 1987).

31. See, e.g., Ybarra v. Texas Dept. of Human Servs., 869 S.W.2d 574, 574 (1993).

32. See, e.g. Holodook v. Spencer, 324 N.E.2d 338 (N.Y. 1974) (holding that child plaintiffs have no cause of action against their parents for negligent supervision).

33. See Fuller v. Studer, 833 P.2d 109 (Idaho 1992); Lyons v. Bruun, No. 973591, 1999 WL 707115 at *1 (Mass. Super. 1999).

34. See Comment, "The 'Reasonable Parent' Standard: An Alternative to Parent-Child Tort Immunity," 47 U. Co. L. Rev. 795, 804–805 (1976) (explaining rationale for immunity in circumstances where parent disciplines her child or otherwise makes decisions to fulfill her duty to care for the child).

35. Holodook, 324 N.E.2d at 346.

36. Id.

37. Indeed, for it to be any other way would likely be a violation of the constitutional doctrine of parental autonomy. Interestingly, there are no cases raising this issue in circumstances where the standard has been applied on the edges, i.e., where it certainly could be argued that a particular parental choice, action, or inaction that resulted in unintended injury to a child was appropriately within the bounds of that autonomy. This is likely because such actions typically are brought with at least the parent's tacit consent; on the other hand, the argument certainly would be feasible if the "reasonable parent" claim that a parent did not act "reasonably" is made by an insurance carrier or a third-party seeking contribution from the parent.

38. Restatement (Second) of Torts, section 895G, comment k, quoted in Broadbent v. Broadbent, 907 P.2d 43, 51 (1995) (C.J. Feldman, specially concurring) (emphasis added).

39. Prosser and Keeton, Torts sec. 122, at 908 [5th ed].

40. 479 P.2d 648 (1971).

41. The Court emphasized that "the possibility that some cases may involve the exercise of parental authority does not justify continuation of a blanket rule of immunity. In many actions, no question of parental control will arise." Id. at 652–653; see also, Goller v. White, 122 N.W.2d 193, 198 (1963) (ending parental immunity except as to those circumstances "(1) [w]here the alleged negligent act involves an exercise of parental authority over the child; and (2) where the alleged negligent act involves an exercise of ordinary parental discretion with respect to the provision of food, clothing, housing, medical and dental services, and other care"); Bang v. Tran, 1997 WL 538739 (Mass. App. Div.) (adopting simplified "reasonable parent" standard from *Gibson* and, like *Gibson*, excluding those "functions which are parental in nature"); Broadbent, 907 P.2d. at 49 (adopting "reasonable prudent parent" standard, but recognizing that it must be interpreted consistent with the right and duty of parents "to raise their children by their own methods and in accordance with their own attitudes and beliefs"); Gross v. Sears Roebuck & Co., 386 A.2d 442, (App. Div. 1978) ("immunity has thus been abrogated except where the negligent act clearly involves the exercise of parental authority, or the provision of food, clothing, housing, medical or dental services, or other care.") The existence of liability insurance, particularly in the context of motor vehicle accidents, is largely cred-

ited for the decision of some jurisdictions to abrogate the traditional immunity doctrine which precluded suits between children and their parents. See Renko v. McLean, 697 A.2d 468, 473–76 (Md. 1997) (discussing the argument for abrogation based upon the wide availability of insurance).

42. Broadbent, 907 P.2d at 45 (1995) (abrogating immunity and holding that two and a half year old child could bring negligence action against his mother for negligent supervision in swimming pool).

43. See, e.g., Nolochek v. Gesuale, 385 N.E.2d 1268 (in state that rejects "reasonable parent" rule, and that does not allow tort of negligent supervision of a child, parent may nevertheless be liable where child engages in "improvident use of a dangerous instrument, at least, if not especially, when the parent is aware of and capable of controlling its use").

44. This is, in fact, a strict liability rule; thus, the plaintiff in such a case need not show negligence. See generally, George C. Christie, James E. Meeks, Ellen S. Pryor, Joseph Sanders, Cases and Materials on the Law of Torts, 3d ed., at 562–568 (discussing doctrine of strict liability for domestic and wild animals, including the "one bite free" rule for domestic pets).

45. Hall v. McBryde, 919 P.2d 910, 912–13 (Colo. App. 1996); Horton v. Reaves, 186 Colo. App. 149, 526 P.2d 304, 308 (1974); Mitchell v. Allstate Insurance Co., 36 Colo. App. 71, 534 P.2d 1235 (1975).

46. Belkin at 94; see also Complaint in same case, on file with author.

47. Curry v. Superior Court, 24 Cal. Rptr.2d 495 (Cal. App. 4 Dist. 1993).

NOTES FOR CHAPTER NINE

The Right to Free Speech

1. John E. Nowak, Ronald D. Rotunda, Constitutional Law 986 (5th ed., 1995).

2. 302 U.S. 319 (1937).

3. Id. at 327.

4. Id.

5. Rodney A. Smolla, Free Speech in an Open Society (Alfred A. Knopf, New York, 1992) at 4.

6. Id. at 6–8.

7. Id. at 6, quoting Justice Holmes in Abrams v. United States, 250 U.S. 616, 630 (1919).

8. Id.

9. See id. at 9–11.

10. Id. at 9, quoting Justice Marshall in Procunier v. Martinez, 416 U.S. 396, 427 (1974) (emphasis in Smolla).

11. See id. at 12–17.

12. 274 U.S. 357 (1927) (concurring with majority's holding that, de-

spite this strong protection for political speech in particular, a statute was constitutional as applied which criminalized the formation of and membership in a political party that advocated the violent overthrow of the government).

13. See Smolla at 14.

14. Id. at 14–16.

15. See id. at 9–10.

16. Id. at 9.

17. Id. at 3–4.

18. Id. at 9–10.

19. Id. at 10.

20. Id. at 50. Smolla distinguishes these "reactive harms" from "physical harms" and "relational harms," both of the latter of which he explains are subject to First Amendment regulation. Id. at 48–49.

21. Id. at 48–49.

22. Indeed, the location of the free speech clause in the very first line of the First Amendment, as well as the clause's uniquely absolute language, has caused important constitutional scholars to agree strongly with Justice Cardozo's description of this doctrine as the "matrix" of American liberty more generally. In this regard, as William Van Alstyne has noted, "the First Amendment, by way of contrast [with others rights, both explicit and 'penumbral'], acknowledges no overriding conditions that would provide any excuse for any Act of Congress abridging the freedom of speech or of the press." William W. Van Alstyne, First Amendment Cases and Materials at 4–5 (2d ed., 1995). While this textual absolutism is not (and arguably could not be) followed in practice, it nevertheless points to the amendment's status as "among the 'preferred' liberties the Constitution enshrines." Id. at 5, n. 8; see also William W. Van Alstyne, "The Second Amendment and the Personal Right to Arms," 43 Duke L. J. 1236, 1254 (noting that "the freedoms of speech and of the press ... are not absolute"); R.A.V. v. City of St. Paul, Minnesota, 505 U.S. 377, 382–83 (1992) (noting that exceptions have been carved out to the right to free speech beginning at least since 1791).

23. See Glendon at 1–17. American children are said to have the right to free speech, but its scope is certainly circumscribed in comparison with that of adults. See, e.g., Bethel School District No. 403 v. Fraser, 478 U.S. 675 (1986) (upholding ruling of school district to discipline student who gave lewd speech at high school assembly); Hazelwood School District v. Kuhlmeier, 484 U.S. 260 (1988) (upholding decision of school district to remove books discussing teen pregnancy and divorce from school newspaper); Ginsberg, 390 U.S. at 629 (upholding statute restricting the ability of minors to obtain pornography).

24. 505 U.S. 377, 382 (1992), citations omitted (finding a state statute unconstitutional which sought to proscribe "hate speech" directed at racial and ethnic minorities); see also id. at 390 (speech may ordinarily not be

"'conditioned upon the sovereign's agreement with what a speaker may intend to say'").

25. Chaplinsky v. New Hampshire, 315 U.S. 568, 571–72 (1942).

26. William W. Van Alstyne, Interpretations of the First Amendment, 24–28, 41–42 (1984).

27. Roth v. United States, 354 U.S. 476 (1957); Jacobellis v. Ohio, 378 U.S. 184 (1964); Miller v. California, 413 U.S. 15 (1973).

28. See New York v. Ferber, 458 U.S. 747, 765–66 (1982). Certain pornography may be "obscene" for children, under the standard of "variable obscenity" that applies to them. In this case, and for children, the pornography would not be deemed "First Amendment" or "protected" speech, in which case the government only would need to demonstrate a "rational basis" to regulate it.

29. Chaplinsky, 315 U.S. at 571–72.

30. Brandenburg v. Ohio, 395 U.S. 444, 449 (1969).

31. Beauharnais v. Illinois, 343 U.S. 250 (1952); New York Times Co. v. Sullivan, 376 U.S. 254 (1964); Gertz v. Robert Welch, Inc., 418 U.S. 323 (1974).

32. See R.A.V., 505 U.S. at 385 (quoting Chaplinsky, 315 U.S. at 572). In R.A.V., Justice Scalia, writing for the Court, noted that statements to the effect that such material is "not within the area of constitutionally protected speech ... must be taken in context," since government is still prohibited by the First Amendment from making content-based distinctions among, for example, speech that constitutes "fighting words." In the R.A.V. case itself, and on these grounds, the Court struck a state statute that would have punished only one category of fighting words, namely that which incited violence because of its appeal to racial and related bigotry. See id. at 381. This position is controversial, even on the Court itself, where four Justices concurred in the result in R.A.V., but disagreed with Scalia that any sort of "fighting words" were within the protections of the First Amendment. See id. at 428 (Stevens, J., concurring).

33. See Playboy, 529 U.S. at 813.

34. Id. (applying "strict scrutiny" for content-based restrictions or bans on speech that is "protected" for adults). "According to the court, when a plausible, less restrictive alternative is offered to a content-based speech restriction, it is the Government's obligation to prove that the alternative will be ineffective to achieve its goals." Id. at 816.

35. R.A.V., 505 U.S. at 377.

36. Dyson v. Stein, 401 U.S. 200, 208 (1971); see also Catherine Ross, "Anything Goes: Examining the State's Interest in Protecting Children from Controversial Speech," 53 Vanderbilt L. Rev. 427, 456 (2000).

37. Dyson, 401 U.S. at 200; ACLU, 521 U.S. at 844.

38. Dyson, 401 U.S. at 208 (J. Douglas dissenting in case involving in part the freedom of the press to possess obscene materials).

39. Id.

40. Id. at 209–10.

41. Terminiello v. City of Chicago, 337 U.S. 1, 4–5 (1949).

42. 529 U.S. 803 (2000).

43. Id. at 817.

44. Id.

45. Id.

46. See, e.g., Jacobellis, 378 U.S. at 195 ("recogniz[ing] the legitimate and indeed exigent interest of States and localities through the Nation in preventing the dissemination of material deemed harmful to children"); Ginsberg, 390 U.S. at 641–42; Playboy, 529 U.S. at 838, J. Breyer, dissenting ("This Court has also recognized that material the First Amendment guarantees adults the right to see may not be suitable for children.")

47. The Court has recognized, for example, that children may "speak" (in all the ways that one might do this) on public school grounds, but that this right is heavily circumscribed by the corresponding right of the school authorities to teach values and to maintain discipline. See, e.g. Tinker v. Des Moines Independent Community School District, 393 U.S. 503, 505, 511 (1969) (while "state-operated schools may not be enclaves of totalitarianism," children's speech on school grounds can be censored where it "materially and substantially interferes with the requirements of appropriate discipline in the operation of the school"); Bethel School District No. 403 v. Fraser, 478 U.S. 675, 680 (1986) ("The undoubted freedom to advocate unpopular and controversial views in schools and classrooms must be balanced against the society's countervailing interest in teaching students the boundaries of socially appropriate behaviour"; thus, where student speech is "plainly offensive ... acutely insulting ... [and] seriously damaging" it may be censored); Hazelwood School District v. Kuhlmeier, 484 U.S. 260, 266 (1988) (school may censor content of student newspaper that is part of journalism curriculum where such newspaper "substantially interfere[s] with the work of the school or impinge[s] upon the rights of other students.") In other areas, as I shall explain, the Court has consistently held that the state may restrict the rights of children under the First Amendment, either because the speech at issue is considered in general to be inappropriate for children, or (ostensibly) to assist parents in their gate-keeping function. See, e.g., Ginsberg, 390 U.S. at 629 (holding that state could restrict rights of children to purchase pornographic magazines both to protect the children themselves from material that might be detrimental to them, and to assist parents in their endeavors to screen the material that their children can see.) Catherine Ross has recently written on the subject of children's free speech rights in her article, "An Emerging Right for Mature Minors to Receive Information," 2 Pa. J. Const. L. 223 (1999).

48. See Davis, Scott, Wadlington, Whitebread at 12 ("Intervention [by the state in matters of child-rearing] is warranted ... when an important interest of the state or of the child is implicated").

49. Thus far, pornography is the only area which the Court has accepted as valid for regulation to protect children.

50. Ginsberg, 390 U.S. at 629 (upholding state statute prohibiting sale of "girlie" magazines to children under seventeen).

51. F.C.C. v. Pacifica Foundation, 438 U.S. 726 (1978) (upholding regulatory order prohibiting "patently offensive" language in radio broadcast; the case was based on a daylight radio broadcast of comedian George Carlin's skit "Filthy Words").

52. The statute at issue, out of the state of Virginia, defined the offending material as that which, "when taken as a whole," was "lacking in serious literary, artistic, political or scientific value for juveniles." American Booksellers Ass'n, Inc. v. Virginia, 484 U.S. 383 (1988). The Court had previously noted jurisdiction in the same case, and had certified two questions to the Virginia Supreme Court, the first involving the particular books that might or might not fall within the ambit of the restriction, as well as the standard that courts would use to determine that question, and the second involving the state's intentions with respect to the enforcement of the prohibition. Id. Ultimately, and based upon the Virginia Supreme Court's responses, the statute was upheld by the Fourth Circuit Court of Appeals, 882 F.2d 125 (4th Cir. 1989) and the United States Supreme Court denied certiorari. 494 U.S. 1056 (1990).

53. See, e.g., Board of Education v. Pico, 457 U.S. 853 (1982) (finding First Amendment violation in school board's removal of certain books from school's library, but noting that board clearly had right to remove books that were obscene or that lacked "educational suitability"); Presidents Council, Dist. 25 v. Community School Bd. No. 25, 457 F.2d 289 (1972) (Circuit Court holding that the school board's removal of a particular book from the junior high school library because it contained "obscenities" and "explicit sexual interludes" did not violate the First Amendment).

54. See ACLU, 521 U.S. at 844.

55. See Playboy, 529 U.S. 803.

56. See Sable Communications of California, Inc. v. F.C.C., 492 U.S. 115 (1989).

57. Also, see ACLU, 521 U.S. at 844 (using this condition, among other things, to find invalid a federal statute designed to shield children from pornography on the Internet).

58. 521 U.S. 844 (1997).

59. 521 U.S. at 849.

60. Id. at 868. The first contested provision, 47 U.S.C.A. sec. 223(a) (Supp. 1997), "prohibits the knowing transmission of obscene or indecent messages to any recipient under 18 years of age." Id. at 859. The second provision, 47 U.S.C.A. sec. 223(d), "prohibits the knowing sending or display of patently offensive messages in a manner that is available to a person under 18 years of age." Id.

61. Vikas Arora, The Communications Decency Act: Congressional Repudiation of "The Right Stuff," 34 Harv. J. on Legis. 473, 486 (1997).

62. See id. at 867–68. In rejecting the Government's analogy to its past zoning decisions, the Court noted that the CDA is not similarly limited to a particular geographic locale, but rather "applies broadly to the entire universe of cyberspace.") Id. at 868. Justice O'Connor, joined by Chief Justice Rehnquist, wrote a separate opinion concurring in the judgment in part and dissenting in part. See id. at 886–897. In her concurrence, she elaborates on the Court's rejection of the zoning analogy, noting that previous zoning laws have been sustained "only if they respect the First Amendment rights of adults and minors." Id. at 887. She concludes that the creation of adult-only zones in cyberspace is a literal impossibility because of its inherently non-physical and "malleable" quality. Id. at 889–90.

63. See id. at 864–66 (discussing and rejecting the applicability of the *Ginsberg* decision to this case). The Court rejected the analogy to *Ginsberg*, and to constitutionality of prohibiting the sale of "girlie" magazines to children, on four ground, including that (1) parents were not in that case themselves barred from providing this material to their children, (2) the statute in that case was limited to commercial transactions, (3) that statute only applied to material that was found to be "utterly without redeeming social importance for minors," and (4) it permitted access to pornography to children who were over seventeen. Id. at 865–66. See also id. at 866 (discussing and rejecting the applicability of the *Pacifica* decision to this case). The Court rejected the applicability of the *Pacifica* decision on the grounds that radio broadcasts traditionally "had received the most limited First Amendment protection"—because "warnings could not adequately protect the listener from unexpected programming content"—and that the regulation at issue in that case was merely one of time, place, and manner, rather than a blanket prohibition on the offending speech. Id. at 866–67.

64. See id. at 870–74 (discussing vagueness of provisions); id. at 874–881 (discussing unconstitutional broadness of provisions); id. at 874–75.

65. Id. at 874–75, citations omitted.

66. Id. at 878.

67. See Arora at 507 ("the two judicial panels who have spoken on the constitutionality of the CDA have relied extensively on libertarian arguments in justifying their decisions.") Vikras's note is particularly useful in parsing out the utilitarian and libertarian arguments for and against the CDA that were made at the time of its passage, and subsequently throughout the litigation that led to the Supreme Court's ultimate decision in the case.

68. Id. at 507–08.

69. Id. at 854–56, 888–89.

70. See Kelly M. Doherty, "www.obscenity.com: An Analysis of Obscen-

ity and Indecency Regulation on the Internet," 32 Akron L. Rev. 259, 296–97 (1999); Kim L. Rappaport, "In the Wake of Reno v. ACLU: The Continued Struggle in Western Constitutional Democracies with Internet Censorship and Freedom of Speech Online," 13 Am. U. Int'l L. Rev. 765 (1998); Amber Jene Sayle, "Net Nation and the Digital Revolution: Regulation of Offensive Material for a New Community," 18 Wis. Int'l L. J. 257, 278–79 (Winter 2000).

71. Playboy, 529 U.S. at 856. It is doubtful also that technology could ever do this properly, since the human mind itself may be incapable of making such distinctions in any meaningful, and certainly objective way. Catherine Ross and others have (appropriately) made much of this apparent impossibility, noting that the definition of such terms as "indecent" and "violent" is too subjective and variable within the culture ever to provide the requisite precision for legal purposes. See Ross "Anything Goes: Examining the States' Interest in Protecting Children from Controversial Speech," at 446–458 (explaining this definitional problem and describing the critique as made by others).

72. Id.

73. See e.g., id. at 850, 852, and 870.

74. Id. at 868.

75. Id. at 870.

76. Id. at 882.

77. Id.

78. As I noted earlier, Justice Kennedy emphasized this point in *Playboy* when he opined that "it denies the potential of th[e new information technology] if we assume the Government is best positioned to make ... choices [for example, about what is "decent" or "indecent"] for us." Playboy, 529 U.S. at 817. ACLU v. Reno, and the passage of the CDA itself, inspired many commentaries. Most were consistent with the Court's ultimate position in the case, and thus of liberal rather that utilitarian or communitarian orientation. See, e.g. Walter J. Dorgan III, "The Cyberworld Cannot Be Confined to Speech That Would Be Suitable for a Sandbox," 29 Seton Hall L. Rev. 286 (1998); Blake T. Bilstad, "Obscenity and Indecency in a Digital Age: The Legal and Political Implications of Cybersmut, Virtual Pornography, and the Communications Decency Act," 13 Santa Clara Computer & High Tech. L. J. 321 (1997); Vikas Akora, "The Communications Decency Act: Congressional Repudiation of the 'Right Stuff,'" 34 Harv. J. on Legis. 473 (1997); Nathan M. Semmel, "Talking Back to Cyber-Mum: Challenging the Communications Decency Act," 14 N.Y.L. Sch. J. Hum. Rts. 533 (1998); Stephen C. Jacques, "Reno v. ACLU: Insulating the Internet, the First Amendment, and the Marketplace of Ideas," 46 Am. U.L. Rev. 1945 (1997). A few, however, did argue that the CDA was or should have been found unconstitutional. See Vickie S. Byrd, "Reno v. ACLU—A Lesson in Juridical Impropriety," 42

How. L.J. 365 (1999) (the logic employed by the U.S. Supreme Court in the case is problematic because it appears that technology drove the decision and not constitutional principles); Rebecca J. Dessoffy, "Salvaging the Communications Decency Act in the Wake of ACLU v. Reno and Shea v. Reno," 45 Clev. St. L. Rev. 271 (1997) (analyzing constitutional problems within the current CDA and evaluating several options to saving the Act).

79. 120 S.Ct. 1878 (2000).

80. Id. at 1893.

81. Id. at 1883 (defining "signal bleed" as imprecise scrambling such that "either or both audio and visual portions of the scrambled programs might be heard or seen").

82. Id.

83. Id. at 1889. The Court goes on at length to scrutinize the particular evidence the government did produce, finding that unless the government it included "evidence on the number of households actually exposed to signal bleed and ... the actual extent of the problem of signal bleed" it could not sustain its compelling interest requirement. Id. at 1889–90. Based upon the fact that the government could not produce such evidence—the best it could do was to produce statistical analyses of probabilities and some anecdotal evidence of signal bleed—the Court concluded that "the Government has failed to establish a pervasive, nationwide problem justifying its nationwide speech ban." Id. at 1891.

84. Id. at 1893.

85. See id. at 1889–1891 (questioning the nature of the government's evidence concerning the numbers of children exposed to "signal bleed" from the pornographic programming, and requiring more than mere anecdotal evidence and statistical analyses to justify the restriction on this speech); and id. at 1890–93 (describing the flaws in the government's arguments that it's restrictions were narrowly tailored).

86. See id. at 1900.

87. See id.

88. Id.

89. Id.

90. The portion of Justice Kennedy's opinion to which I refer in this instance is that in which he states that the Court in *Playboy* could not allow itself to "be influenced ... by the perception that the regulation question is not a major one because the speech is not very important. The history of the law of free expression [to] be one of vindication in cases involving speech that many citizens may find shabby, offensive, or even ugly." Id. at 1893.

91. Ross "Anything Goes: Examining the States' Interest in Protecting Children from Controversial Speech," at 455.

92. Id. at n. 136.

93. Id. at 455.

94. Id. at 457. The Court's only decision in a case that involved a "hate crimes" statute was *R.A.V.*, which involved an ordinance that providing that:

> Whoever places on public or private property a symbol, object, appellation, characterization, or graffiti, including, but not limited to, a burning cross or Nazi swastika, which one knows or has reasonable grounds to know arouses anger, alarm or resentment in others on the basis of race, color, creed, religion or gender commits disorderly conduct and shall be guilty of a misdemeanor.

Id. at 380, quoting St. Paul Bias-Motivated Crime Ordinance, St. Paul, Minn., Legis. Code sec. 292.02 (1990). Despite its language, the Court did not have occasion to address the broader issue whether such a "hate crime" law was constitutional. Rather, because the Minnesota Supreme Court had previously interpreted the ordinance only to apply to "fighting words" that do or may "arouse[] anger, alarm or resentment in others on the basis of race, color, creed, religion or gender," the Court found that it only had discretion to address the narrower issue whether the government could constitutionally make content-based distinctions among otherwise unprotected "fighting words." Id. Ultimately, the answer was "no."

95. Jacobellis v. Ohio, 378 U.S. 184 (1964).

96. Interestingly, the situation in Europe might be said to be exactly the opposite. That is, it appears to be the case that Europeans are much more likely to bar (and generally to deplore) violent content than they are to bar (or to deplore) what Americans call pornography. Indeed, Europeans often marvel at what they see as the American paradox of extraordinary shamelessness with respect to violence, and at the same time extraordinary reluctance about sexuality.

97. 90 F.Supp.2d 798 (W.D. Kentucky 2000). The federal district court in this diversity case was bound by state law. This case is one of the recent spate of school shootings, culminating in the Columbine incident, which has so mesmerized the country, and which has revealed the depth and prevalence of epidemic that is at issue in this book.

98. Meow Media, 90 F.Supp. at 799–801.

99. Id. The plaintiffs also filed strict liability and RICO claims. Id. at 800.

100. Id. at 800.

101. Id.

102. Id. at 801.

103. Id.

104. To state a viable claim in negligence in most, if not all, jurisdictions including Kentucky, a plaintiff must establish facts tending to show that the defendant owed her a duty of care, that this duty was breached, and that the breach caused a compensable injury. See id. at 802.

105. Id. at 803–04.

106. Id. at 803.

107. Id.

108. Id.

109. See id. at 805 (noting that "[o]ther courts across the country have also refused to impose a duty on defendants in like situations," and citing the decisions in Watters v. TSR, Inc., 904 F.2d 378 (6th Cir. 1990) (rejecting suit seeking to hold producers of game called Dungeons & Dragons responsible for child's suicide); McCollum v. Columbia Broadcasting Systems, Inc., 202 Cal.App.3d 989 (1988) (rejecting suit seeking to hold Ozzy Osbourne's song, "Suicide Solution" partially responsible for a child's suicide); Zamora v. CBS, 480 F.Sup. 199 (S.D. Fla. 1979) (rejecting suit seeking to hold television violence responsible for plaintiff's sociopathic personality and murder of neighbor); Davidson v. Time Warner, Inc., 1997 WL 405907 (S.D. Tex. 1977) (rejecting suit seeking to hold producers of rap song about "cop killings" responsible for killing of police officer); Sakon v. Pepsico, Inc., 553 So.2d 163 (Fla. 1989) (rejecting suit seeking to hold producers of television commercial responsible for child's commission of stunt portrayed in that commercial).

110. The court in *Meow Media* acknowledged that it was making a decision "as a matter of law" on both the duty question and the foreseeability issue. See id. at 803. There is nothing incorrect about this; in fact, it is standard negligence doctrine that the question whether the defendant owes a duty to the plaintiff is "a matter of policy" and thus, also a matter of law. Of course, it is also standard civil procedure doctrine that courts reviewing motions to dismiss must determine "as a matter of law" whether reasonable jurors could disagree on the facts.

111. Id. at 806, quoting Watters v. TSR, Inc., 904 F.2d 378, 383 (6th Cir. 1990).

112. Id. at 805, quoting McCollum v. CBS, Inc., 202 Cal.App. 3d 989, 1005–06 (1988).

113. Id.

114. Id.

115. 480 F.Supp. 199 (S.D. Fla. 1979) (case in which child sued television station charging that violent programming caused him to become "desensitized to violent behavior," to develop a "sociopathic personality," and to kill his neighbor).

116. Zamora, 480 F.Supp. at 202 (S.D.Fla. 1979).

117. See Meow Media, 90 F.Supp.2d at 805; see also Watters, 715 F.Supp. 819 (W.D. Ky. 1989); Waller v. Osbourne, 763 F.Supp. 1144 (M.D. Ga. 1991); Bill v. Superior Court, 137 Cal.App. 3d 1002 (1982).

THE CONSTITUTION'S ROCKWELLIAN IMAGE OF LIFE IN CONTEMPORARY AMERICA

1. Transcript, Larry King Live, August 8, 2000, CNN.com transcripts, www.cnn.com, visited on Aug. 9, 2000, at 15. This was a "rush transcript." Id. Thus, it "may not be in its final form and may be updated." Id.

2. Dyson, 401 U.S. at 208.

3. Id.

4. Charles Dickens, Oliver Twist. The complete quotation is: "If the law supposes that ... the law is a ass, a idiot." Available at http://www. bartleby.com/100/470.22.html (Bartlett's Quotations).

5. See, e.g., Davis, Scott, Wadlington, Whitebread at 1–2 (describing the previous sanctity of the parental role and this most recent intrusion into that sanctity, including in the context of a law passed by the Massachusetts Colony in 1672).

6. See, e.g., Alaska St. 47.17.290(2) (Michie 1998) ("'Child abuse or neglect' means the ... mental injury ... of a child under the age of 18 ...;' 'mental injury' means an injury to the emotional well-being, or intellectual or psychological capacity of a child, as evidenced by an observable and substantial impairment in the child's ability to function ..."); Ky. Rev. Stat. Ann. (Banks-Baldwin 1995 & Supp. 1998) ("'Abused or neglected child' means a child whose health or welfare is harmed or threatened with harm when his parent ... inflicts ... emotional injury, ... creates ... a risk of ... emotional injury.").

7. According to Catherine Ross, for example, "[c]onfronted with the incantation that the state aims to safeguard children, courts at every level, including the Supreme Court, have regularly failed to scrutinize the interest alleged by the government." Ross, "Anything Goes: Examining the States' Interest in Protecting Children from Controversial Speech," at 429. Ross further notes that "[t]his lack of analysis is all the more striking because the speech at issue ... is protected under the Constitution." Id.

8. Id. at 433; see also id. at n. 19 (citing others in the legal academy who have made a similar argument).

9. Id.

10. Id. Ross herself is keenly interested in the scope of the free speech rights of children. See Catherine J. Ross, "An Emerging Right for Mature Minors to Receive Information," 2 U. Pa. J. Const. L. 223 (1999).

11. Chaplinsky, 315 U.S. at 571–72.

12. The fact that this would reflect majoritarian sentiment, and thus that minority or divergent viewpoints would be restricted rather than protected, is not inconsistent with the doctrine. In *Jacobellis*, for example, the Court explains that "deviation[s] from society's standards of de-

cency" may be "squared with the guarantees of the First ... Amendment[]." Jacobellis, 378 U.S. at 192. This notion comes out of Roth v. United States, 354 U.S. 476 (1957), which incorporates "contemporary community standards" into its obscenity test, in an effort to "achieve a sensible accommodation between the public interest ... and protection of genuine rights of free expression." Jacobellis, 378 U.S. at 203–04, J. Harlan, dissenting.

13. See Zakaria at 22 (describing an "illiberal democracy" as a government which is elected and even re-elected democratically, but which "routinely ignor[es] constitutional limits on their power and depriv[es] their citizens of basic rights and freedoms" as Americans would define them).

14. This expression comes out of the Justice's concurrence in *Jacobellis*. Specifically, Stewart wrote that

> under the First and Fourteenth Amendments criminal laws in this area are constitutionally limited to hard-core pornography. I shall not today attempt further to define the kinds of material I understand to be embraced within that shorthand description; and perhaps I could never succeed in intelligibly doing so. But I know it when I see it, and the motion picture involved in this case is not that.

Jacobellis, 378 U.S. at 197.

15. Id. at 187 (citing majority opinion).

NOTES TO CHAPTER ELEVEN

The Role and Effectiveness of Religion and Communitarianism

1. There has also been a spate of recommendations for tightening security and discipline in the schools. For example, one reporter notes that "[u]rged on by the President, many schools have adopted uniforms—or at least require tucked-in shirts, which can't hide pistols. Some districts have purchased surveillance cameras or fancy fire alarms that guard against pranks." John Cloud, "What Can the Schools Do?," Time, May 3, 1999 at 39. Also, in the immediate aftermath of the tragedy at Columbine High School, the government ordered and the FBI subsequently produced a "profile" of the teenager who is most likely to follow in Harris and Klebold's footsteps. See, e.g., Lenny Savino, "FBI offers tips on detecting threats at school," The News & Observer, Sept. 7, 2000, at 8A. While it certainly is useful for the authorities, including school authorities, to have a better sense of the children in the community who may be dangerous to themselves and others, this sense unfortunately does nothing to solve or to cure the underlying problems that make the children

dysfunctional. That is, as a result of this profile, the authorities may be able to avert another school shooting (which is obviously no small thing) but the profile and the vigilance of the authorities in this respect will not make the children well. That this is true is evident in the conclusions of this same FBI report, which identifies among the "common threads ... [it] found among school shooters" a series of factors with a complex, and generally early etiology: low tolerance for frustration; poor coping skills; inability to bounce back from a frustrating or disappointing experience; resentment over real or perceived injustices; depression; narcissism; alienation; intolerance; lack of trust; negative role models; unusual interest in sensational violence; fascination with violence-filled entertainment; turbulent parent-child relationship; parents' refusal to recognize or acknowledge problems in their children; family lacks closeness; no limits or monitoring of television and Internet; student is detached from school, students and teachers; and behavior is unyielding and insensitive to others. Id.

2. Communitarianism has been defined as

a sociological perspective focused on balancing personal autonomy and rights with the common good and shared interests. Communitarians contend that much of human behavior is—and should be— "associative, " that is, guided by moral conscience and informal social bonding in one's community. From a communitarian view, the goal of minimizing harmful behavior ... can only be attained if communities provide nurturing environments that encourage responsible and protective behavior. This is the only approach that produces, in individuals, a tendency and a desire to make responsible choices; and thereby accomplishes the objective at a minimal societal cost.

Nancy Kubasek and Melissa Hinds, "The Communitarian Case Against Prosecutions for Prenatal Drug Abuse," 22 Women's Rts. L. Rep. 1 (Fall/Winter 2000) at 2.

3. See "Remarks by the President and the First Lady to the Columbine High School Community," White House Press Release, May 20, 1999, http://www.pub.whitehouse.gov/urires/l...di://oma.eop.gov.us/1999/5/21/22.text. 1, visited on Nov. 2, 1999.

4. The Clintons were joined in their sentiments by conservatives including Ohio Representative James Trafiant, who "used Littleton to try to revive the idea of prayer in schools, which the Supreme Court has ruled illegal about 38 times." Cloud at 38.

5. On the causes of Columbine, see, e.g. "President's Remarks at Columbine," at 5 (suggesting that they include "hatred and distrust [which ...] distort the mind or harden the heart"; individual differences which today divide us because they are "far more important" than "what we have in

common"; parents and children [who are not sufficiently] involved in each other's lives so that they do not "share hopes and dreams, love and respect, a strong sense of right and wrong"; a lack of mutual respect among students who "belong to different groups, or come from different faiths, or races, or backgrounds"; "schools and houses of worship, and communities, [that are not] connected to all our children"; and a "society [which does not adequately] guard[] our children ... against violent influences and weapons that can break the dam of decency and humanity in the most vulnerable of children.") On the solutions to Columbine, see, e.g., id. at 5 ("we must walk by faith, not by sight."); id ("life is a struggle against every person's own smallness and fear and anger ... the struggle to be human is something that must be a daily source of joy to you, so you can get rid of your fears and let go of your rage, and minimize the chance that something like this will happen again."); "Hillary Clinton's Remarks at Columbine" at 2 ("imagine if every adult in America began looking at his or her own personal life, professional life and public life with the view toward making sure that whatever we do is good for children."); "President's Remarks at Columbine" at 5 ("You can help us to build a better future for all our children, ... [a] future where students respect each other even if they all belong to different groups, or come from different faiths, or races, or backgrounds); "Hillary Clinton's Remarks at Columbine" at 2 ("Imagine what our country could accomplish if everyone acted as your principal described you, as a family—members of the human family, as well as the Columbine family; the American family—members of a community and a nation that was really committed to making sure that we helped each other, we cared about each other, we reached out to one another.").

6. See "Hillary Clinton's Remarks at Columbine" at 2.

7. Id.

8. See "President's Remarks at Columbine" at 6 (suggesting that the White House would seek legislatively to address the extent to which children had access to handguns, and to enable the public authorities to identify and help troubled children before they commit violent acts).

9. I say only "some" religions because they are not all alike in their fealty to group based thinking, i.e., some religions are focused upon the individual rather than the group. For example, in her book, all about love: new visions, bell hooks writes that "[o]rganized religion has failed to satisfy spiritual hunger because it has accommodated secular demands, interpreting spiritual life in ways that uphold the values of a production-centered commodity culture. This is as true of the Christian church as it is of New Age spirituality.... The basic interdependency of life is ignored so that separateness and individual gain can be deified." Id. at 72–73.

10. Adrien Katherine Wing at 297–98.

11. Id. at 301.

12. Glendon at 14.

13. Leach at 3.

14. Id.

15. Id.

16. Id. at 3–4.

17. Peters at 2.

18. Id.

19. Id. at 11; see also id. at 2–12 (elaborating on this general point).

20. See id. at 3 (introducing this notion of a "covenant" to protect the children's interests).

21. In all fairness to Peters, it is clear that he does not imagine his idea to be a panacea. Indeed, he understands that its success is limited by its voluntary nature.

WHERE LIBERALISM YIELDS TO COMMUNITARIANISM IN THE LAW

1. As I suggested in Part II, I do not believe that any complete law-based solution to Columbine could withstand constitutional scrutiny.

2. Prince v. Massachusetts, 321 U.S. 158, 165 (1944).

3. Lawrence A. Cremin, American Education: The National Experience, 1783–1876, at 148 (1980). With respect to the "provincial era" that preceded the nation's founding, Cremin notes that the "colonists had long manifested a commitment to education as an instrument of individual and social development, and they had increasingly expressed that commitment during th[at period] in their support and patronage of schools and colleges." Id. (emphasis added).

4. John W. Yolton, "Locke: Education for Virtue," in Amelie Oksenberg Rorty, Ed., Philosophers on Education, (Routledge, New York, 1998) at 177.

5. Id. at 180–81.

6. Id. at 173.

7. Cremin at 148.

8. Benjamin Franklin developed and championed a "utilitarian curriculum" for the schools "that would make respectable those educational values consistent with the needs of a flexible, changing society." Abraham Blinderman, American Writers on Education before 1865 (Twayne Publishers, Boston, 1975) at 49–56.

9. See Blinderman at 56.

10. According to Cremin, "John Adams proffered ... advice [similar to that which was given by George Washington on the subject] in his inaugural address, despite his growing disenchantment by the 1790s with his earlier hopes for the perfectability of mankind [through education.]" Cremin at 103.

11. In one of his last speeches as President, George Washington addressed the question of the goals of a public education:

> It is substantially true ... that virtue or morality is a necessary spring of popular government. The rule indeed extends with more or less force to every species of free government. Who that is a sincere friend to it can look with indifference upon attempts to shake the foundation of the fabric? Promote then as an object of primary importance institutions for the general diffusion of knowledge. In proportion as the structure of a government gives force to public opinion, it is essential that public opinion should be enlightened.

Cremin at 103. Washington, like Franklin and Rush, believed that universal education was an important objective, but interestingly, "he was concerned more with national education than with universal education." Blinderman at 61. Thus, beginning in 1775, Washington "urged the establishment of a national university." Id. According to Blinderman, it was at this university that Washington expected that "leaders would be prepared; instructed in the science of government, [and] the graduates would in turn educate the future guardians of American liberty." Id. Despite this focus on higher education, Washington was not absent from the discussion of elementary and universal education. For example, on the issue of funding, he shared the view of Jefferson and James Madison that while public education was important, the government must not lend its support parochial schools since this policy would be "impolitic ... to the disquiet of a respectable minority." Id. at 62.

12. Abraham Blinderman writes that, among other things, "Franklin, Jefferson, and John Adams strongly advocated public education as a deterrent to war." Id. at 49. Because securing the new democracy was their ultimate objective, and because this democracy itself was created for the purpose of assuring individual fulfillment within the bounds that are possible in a governmentally-ordered society (or post-natural state), it could be argued that the schools are not communitarian in the true or formal sense of that term. This logic is attractive but assailable in the end, simply because the schools as conceived by the founders (and their successors who implemented their ideas) were intended specifically to serve as the institution that would bind the society together by indoctrinating the children (and young adults) in the lessons of the community. That these lessons included and continue to include the value of individualism to the community makes it no less of a communitarian enterprise.

13. Blinderman at 49 (quoting Franklin).

14. Id.

15. Id. at 49–56.

16. Id. at 49–50.

17. Id. at 53.

18. Id. at 51–52.

19. Id. at 52.

20. Id.

21. Id. at 56.

22. Id. at 57.

23. Id.

24. Id.

25. There is, of course, a notable exception to this in New England's strong history of quasi-public education for the public good.

26. James B. Conant, Thomas Jefferson and the Development of American Public Education (University of California Press, 1962) at 5.

27. Lee E. Teitelbaum, "Family History and Family Law," 1985 Wis. L. Rev. 1135, 1150–52.

28. Id.

29. Id., quoting the "Twenty-seventh Annual Report of the Trustees of the Public Schools Society of New York" at 15–16 (1932), reprinted in 1 Children and Youth in America: A Documentary History 260 (Robert Bremner, ed. 1970).

30. Id.; see also Davis, Scott, Wadlington, Whitebread at 27 (discussing child labor law "as part of a comprehensive policy that also included compulsory education requirements").

31. As I have explained previously,

> "Americanization" may be defined as the process of becoming American or "Americanized." ... In the legal literature, the words "Americanize" and "Americanization" are most often used in connection with immigrants; specifically, this term usually refers to the process of learning the English language and American cultural behaviors.... The term "Americanization" itself is controversial. Some believe that it accurately, poignantly, and with utmost good will describes the process of acculturating immigrants. Like Barbara Jordan, they believe that although the "word earned a bad reputation when it was stolen by racists and xenophobes in the 1920s ... [I]t is our word, and we are taking it back." ... Others believe that conservative anti-immigration forces stole the word forever, and thus that it cannot be resuscitated in any useful—i.e., non-racist–sense. Even when viewed in the best light as defining "the process of integration by which immigrants become part of our communities and by which ... the nation learn[s] from and adapt[s] to their presence," ... the term necessarily begs loaded questions including, acculturation into what and just how much acculturation do we require?

Coleman, The Seattle Compromise at n. 242.

32. John J. Miller, The Unmaking of Americans: How Multiculturalism has Undermined America's Assimilation Ethic, at 50–51 (1998).

33. Id. at 52–53 (quoting Hartmann).

34. Id.

35. See Coleman, The Seattle Compromise at 778–779.

36. 262 U.S. 390, 402 (1923). On its facts, the case involved the question whether parents could choose to include the teaching of German in their children's private schools curriculum.

37. Id. The notable exception to this rule is, of course, the imposition of requirements that violate the Establishment Clause. See, e.g., Epperson v. Arkansas, 393 U.S. 97 (1968) (states may not forbid the teaching of evolution in the public schools); Edwards v. Aguillard, 482 U.S. 578 (1987) (states may not mandate the teaching of creationism). Relatedly, and also on Establishment Clause grounds, the Supreme Court has intervened to prevent the allocation of public funds to public school programs that were characterized as advancing a particular religious viewpoint. See, e.g., Lemon v. Kurtzman, 403 U.S. 602 (1971); Committee for Public Education and Religious Liberty v. Nyquist, 413 U.S. 756 (1973). And, the courts since *Meyer* have accepted that parents may enroll their children in the public schools and at the same time cause them to be excluded from certain aspects of the curriculum, for example, sex education. See Davis, Scott, Wadlington, Whitebread at 46 (discussing some of these cases and the doctrine that has emerged as a result).

38. Meyer, 262 U.S. at 401; see also Pierce v. Society of Sisters, 268 U.S. 510 (1925) (holding that state could not require that children attend only public schools, but that it did have the right to regulate the curriculum of all schools, including the private schools, to assure that the objectives of compulsory education laws were met.) Again, the Establishment Clause is the important exception to the general rule that the state may prescribe the curriculum for all schools, including the private schools.

39. Meyer, 262 U.S. at 402.

40. Id. at 402. The only aspect of the state's plan that the Court refused to condone was the means it used to achieve these ends, namely prohibiting the teaching of the German language in all schools, including specifically in the private schools, since there was no evidence that such an education would be harmful to American children in peacetime. Id. at 403.

41. Board of Education v. Pico, 457 U.S. 853 (1982) (the law supports the "absolute discretion" of the state in the development of the public schools' curriculum). See also, Pierce v. Society of Sisters, 268 U.S. 510 (1925) (confirming the authority of the state "reasonably to regulate all schools, to inspect, supervise and examine them, their teachers and pupils; to require that all children of proper age attend some school and that teachers shall be of good moral character and patriotic disposition, that certain studies plainly essential to good citizenship must be taught, and that nothing be taught which is manifestly inimical to the public welfare").

42. Pierce, 268 U.S. at 534. In *Pierce*, the Court held that states do not have "the general power to standardize [their] children by forcing them to accept instruction from public teachers only." Id. at 535. In other words,

parents could choose to send their children to private school, so long as these schools satisfied the state's curricular requirements otherwise. See id.

43. 347 U.S. 483, 493 (1954).

44. 478 U.S. 675 (1986), citing C. Beard & M. Beard, New Basic History of the United States 228 (1968).

45. Id. at 685.

46. Id. at 683, citing Tinker, 393 U.S., at 508. See also, Plyler v. Doe, 457 U.S. 202, 221 (1982) ("We have recognized 'the public schools as ... the primary vehicle for transmitting 'the values on which our society rests'... education has a fundamental role in maintaining the fabric of our society.").

47. 406 U.S. 205 (1972).

48. Id. at 219.

49. Id. at 218.

50. Id.

51. Id.

52. Id. at 22.

53. Id.

54. Id. at 235.

55. 827 F.2d 1058 (6th Cir. 1987), cert. denied, 484 U.S. 1066 (1988). For a more thorough discussion of the *Mozert* case, see generally Stephen Bates, Battleground: One of Mother's Crusade, the Religious Right, and The Struggle for Control of Our Classrooms (Poseidon Press, New York, 1993). The *Mozert* decision became known in the media as the "Scopes II" case because it also examined the content of public school text books with respect to the theory of evolution. In addition, the "proximate venue of the two cases" led to it being referred to as "Scopes II." Janet Kalt-O'Bannon, "Scientific Dating and the Law: Establishing the Age of Old Objects for Legal Purposes," 63 U.M.K.C.L. Rev. 93, n. 296 (Fall 1994). The first Scopes case involved a review of a state law banning the teaching of evolution, and the decision by a state court that the law was a valid regulation of the public schools' curriculum. Scopes v. State, 289 S.W. 363 (Tenn. 1927).

56. Mozert, 827 F.2d at 1061.

57. Id. at 1060-62.

58. Id. at 1062.

59. There is a significant argument that the parents' free exercise rights were in fact substantially burdened by the textbooks and the manner in which they were to be used by the teachers. Indeed, particularly given that the children in question were in elementary school and thus especially subject to outside influence, I find rather weak the contrary albeit prevailing argument that the books merely "exposed" the students to new ideas but did not "indoctrinate" them in any manner. This is particularly so given that the books were intended by the state expressly to fulfill the "character educa-

tion" requirement of its relevant statute. Id. at 1060. See also, Stanley Fish, "Mission Impossible: Settling the Just Bounds between Church and State," 97 Colum. L. Rev. 2255, 2288–2300 (discussing the decision in *Mozert*). In any event, what is clear is that the Court did not find the burden on the parents' right to free exercise to be "undue." Mozert, 827 F.2d at 1070 (acknowledging only that the children "'could' or 'might' come to conclusions that were contrary to the teachings of their and their parents religious beliefs.") In the end, the result in *Mozert* is correct not because of this dubious characterization of the materials as "merely exposing" the children to assimilative values, but because the government has a compelling interest in the inculcation of those values. What the parents sought—accommodation of their perspective within the public schools system—was impossible given this objective.

60. Id. at 1060, citing Tennesee Code Annotated (TCA) 49-6-1007 (1986 Supp).

61. Bethel School District v. Fraser, 478 U.S. 675, 681 (1986). As a doctrinal matter, if the majority had found that the textbooks constituted an undue burden on the parents' right freely to exercise their religion (that is, had the court agreed with the parents that the books indoctrinated their children in, rather than merely exposed them to, intrusive values) this interest would have had to be compelling. This scenario was played out in the *Mozert* dissent, which—based on the decision in *Fraser*, and assuming the existence of an undue burden on the plaintiffs—did find that the government had a compelling state interest in in "teach[ing] the students how to think critically about complex and controversial subjects and to develop their own ideas and make judgments about these subjects." Id. at 1070. In particular, the dissent emphasized the compelling state interest in "[t]eaching students about complex and controversial social and moral issues," noting that these subjects are "just as essential for preparing public school students for citizenship and self-government as inculcating in the students the habits and manners of civility." Id. at 1071. The dissent also noted that the state has a compelling interest in "avoiding religious divisiveness" which would be promoted by permitting students to opt out of core subjects for religious reasons. Id. at 1072. Finally, the dissent found that the state has a compelling interest in "avoiding disruption in the classroom," and that the parents' request that their children be permitted to opt out of the reading portion of the day would cause such disruption since the curriculum was integrated. Id.

62. Mozert, 872 F.2d at 1062 (setting out the context for this quotation).

63. President '96: Issues, http://www.pres96.com/iss8.htm, visited on Sept. 3, 2001.

64. Id.

65. For a discussion of the equal protection right to access public education if it exists, see Plyler v. Doe, 457 U.S. 202 (1982).

CURRICULUM REFORM AS AN ANTIDOTE TO COLUMBINE

1. "Final Report, Bipartisan Working Group on Youth Violence," 106th Congress, Nov. 17, 1999.

2. Id.

3. Id.

4. Id.

5. Id.

6. Id.; see also H.R. 1944, 107th Congress, 1st Session, May 22, 2001 (legislation entitled "A Bill To provide dollars to the classroom," which includes money for classroom activities and services generally, but also for a lengthening of the school day and year, the reduction of pupil:teacher ratios, civics lessons, and after-school programs); H.R. 228, 107th Congress, 1st Session, January 6, 2001 (legislation entitled "A Bill To improve character education programs," which proposes the establishment of grants to develop character-based components for a model curriculum); S. 311, 107th Congress, 1st Session, February 13, 2001 (legislation entitled "A Bill To amend the Elementary and Secondary Education Act of 1965 to provide for partnerships in character education," which is a companion to H.R. 228, supra); H.R. 1118, 107th Congress, 1st Session, March 20, 2001 (legislation entitled "A Bill To establish comprehensive early childhood education programs, early childhood education staff development programs, model Federal Government early childhood education programs, and for other purposes," including an emphasis on funding lower income and minority populations); S. 157, 107th Congress, 1st Session, January 23, 2001 (legislation entitled "A Bill To establish a program to help States expand the existing education system to include at least 1 year of early education preceding the year a child enters kindergarten"); H.R. 613, 107th Congress, 1st Session, February 14, 2001 (legislation entitled "A Bill To provide a grant to develop initiatives and disseminate information about character education, and a grant to research character education").

7. See, e.g., H.R. 228, 107th Congress, 1st Session, January 6, 2001 (legislation entitled "A Bill To improve character education programs"); S. 311, 107th Congress, 1st Session, February 13, 2001 (legislation entitled "A Bill To amend the Elementary and Secondary Education Act of 1965 to provide for partnerships in character education"); Senate Bill 898, General Assembly of North Carolina, Session 2001 (legislation entitled "The Student Citizen Act of 2001, providing for training in courage, good judgment, integrity, kindness, perseverance, respect, responsibility, and self-discipline, as well as in respect for school personnel, responsibility for school safety, and service to others"); The Children's Book of Virtues, edited by William J. Bennett, in The Children's Treasury of Virtues, edited by William J. Bennett (Simon & Schuster, New York, 1995) (setting out the following virtues:

courage and perseverance; responsibility, work, and self-discipline; compassion and faith; and honesty, loyalty, and friendship).

8. Garbarino at 83.

9. Id.

10. In Jacobson v. Massachusetts, 197 U.S. 11 (1905), the Supreme Court upheld that state's right to require that public school children be vaccinated against certain diseases. The Court wrote that the state has "a general authority to require immunizations in the interest of public safety." Timothy J. Aspinwall, "Religious Exemptions to Childhood Immunization Statutes: Reaching for a More Optimal Balance Between Religious Freedom and Public Health," 29 Loy. U. Chi. L.J. 109, 117 (Fall 1997).

11. Bennett, The Children's Book of Virtues, at 5. For a discussion of Bennett's conservative credentials, see www.mediatransparency.org/people/wbennett/htm, visited on Aug. 17, 2001. Bennett is widely recognized as

> one of the prime movers of the new right wing movement. Subsidized as a Distinguished Fellow at the Heritage Foundation, Bennett was Secretary of Education in the Reagan Administration, and later he served as national drug czar, and has written numerous pessimistic books about American culture, appearing frequently on television (he's a favorite of Tim Russert and NBC's Meet The Press), and speaking regularly at any number of right wing organizations, as well as serving on many of their boards of directors. He also has very close ties to the Republican Party. Besides serving in the Reagan Administration, Bennett is quoted in a number of national magazines (1999) as editing or writing George W. Bush speeches, and he nearly became the chairman of the Republican National Committee a few years ago.

Id.

12. Bennett, The Children's Book of Virtues at 5.

13. Id. at 6.

14. Id.

15. Bennett, The Children's Treasury of Virtues, at xiii. This anthology contains the previously published The Children's Book of Virtues (1995), The Children's Book of Heroes (1997), and The Children's Book of America (1998), all edited by Bennett and published by Simon & Schuster in New York.

16. I restate the "ground rules" in the negative to emphasize that the principal threshold obstacle to a viable conversation about character education may be the fact that the parties have tended to come to the table with this erroneous sense of individual entitlement.

17. See, e.g. Tracy Dell'Angela, "Reaction is Mixed to Diversity Policy," Chicago Tribune, June 22, 2000, at 5 (discussing multicultural curriculum proposals and problems associated with their development or implementation); Larry Barszewski, "Expansion Sought in History Lessons," Sun-Sentinel (Fort Lauderdale), Aug. 13, 1996, at 3B (same); Maria Newman, "Old

Debate Again Divides the Schools," The New York Times, Feb. 14, 1995, at 3 (same); John Hildebrand, "State Plan to Revamp Curriculum Draws Fire," Newsday, Nov. 20, 1993, at 8 (same).

18. See generally, The Ten Commandments, Exodus 20:1–20; Deuteronomy 5:1–22, in The Small Catechism of Martin Luther, Part One: The Ten Commandments, http://www.mit.edu:8001/afs/asthena.../luther-catechism-1-decalogue.html, visited on July 16, 2001; and id., The First Commandment ("Thou shalt have no other gods before me"); id., The Second Commandment ("Thou shalt not take the name of the Lord thy God in vain"); id., The Third Commandment ("Remember the Sabbath day, to keep it holy). My statement in this respect assumes that the Commandments would not be integrated into the curriculum along with the related texts of other religions for exposure or comparative purposes; there is little controversy that this approach, which does not "prefer" any one of the religions that would be explores, would be constitutionally permissible. Rather, it assumes that the purpose of the incorporation of the Commandments into the curriculum would be to expose and thus to indoctrinate the children to its special status among religions in the United States. This is what the American community would not and constitutionally could not agree to.

19. See, e.g., Mozert, 827 F.2d at 1060–61 (describing this debate).

20. See Mozert, 827 F.2d 1060–61 (describing the plaintiffs' series of disagreements with the textbook series, and including amongst those disagreements the inclusion as they saw it of satanism alongside other religions). As I already have indicated, *Mozert* is a very interesting case in many ways. See id. (setting out my principal discussion of the case). It is an extraordinary subject for classroom discussion, particularly as a means to challenge those students who are convinced that they are "good" or "absolute" multiculturalists, and thus tolerant and even respectful of all individual difference. At least by the end of the session if not before, they all find themselves to be extremely intolerant of Vicki Frost. Given that she is intolerant of tolerance, this reaction is logical, and thus not entirely surprising. What may be surprising, at least to them initially, is that their own intolerance goes quite a lot farther, as they find themselves agreeing with Frost with respect to certain aspects of the County's curriculum. Thus, as several have exclaimed over the years, "I am tolerant, but Vicki Frost *and* Satanism are over the edge." I previously have joined others including especially Stanley Fish in discussing the ultimate point that this exclamation makes, that "there is no such thing as a pure multiculturalist" because everyone has some boundary that they would not allow or suggest to be crossed. See Stanley Fish, "Boutique Multiculturalism," in Arthur M. Melzer, Ed., Multiculturalism and American Democracy (1998).

21. This particular version of The Golden Rule comes from Luke 6:31, The Holy Bible (Holman Bible Publishers, Nashville 1982) at 909. In this

Christian text, the Rule also is found at Matthew 7:12 at 858 ("So whatever you wish that men would do to you, do so to them; for this is the law and the prophets.").

22. The fact that the principle finds itself in the doctrine of many if not all of these religions is not happenstance. See Steven K. Green, Justice David Joshiah Brewer and the "Christian Nation" Maxim, 63 Alb. L. Rev. 427 (1999), quoting Justice David Josiah Brewer ("[T]hat on which all religions rest is the Golden Rule. Upon that, Protestant and Catholic, Christian and Jew, Mohammedan and Buddhist, follower of Confucius and believer in Sintoism, can meet and in it find a working basis. It is, in fact, the foundation upon which all true religion must rest.").

23. See Martin Luther: Small Catechism, Part I: The Ten Commandments (setting out the text of The Ten Commandments, including the Fifth—"Thou shalt not kill"—the Seventh—"Thou shalt not steal"—and the Eighth—"Thou shalt not bear false witness against thy neighbor").

24. See Bennett, The Book of Virtues, passim.

25. See, e.g., Bennett, The Book of Virtues at 19 (using "The Tortoise and the Hare" to illustrate perseverance); id. at 76 (using "The Lion and the Mouse" to illustrate compassion); id. at 100 (using "The Boy who Cried 'Wolf'" to illustrate honesty).

26. See, e.g., id. at 63 ("A Child's Prayer" which refers to the "Lord"); id. at 66 ("The Sermon to the Birds" which refers to "God"); id. at 68 ("Someone Sees You" which refers to the judgment "from above"); id. at 70 ("The Honest Disciple" which refers to "God").

27. In his book, The Educated Child: A Parent's Guide from Preschool through Eighth Grade (The Free Press, New York, 1999), Bennett focuses also on "Character Education in the Early Years," including on the need for "[g]oing to the house of God." Id. at 71. It may be that in the context of the public schools, he imagines the propriety of de-linking religion from education, however, it is clear that he views the total education of a child as involving religion.

28. Indeed, the fact that there are "tried and true" existing curricula allows the cynicism that at least some contemporary legislative proposals, for example for extensive grants to research and develop ostensibly new models, are either ignorant or disingenuous. See, e.g. H.R. 613, 107th Congress, 1st Session, February 14, 2001 (legislation entitled "A Bill To provide a grant to develop initiatives and disseminate information about character education, and a grant to research character education").

29. Mash & Wolfe at 31, 306–07.

30. Garbarino at 83; Leach at 31.

31. Leach at 132.

32. Id. at 135.

33. Id. at 146–147.

34. Id. at 147 (emphasis added).

35. Rosemond at 163.

36. George W. Bush's official Presidential Election website, for example, stated that:

> Everyone agrees there is a problem in these empty, unsupervised hours after school. But those hours should not only be filled with sports and play, they should include lessons in responsibility and character. The federal government already funds after-school programs. But charities and faith-based organizations are prevented from participating. In my administration they will be invited to participate. We will empower parents with more choices in after-school programs.

See georgewbush.com, http://www.georgewbush.com/issues/afterschoolenrichment.html, visited on Sept. 3, 2001.

37. See Mike Hendricks, "Those Lazy, Hazy, Crazy Days," The Kansas City Star, Aug. 18, 2000, at B1; Thomas C. Palmer, "Is Summer Obsolete?," The Boston Globe, July 12, 1992, at 65.

38. See Joan Beck, "Why we should end summer-long breaks for school children," Chicago Tribune, Aug. 25, 1994, at 29; Dennis Kelly, "A 1-year dip in year-round school growth," USA Today, Jan. 3, 1994 at 1D.

39. See E.J. Anderson, "District Moves up Start Date; Year-Round Students will begin in July," The Arizona Republic, Jan. 20, 1995; "We love our year-round schools," USA Today, July 21, 1995, at 12A.

40. See, e.g., Charles W. Fowler, "In Defense of America's Public Schools," The New York Times, June 5, 1983, at 26; Alan Lupo, Editorial, The Boston Globe, May 30, 1990, at 11.

41. See, e.g., S. 157, 107th Congress, 1st Session, January 23, 2001 (legislation entitled "A Bill To establish a program to help States expand the existing education system to include at least 1 year of early education preceding the year a child enters kindergarten," which is laudable in its inclusion of all children and in its proposal fully to fund this extension, but ineffectual for present purposes because it focuses exclusively on academic preparedness).

42. See Tom Nankivell, "Parental subsidies discriminate against childless," The Canberra Times, June 23, 2000, at 11; Jerry Carroll, "Adults Only," The San Francisco Chronicle, Feb. 26, 1995, at 5/z3; Julie K. L. Dam, "All Kidding Aside: Childless by Choice," People, April 2, 2001, at 105.

43. See, e.g., Michael A. Fletcher, "As Stakes Rise, School Groups Put Exams to the Test: Critics Decry Heavy Reliance on Standardized Measures," The Washington Post, July 9, 2001, at A1 (noting that "the emphasis on testing is leading teachers to steal time from the curriculum to prepare their students for the tests.")

FEDERALIZING THE SOLUTION TO A NATIONAL EPIDEMIC

1. Public Law 96-88 Sec. 319. State and Local Government Control of Education. The relevant parts of Section 319(a) provide in general that

(1) Congress is interested in promoting State and local government reform efforts in education.

(2) In Public Law 96-88 the Congress found that education is fundamental to the development of individual citizens and the progress of the Nation.

(3) In Public Law 96-88 the Congress found that in our Federal system the responsibility for education is reserved respectively to the States and the local school systems and other instrumentalities of the States.

(4) In Public Law 96-88 the Congress declared the purpose of the Department of Education was to supplement and complement the efforts of States, the local school systems, and other instrumentalities of the States, the private sector, public and private educational institutions, public and private nonprofit educational research institutions, community based organizations, parents and schools to improve the quality of education.

(5) With the establishment of the Department of Education, Congress intended to protect the rights of State and local governments and public and private educational institutions in the areas of educational policies and administration of programs and to strengthen and improve the control of such governments and institutions over their own educational programs and policies.

(6) Public Law 96-88 specified that the establishment of the Department of Education shall not increase the authority of the Federal Government over education or diminish the responsibility for education which is reserved to the States and local school systems and other instrumentalities of the States.

Most specifically, Section 319(a)(7) provides that

no provision of a program administered by the Secretary or by any other officer of the Department of Health, Education, and Welfare shall be construed to authorize the Secretary or any such officer to exercise any direction, supervision, or control over the curriculum, program of instruction, administration, or personnel of any educational institution, school, or school system, over any accrediting agency or association or over the selection or content of library resources, textbooks, or other instructional materials by any educational institution or school system.

And Section 319(b), entitled "Reaffirmation," provides that

> [t]he Congress agrees and reaffirms that the responsibility for control of education is reserved to the States and local school systems and other instrumentalities of the States and that no action shall be taken under the provisions of this Act by the Federal Government which would, directly or indirectly, impose standards or requirements of any kind through the promulgation of rules, regulations, provision of financial assistance and otherwise, which would reduce, modify, or undercut State and local responsibility for control of education.

2. Dary Matera, A Cry For Character: How a Group of Students Cleaned up Their Rowdy School and Spawned a Wildfire Antidote to the Columbine Effect (Prentice Hall Press, 2001) (commenting on the "blight of violence that staggers America's schools," how this blight affected one high school in suburban Chicago—Mundelein High—and how a student-initiated program of "character education" changed important aspects of that toxic environment.)

3. 457 U.S. 202, 221 (1982).

4. Thus, for example, in 1997 in Ohio,

> a statewide total of more than $10 billion in local, state, and federal funds was spent on primary and secondary education. The federal government's contribution was approximately six percent of that total. Considering only the combined state and local revenues of the districts, the state contribution was about 43.8 percent, and the local share was about 56.2 percent.... The Ohio school-funding system's reliance on local revenue, chiefly in the form of local property taxes, is one aspect of the overall system with deep historical roots. In Ohio, as in many other states, the tradition of using local property taxes as the primary means to fund public schools has been entrenched since early statehood.

DeRolph v. State, 89 Ohio St.3d 1, 7–8 (2000).

5. Id. at 26–27.

6. Id. at 8.

7. Leandro v. North Carolina, 346 N.C. 336, 488 S.E.2d 249 (1997).

8. Id. at 255.

9. Id. at 256.

10. General Assembly of North Carolina, Session 2001, Senate Bill 898, The Student Citizen Act of 2001, April 5, 2001, at Section 6 (2).

11. David Tyack, "Introduction," School: The Story of American Public Education (Beacon Press, Boston, 2001) at 1–2.

12. Id. at 2.

13. Id.

14. See generally Kan. State Bd. Of Educ., Kansas Curricular Standards for Science Education (1999), http://www.ksbe.state.ks.us/outcomes/sci-

ence_12799.html (outlining the standards adopted, including the limit on the teaching of evolution). For a discussion of this decision, see Douglas E. Stewart, Jr., "Going Back in Time: How the Kansas Board of Education's Removal of Evolution from the State Curriculum Violates the First Amendment's Establishment Clause," 20 Rev. Lit. 549 (Spring 2001); Marjorie George, "And Then God Created Kansas? The Evolution/Creationism Debate in America's Public Schools," 149 U. Penn. L. Rev. 843 (Jan. 2001); Robert Vaught, "The Debate over Evolution: A Constitutional Analysis of the Kansas State Board of Education," 48 Kan. L. Rev. 1013 (June 2000).

15. Tyack at 2 (quoting Thomas Bender as describing the debate about schooling as a battle to define "the public culture.")

16. See, e.g., Richard W. Riley, "The Role of the Federal Government in Education—Supporting a National Desire for Support for State and Local Education," in Symposium: Reading, Writing, and Reform, the Roles of State and Federal Government in Education, 17 St. Louis L. Rev. 29, 32 (1997) (arguing that "the goal of [the federal role in education] is to supplement and support local and state efforts to improve education," and that a national achievement test would be consistent with that goal); Faber at 466 (noting that, despite the lack of evidence that local control of curricular matters is important to children's intellectual and emotional success, "[t]here appears to be no real possibility that the local school district will disappear completely from the American educational scene within the foreseeable future. It is too entrenched by tradition and too well accepted by American culture.")

17. John Ashcroft, "The President's National Testing Proposal Had to be Stopped," in Symposium, Reading, Writing, and Reform: The Roles of State and Federal Government in Education, 17 St. Louis U. Publ. L. Rev. 1, 15 (1977).

18. Carl F. Kaestle, "Introduction, Part One: 1770–1900, The Common School," in School: The Story of American Public Education (Beacon Press, Boston, 2001) at 12.

19. Conant at 37.

20. Id.

21. Id. at 11–12.

22. Id. at 12.

23. See id. (noting that parents "were responsible" for any education that did exist at the time as well as for the basic decision whether or not formally to educate their children).

24. Ellwood Cubberley, Public Education in the United States (1989) (noting the relative exceptional nature of the New England schools at the time).

25. Blinderman at 64.

26. Tyack at 1–2.

27. Conant at 38–39. According to Conant, Horace Mann in particular is cited for having "grasped the significance of the old Puritan tradition,

strengthened it, and proclaimed it widely throughout the nation. It became the pattern of American public education." Id. at 39. There were two principal reasons for this slow national progression toward universal, mandatory public education. The first was a sense in the legislatures before that time that only propertied men (and their sons) were entitled or qualified to receive an education. Id. Because these individuals could afford a private education, there was no need for a system of free public education. Id. Thus, for example, Jefferson's proposal for free public education for children whose parents could not afford a private education was quite revolutionary, since the wealthier classes were not interested in being taxed to assure the education of the poor. The second reason was based in the culturally prevalent view, supported by the law, that children belonged absolutely to their fathers who were free to determine their fate. As Jefferson noted in 1817, in support of his draft "Act for Establishing Elementary Schools," "It is better to tolerate the rare instance of a parent refusing to let his child be [freely] educated, than to shock the common feelings and ideas by the public asportation and education of the infant against the will of the father." Id.

The history of public elementary education in Virginia is illustrative of this nineteenth century struggle between the interests of the state in establishing universal public education and those of wealthier citizens and parents in assuring that the state did not impose the requirement upon its unwilling (adult) citizens:

> The Virginia legislature in 1796 had passed a bill that purported to provide [free elementary education for all], but it was a fraud, for as Jefferson wrote in his autobiography: "And in the elementary bill, they inserted a provision which completely defeated it; for they left it to the court of each county to determine for itself, when this act should be carried into execution, within their county. One provision of the bill was, that the expenses of these schools should be borne by the inhabitants of the country, every one in proportion to his general tax rate. This would throw on wealth the education of the poor; and the justices, being generally of the more wealthy class, were unwilling to incur that burden, and I believe it was not suffered to commence in a single county."

Id. at 29–30. The legislature of that state did not act to remove this political obstacle until 1818, when it allocated funds to pay for the education of "poor children." Id. at 30. But again, as Conant notes, this legislation did nothing to assure the universal education of children in that state. As I have already noted above, those children who did not qualify as "poor," or whose parents did not want them to be educated, were not guaranteed a public education in Virginia until the 1860s.

Other states across the young nation had a similarly progressive history with respect to the establishment of public education. For example, the state of New York as early as 1795 "encourage[d] local communities to establish public schools," in part by providing some assistance for students who could not afford to pay the otherwise mandatory tuition. Id. at 33. This tuition-based system lasted throughout the first half of the nineteenth century. Id.

28. Id. Tenth Amendment provides in relevant part that "the powers not delegated to the United States are reserved to the States."

29. Tyack at 4.

30. Id.

31. Id.

32. Kaestle at 11 (providing the quote).

33. According to Conant, when Thomas Jefferson proposed in 1779 that Virginia adopt a plan that would provide at least three free years of public elementary education to "all the children (rich and poor alike)," the notion of requiring school attendance was "far too radical to be accepted [at that time] or for many, many years." Conant at 5 (1962).

34. Kaestle at 12.

35. See id. (noting that parents "were responsible" for any education that did exist at the time as well as for the basic decision whether or not formally to educate their children).

36. Jefferson himself did spend quite a lot of time imagining all of this. What ought to be clear, however, is that even if his musings suggest a penchant for local control—a position which may be disputed—this hardly amounts to the establishment of local control as a "cornerstone" of public education at the time.

37. Cubberley at 78.

38. Blinderman at 57.

39. See Richard W. Garnett, "The Story of Henry Adams's Soul: Education and the Expression of Associations," 85 Minn. L. Rev. 1841, 1874 (June, 2001).

40. Blinderman at 49–56.

41. Id.

42. Riley at 31 (citations omitted).

43. See generally Thomas Jefferson, "A Bill for the More General Diffusion of Knowledge" (introduced in the Virginia legislature in 1779).

44. See also Riley at 31 (noting that "George Washington advocated a national university to promote learning and virtue among potential statesmen"); and id. (noting that "Benjamin Rush, one of the Revolutionary leaders, proposed a national system of education that he hoped [also] would fulfill the needs of the new democracy. He believed, along with others like James Madison and John Adams, that the best security for the new nation lay in a proper form of education.") The fact that the evidence of the intent of the nation's founders is largely directed toward higher education dilutes somewhat its persuasive value with respect to elementary and secondary education, since local communities and certainly parents are more likely to be concerned about the nature of the education provided to their young chil-

dren than they are about that which is afforded to their adult offspring. Nevertheless, and to the extent that the views of the framers continue to be considered in the contemporary discussion about "local control," it is essential to understand both their objectives in thinking about public education, and the cultural obstacle they faced in imagining a broader application of those objectives beyond (and below) the university level.

45. Blinderman at 50; Riley at 31 (noting the complete silence of the Constitution on the subject). On the absence of specific discussion of public education at the Convention, Blinderman writes that

[p]erhaps [it] might have been discussed [there] had the more radical revolutionary leaders, namely, Jefferson, John Adams, Thomas Paine, John Hancock, Samuel Adams, Christopher Gadsden, Patrick Henry, and Willy Jones, been present at the proceedings, but [Benjamin] Franklin's silence on education in Philadelphia was an understandable intentional or unwitting oversight which is insignificant when compared with his exemplary participation in the educational and cultural life of the new nation.

Id.

46. Id.

47. Cubberley at 78.

48. Riley at 31 (discussing the use of the General Welfare Clause and the spending power to accomplish federal ends in otherwise state-run public education programs).

49. See id.

50. U.S. Const., Art. I, Sec. 8.

51. Riley at 32, n. 7 (quoting Alexander Hamilton's Report on Manufactures.) Hamilton's perspective on this was certainly shared by others at the time, including perhaps most notably Thomas Jefferson whose views in this respect I already have discussed.

52. Id. at 31–32.

53. Teitelbaum at 1150–52 (quoting the "Twenty-Seventh Annual Report of the Trustees of the Public Schools Society of New York").

54. Id.

55. 262 U.S. 390 (1923).

56. See, e.g., L.K. Beale, "Charter Schools, Common Schools, and the Washington State Constitution," 72 Wash. L. Rev. 535, 541 (April, 1997).

57. See, e.g., Code of Alabama Section 16-6B-2(b); 2 - O.C.G.A. Section 20-2-140 (2000) (Georgia); North Carolina General Statutes 115C-85, et seq. (providing for state rather than local control of "the free public school system," and specifically of such matters as textbook selection, and curriculum content standards).

58. See, e.g., North Carolina General Statutes 115C-12(9a) (providing for control of curriculum by state board of education which itself is to "in-

volve and survey a representative sample of parents, teachers, and the public to help determine academic content standard priorities and usefulness of the content standards.")

59. Ashcroft at 1.

60. Governor Terry E. Branstad, "Quality Education Results from State and Local Innovations," in Symposium, Reading, Writing, and Reform: The Roles of State and Federal Government in Education, 17 St. Louis Pub. L. Rev. 73, 77 (1997).

61. Ashcroft at 13. Ashcroft was apparently content to rely on this classic and conclusory rhetoric, as his article is empty of supportive data or explanations apart from his reference to the intent of the "nation's founders." As I will explain below, his proffer of data indicating that children do better when their parents are involved with their education does not support the traditional view that local control of the curriculum of the schools by parents, teachers, and school boards is what leads to students' academic success. Indeed, this data merely suggests (convincingly) that children whose parents are involved with their education tend to do better in school, no matter where the locus of control of the curriculum lies. Even a generous reading of Ashcroft's article fails to yield anything of greater substance. Apart from the data concerning parental involvement, the only support Ashcroft lends to his own rhetoric in favor of local control is "our nation's history." Id. at 17.

62. Faber at 468.

63. The national government obviously would have to be committed to creating good schools in the way that I have defined them above for this supposition to be valid. However, this is no different from the commitment that local school boards must make to assure the success of their programs.

64. 827 F.2d at 1062.

65. Faber at 459.

66. See Rebecca Winters, "Vouchers: More Heat than Light," Time, Oct. 9, 2000, at 76 (noting that education was is a "top priority" for both G.W. Bush and Al Gore, with much attention focused on the issue of school vouchers); Susan Page, "Why good times, the Internet, again boomers, peace abroad and President Clinton could decide who wins your vote," USA TODAY, Sept. 7, 2000, at 1A (commenting that jobs in the new economy require more knowledge, expertise and training than jobs of the old economy, thus making education a top priority for many).

67. See Faber at 459 ("While these positive characteristics can create an atmosphere conducive to increased student achievement, administrative fiat from either the state or the school district level cannot command these factors into existence.").

68. Id.

69. See "Parental Involvement Is as Easy as PIE!," Education World: The Educator's Best Friend, at wysiwyg://9/http://www.education-world.com/

a_curr/curr030.shtml, visited on Sept. 5, 2001 (describing the research on the impact of parental involvement in education, and in particular the sorts of involvement that are critical to the children's success.)

70. John Hartmire, "At the Heart of a Historic Movement," Newsweek, July 24, 2000, at 12.

71. Id.

72. New Jersey v. T.L.O., 469 U.S. 325 (1985), quoting Ingraham v. Wright, 430 U.S. 651, 662 (1977).

NOTES FOR

Conclusion

1. Doriane Lambelet Coleman, "Columbine (almost) revisited," The Boston Globe, Dec. 3, 2001.

2. H.R. 1118, 107th Congress, 1st Session, "A Bill To establish comprehensive early childhood education programs, early childhood education staff development programs, model Federal Government early childhood education programs, and for other purposes," March 20, 2001.

3. Id. at Section 2(3).

4. Id. at Section 4(a).

5. Id. at Section 101(b)(2)(A).

6. Id. at Section 101(b)(2)(E).

7. Id. at Section 201.

8. Id. at Section 204(a).

9. Of course, proponents of "parents rights" and "local control" of public education who have historically fought and continue still to fight against all efforts to diminish the moral authority of parents over their children will simply dismiss my entire argument as yet another such attempt. I have sought in this book to achieve some common ground with this group in hopes that they might see that we can if we act in good faith agree on the essential principles that would govern any reform of the system of public education. For example I have sought to show that many of their values are shared and especially that they are "good" in child development terms and thus would form part of any such reform. Nevertheless, and despite this common ground, I am not overly optimistic. I expect their usual categorical rejection of other important aspects of my project—especially the notion of federalizing those reforms—and I proceed on the assumption that other proponents of public education historically have used as the basis for their own work, namely that public education is by definition a majoritarian and communitarian enterprise, and they are in the minority.

10. Coleman, "Columbine (almost) revisited."

11. Edelman at 94.

12. Glendon at x.

13. Benjamin N. Cardozo, Chief Justice, Court of Appeals, State of New York, "What Medicine Can Do For Law," The Anniversary Discourse delivered before The New York Academy of Medicine, Nov. 1, 1928, New York and London, Harper & Brothers Publishers, 1930, at 6.

Index

371.7   Coleman, Doriane
Col   Lambelet.

        Fixing Columbine.

		DATE		
2/9th/06				
12/12				